THE CONSULTANT:

JAY MALKOUN's reputation precedes him. He is an Australian Lebanese man who has lived a large life more authentically than any film character. He has been a mixed-martial-arts champion, worked with Triads, and mixed with royalty, gangsters, tycoons and the 'old money' establishment. He has bred world-class Arabian horses, owned fast exotic cars and boats, nightclubs and strip clubs. Equally, during his time in Pentridge Prison, Jay navigated – and dominated – the notorious Victorian prison culture. He rebuilt his life after prison, and then he became the Victorian state leader of The Comancheros, the most feared and respected motorcycle club in Australia. All the while, he negotiated and mediated high value underworld and corporate deals in Australia and world-wide, 'The Consultant' called up to mediate when the laws of the land are slow or inadequate.

THE CONSULTANT:

A memoir of a former bikie, heroin trafficker and underworld fixer

JAY MALKOUN

PENGUIN BOOKS

PENGUIN BOOKS

UK | USA | Canada | Ireland | Australia
India | New Zealand | South Africa | China

Penguin Books is part of the Penguin Random House group of companies
whose addresses can be found at global.penguinrandomhouse.com.

Penguin
Random House
Australia

First published by Penguin Books, 2024

Cover design by Alex Ross Creative © Penguin Random House Australia Pty Ltd
Front cover portrait © Vincent Fantauzzo
Back cover image from author's collection.
All picture section photos from author's collection unless stated otherwise.
Typeset in Bembo Std by Midland Typesetters, Australia

Printed and bound in Australia by Griffin Press, an accredited
ISO AS/NZ 14001 Environmental Management Systems printer.

NATIONAL
LIBRARY
OF AUSTRALIA

A catalogue record for this
book is available from the
National Library of Australia

ISBN 978 1 76134 167 0

penguin.com.au

FSC
www.fsc.org

MIX
Paper | Supporting
responsible forestry
FSC® C018684

*We at Penguin Random House Australia acknowledge that Aboriginal and Torres Strait Islander
peoples are the first storytellers and Traditional Custodians of the land on which we live and work.
We honour Aboriginal and Torres Strait Islander peoples' continuous connection to Country,
waters, skies and communities. We celebrate Aboriginal and Torres Strait Islander stories,
traditions and living cultures; and we pay our respects to Elders past and present.*

For my children Laila, Jada and Romeo, who mean the world to me and have taught me all about resilience, patience and the power of love

CONTENTS

PREFACE

CHARISMATIC, THE KIND THAT a room turns to see; charming, as in pulling the trees from the birds; funny, because he loves to laugh, and because his twist on a worldview is dog-bite-cynical; generous, in the way of a life-saving gift that's never mentioned again; kind to all animals, which is why all animals love him; confident, in the way of a man who knows how to fight well and doesn't mind doing it; athletic, because if you can play it, he's good at it, and if it has wheels, he can ride or drive it; a diplomat, preferring compromise to confrontation; a leader, a man that hard men will follow into battle or, even more impressively, into peace; a designer, from base home-build to impeccable interior decor; a restaurateur, whose clientele included the high-net-worthy and the mighty cool; a producer, who brought a blind tenor with an angel's voice to audiences across Australia; a horse-breeder in a king's stable;

an autodidact, always asking for the best answers to the hardest questions; a manager, keeping the tension of ambition's dissent at bay, while inspiring the best from his staff; loyal, because once given from his heart, his loyalty can't be broken; brave, in the way that only a brave man will stand up to thugs and gangsters and stop them tormenting young offenders in prison; honest, with the kind of honesty that people call ruthless; caring, as in the one in a friendship who keeps the contact alive by checking in regularly; reliable, because if he says he'll do it, it's already done; beloved, as there are so many people who love him deeply; unique, because there is no-one in any of our lives like him; authentic, because he is the same man on the inside, with the same cheeky twinkle in his eyes on the outside, that I met in prison thirty years ago; a good son; a good father; a good friend; my best friend: Amad Jay Malkoun.

Gregory David Roberts
Jamaica, March 2024

1

ANOTHER BEAUTIFUL DAY
IN PARADISE

1 MARCH 2019 WAS just another day: breakfast, school run, quick gym session – a run-of-the-mill Friday morning in sunny Athens. Until they blew up my car and me along with it.

Let's rewind a little. That morning I'd started the day in my family villa in the Greek beachside suburb of Glyfada. Up early, earlier than usual, I felt strong, aggressive, healthy, ready for another day of single-parent challenges. I tinkered around for a bit, checked this and that, then woke the kids and got them ready for school.

We had our routine: uniforms on, washed and ironed the night before while they did their homework, teeth brushed, faces washed, down to the lock-up garage, bags in the boot of the Merc, then a moment for prayer.

I would say my prayers as soon as we jumped into the car. It was about a three-minute process and the kids would

1

respectfully wait until I finished before bombarding me with requests. These were the same three prayers I've been saying every day since 1987, the year I was incarcerated. They were given to me by my mother, and I believe they've protected me well over the years. Most of the time I say them quietly, part of the ongoing conversation with God I've been having since I was a child growing up in Melbourne.

On this day, however, I decided to say my prayers out loud. This marked the first time Laila, Jada and Romeo heard me speak the words I usually recited under my breath. All three of them quietly joined me and repeated the prayers as I offered them. It was an empowering feeling to watch my children reciting the prayers of their own accord.

I'm doing something right, I thought. *These kids get it.*

A beautiful moment, looking back, but there was no time to reflect on it. We had to get on the road. A quick first stop at the Glyfada bakery for my coffee and a morning snack for the kids to have in the car on our way to school drop-off.

Greek bakeries are amazing, with a great selection of food, including the most delicious bread and croissants. The lifestyle in Greece has a lot going for it. People eat well, party hard and drive like crazy.

Driving in Greece is fun, and back then everybody treated the road with about as much respect as a rally driver, yet there were remarkably few accidents. Driving at high speed was just part of the culture. I remember one time I was pulled over going 178 kph on a motorway with a limit of 100 kph. The cops got out of the car and explained to me that if I'd been doing 120 to 130 kph, they wouldn't have stopped me, but going nearly double the limit was too much to ignore. I apologised and explained that I thought I was only doing 140 kph, but since I was driving a very fast and sophisticated car, it must have been going faster than I thought. They thought that was fair enough and fined me €20 for speeding. End of story. All the while, other motorists were flying by at excessive speeds and beeping their horns. I loved that about Greece – no-one gave a fuck.

I pushed the pedal down and we raced along to the school. As I pulled into the car park, I heard a loud screeching noise start up from the right side of the bonnet. I quickly turned off the engine and rushed the kids out of the car. My brand-new Mercedes-AMG had never made this sound before. I'd never heard any car make a noise like this. I was a bit panicked that something was seriously wrong with my motor, a very fucking beautiful one that I was already very attached to.

I waited a few minutes before I started the car, and all seemed okay. The ignition sparked and the low, proud roar of the engine sounded as it should. I made a mental note to take it to the dealership for a check-up, relaxed into the leather seat, hit the gas and took off to the gym, my usual second stop of the day. I gave the weird sound from under the bonnet no more thought.

I had a lot of things on my mind that morning, but the notion that the noise could be a danger to me wasn't one of them. Day to day, I kept my eyes open for threats, even while I worked out at the gym and tried to relax. The life I'd led meant that there was always the possibility of violence around the corner – but just because death might come for you at any minute, that's no excuse not to live your life. I'd just finished up with training, was distracted, my mind on the day ahead, when I climbed behind the wheel of my Merc, put my foot on the brake to start the ignition with the door still open and reached for the starter button, and the car bomb exploded.

There was a time, not long before that day, when a would-be hitman would have had to try a lot harder to get at me than a car bomb. It's a cowardly way to hit a target, but I suppose it's relatively safe for them. In those days – these days – I am a legitimate businessman, but I haven't always been.

I'd only recently stopped carrying my bit everywhere, a Glock 17. Beautiful gun, mid-sized, fast and accurate, and easy to conceal. Even though I wasn't playing up in my new life in Greece, I still felt the need to carry a gun. You would be surprised to learn that in some ways Greece is still the wild west. Not much in the way of CCTV or traffic cameras. A police force starved of resources, where cops get an average of a thousand euros a month. Barely enough to live on. Not enough to get shot for. They mostly stay out of the way then clean up the blood and the bodies. Killers all around are coming across the borders of even more chaotic countries (Romania and Albania). Cunts get bowled all the time. Mostly as an underworld hit, but also for good old-fashioned armed robbery. You would be mad to not pack a gun.

I used to carry it around everywhere in my man bag as a bit of insurance. That was until a recent incident where Laila had tried to grab something out of the bag and almost got hold of the Glock before I stopped her.

Now, I kept the bit in the safe in my house, and only pulled it out for special catch-ups with old friends and certain acquaintances. The sort of people who knew the lay of the land and that I was tooled-up, or at least understood that I usually was. Maybe it was with that assumption – the common knowledge that I was armed and dangerous – that my assassin thought to hit me from a safe distance.

Certain instincts that I picked up during ten years in prison had never left me. After more than twenty years in the outside world, I had never stopped sizing up strangers, never stopped watching for a hidden weapon, never sat in any room with my back to the door. That was until I became a single dad to three children.

Seriously. As a parent to young kids, especially as a solo parent, you don't have time to scratch yourself. You have three little people hanging off you all the time who need 400 per cent of your attention twenty-four hours a day.

Being a dad is so fucking overwhelming. I'd get up, cook the kids their lunch, drive them to school, pick them up, feed them, bathe them (because they were too little to bathe them-selves), fetch their pyjamas, get them into bed, try and get a little bit of work done before they woke up again in a few hours screaming for breakfast. From dawn until 9.30 pm, I'd be lucky to find time to fit in a cup of coffee.

So, when every moment of your life is consumed by caring for your family, when your kids are your number one priority, you start to drop the ball every now and then, stop seeing the signs – the same face more than once in a day, the same car in the distance behind you. Every parent knows the feeling of not having a moment to yourself. It's totally normal to be distracted. The problem was that for someone in my situation, it meant that I didn't notice that someone had been following me for days before the bombing. Or that most of the Aussie gangsters and associated tourists had either been murdered or quietly disappeared from Athens as an underworld war kicked off just below the surface. At this point I was so far removed from that world that I had no idea there was an issue, until I got into my car and, before I even had time to close the door and hit the ignition, it exploded into flames. Mea culpa, bro; I should have seen it coming. Really dropped the ball on that one.

I knew straight away it was a bomb. The airbag pushed my head back and against the seat of the car. It ballooned into action in sync with the bomb, and then disintegrated as quickly as it had appeared. The airbag did its job and protected my face, so the blast didn't knock me out. I stayed conscious and saw it all happen in real time. My instincts screamed that the danger had only just begun.

The car landed with a heavy thud, and when I felt the shock in the suspension, I realised it must have been lifted airborne from the force of the explosion. My ears were fucked from the pressure of the blast, the ringing in them so loud that it blocked out all other sounds, but I could see through the smoke and debris. I reached up and felt my ears were bleeding. Nose too, although I could smell the smoke, which confused my senses. First the intense smell of the flaming wreck – burning rubber and chrome. Then an unbearable stench of burning flesh hit me. I looked down at my legs and saw that the skin there was engulfed in flames. The car was fucked and on fire, and my legs were fucked and burning. But that wasn't the most urgent problem.

Fuck, there's going to be a shooter for sure, was my initial thought. If the bomb had only torn a few strips off me, then any professional killer would have to finish the job with a tool. No chance I was going to let that happen. I wasn't going to die that day. The thoughts running through my head weren't of my wounds or burns, but my kids. *I've got kids to look after. Can't let my family down.* My body had taken a hit, but in my mind I grew twelve feet tall, ready to take on anything in order to survive. The adrenaline had kicked in hard – I felt no pain, only clarity. My thoughts were calm. I knew that I was at war and what I had to do. This would be a defining moment.

Most would cower, frozen from fear, and just surrender to their fate. That wasn't me though. That would never be me. I had too many responsibilities to just give up and die. Shit to do, people to look after. Starting with the shooter I knew would be coming for me.

My car door was hanging open, so I stuck my head out and looked around for a gunman. He would be easy to spot – some blacked-out cunt in a cap worn low to mask his identity running my way with a pistol, ready to pump a clip into me as quick as possible then keep moving. I would have to give him my right side, give him a low profile to shoot at, shield my head with my arm and hope for the best. There was no-one to be seen, but that could change any second.

I knew there was no more vulnerable position to be in when you're under fire than behind the wheel of a car, so I made myself move. First, I needed to get clear of the burning wreckage. In order to extract myself from the vehicle, I swung my body around into the exit position, pulled my legs out then braced my arms against the doorframe so I could use my upper-body strength to pull myself out, all while digging my right knee into the door.

In that position, wedged between the door and the car, I could sort of balance on my left leg but instantly realised something was wrong. When I tried to stand, I felt I was not at my usual height. Somehow, I was shorter, significantly shorter. I looked down at my leg and saw I was standing not on my foot but on my shin bone, just above the ankle. My legs were completely mangled and my feet were totally fucked. The blast had ripped through my lower legs and broken both of them off where the ankles met the foot. Now just a bloody mess where meat and bone hit the raw road.

One foot was blown to the side and hung limp – it was hanging on by just a bit of skin. So walking wasn't an option, but I figured I could sort of crawl. I hauled myself out and onto the path and started inching away from the wreck.

That was all I could do. If or when the shooter came, I couldn't attack or defend myself. I'd been shot at enough times to know that if you can't get to cover, the best thing to do is make yourself a moving target. I would have to duck and weave and hopefully the noise and commotion would save me.

Visibility was fucked through the flames and thick smoke all around me, but I could make out a strange guy approaching.

He had his phone out, filming me, with a look of fear on his face.

This is it, I thought. Because I didn't know this man and he was clearly panicked, I took him to be the shooter – a young kid, in over his head, too late to back out now. I'd seen plenty like him before.

But he wasn't a killer, just a passer-by. I yelled to him to come and move me. I needed to put as much distance between me and the wreck as possible. He grabbed me and started dragging me away, making my bare bones scrape against the road. He was a skinny guy and couldn't really lift me, so he wasn't that helpful.

Seconds later a person on a moped stopped, and I thought that this would be the bullet for sure, because it was standard operating procedure for Greek gangland shooters to ride up on scooters. I motioned to the first guy to be careful – this new bloke could be an executioner – and recoiled from him, resisting being moved towards the scooter rider. But again, no, not a killer, just a passing student who had stopped to help. Together they picked me up and carried me out into the middle of the road. Fuck knows why they thought that was the best place to put me! They were distressed. Me? I was focused.

There's a video of it, taken of me lying burnt and bleeding on the street calmly working it out in my head. Because I'd realised that there was no shooter. Nobody was waiting to take that final step and make sure I was dead.

I'd realised that my enemies had one big chance to take me out and they'd missed. The question was, who had done it?

Who was crazy enough to have a crack at me with explosives in the middle of the day? But still dumb enough to fuck it up so badly? While my body lay there bleeding, my mind ran a mile a minute with potential suspects.

Fuck, I thought, *it's that woman from earlier, from the gym, the wife of the Hells Angels president; she was acting strange.* Usually, she would be all over me with greetings and kisses, but this morning she had shrugged at me. As I'd walked in her direction to say hi, she'd turned and ignored me.

Hmm, strange, I'd thought, and instantly my intuition kicked in and I made a mental note to grab my gun and start carrying it again, just in case. Of course, this didn't help me now that someone had come for me that very day.

Had she known something was about to go down? Was this a Hells Angels hit? Those cunts probably backed up over the murder of Wayne Schneider while I was in his apartment in Thailand. Or maybe that Hells Angels crew in Germany had got paid a bit more to get me in retaliation for that $16M recovery. Either way, for a moment I was convinced it was the Hells Angels. I knew I would have to back up and respond with similar violence.

This will become a global war, I fantasised for a moment. *I'm going to hit those cunts all over the world.*

These thoughts were racing through my head, then I remembered there were others who bore a grudge and who had the capacity to have a crack. Maybe it wasn't the Angels at all. The more I thought about it, the less likely it seemed. The Angels would not have failed on a hit, no chance. They had too much access, too many willing members with tools ready to go, to fumble a kill this badly. They were professionals, and this hit was amateur hour.

The bomber was probably someone out of their league, contracting out a hit. Anyone can be a sick cunt these days, you just need to have bank (money) and a connect to the underworld. Look at the mayhem and destruction Carl Williams caused in Melbourne. Nothing special about that bloke. Some would even say a flop. But he had money and a connect. Rest is history.

Whoever it was, I thought maybe they wanted to make a statement. A car bomb is certainly a loud statement. If you are successful. Otherwise, you're a stupid cunt that fucked that up and should have spent a few more bucks to get it right. That's probably why no-one was putting their hand up for it.

Definitely couldn't be Aussies. Aussie gangsters want to be famous, infamous. Cunts can't wait to brag about anything and everything. If an Aussie was behind this, they'd already be on the scene, signing autographs and posting on Instagram.

Greeks for sure were a possibility just on the fact that this job had been fucked up. If there is a short cut or cheaper option, you can bet the Greeks will choose that path.

Even if it were Greeks outsourcing their hit to complete flops, this was a dangerous situation. I told myself, *I'm not in the clear yet. Killers don't like to leave a job unfinished, especially if the target has the capacity to also get shit done. That will be a problem for the killers. Retaliation will definitely be on the table. I need to get myself back up and about as quickly as possible to get on with it. Can't be lying around waiting for a second crack at me.*

I looked down at my right foot and consciously decided that it would have to go. A quick amputation and one of those bionic feet and I'd be up and about in no time. I'd seen the photos and articles about American soldiers who had lost a lower leg in Afghanistan or Iraq and were back in combat in no time. That would be me, I decided. I had bank, and loyal, capable men around me; we could run the ball up on this and cause carnage. All these thoughts and many more were sprinting through my mind as I lay on the road.

Eventually, medics arrived and I was literally thrown on a stretcher and into the ambulance, and taken to the closest hospital, where the surgeons were waiting to receive me on the footpath outside the emergency department.

They immediately went to work, asking me for the date and my name – the usual questions to ascertain if I'd received head injuries – while cutting my clothes off me and assessing the damage. They wanted to put me out and start surgery.

I resisted. Before anything else I had to arrange to have my children looked after. My phone was lost in the car, but through a doctor I spoke to a woman from the Australian embassy, and I managed to give enough details so she could locate my children and their mother, Samantha.

Sam was fearless and would do whatever was needed to get to her children and protect them. I knew she would go into soldier mode instantly and be all over having the kids collected from school and looked after.

The embassy lady called back and confirmed both mother and school had been contacted and that the kids were being looked after. Turns out my trusted offsider Cain – my main guy in Greece – went to the school with his wife and picked up my kids. My sister-in-law Jasmine flew in the same day from London to be with my children before I was put under. My brother Joe took twenty-four hours to get to me as did Samantha and others from Australia. My best friend Greg 'Doc' Roberts flew in from Jamaica. Over the next couple of days I had other friends fly in, and many others called offering support, such as LK and Baz, two of my more well-connected friends, who arranged a medivac plane to fly me to Turkey. Baz was also a Como and former acting national president, but like me, he'd left Australia with his family to get away from the bikie world and the negative impact it has on your family. But I didn't want medical treatment in Turkey; I wanted to stay in Greece, as I wasn't ready to bail when so much needed to be done.

Cain was with me in my room. He managed all of the noise and kept reporters and anyone else away. Tooled up at all times, he had a no visitors policy, was willing to enforce it and capable of doing so. For the first thirty-two hours after the bomb Cain did not sleep. He was pumped on adrenaline and the desire to hurt someone. The police put two guards on me, but they kept their distance in fear of further attacks. Cain brought in two former navy SEALs to do their jobs instead – with Cain there, nobody who wanted me dead would even come close to a chance.

If anything was going to kill me at that point, it was the hospital. It was old, run-down and filthy. The kind of place you are more likely to cop an infection and die in than recover. A full centimetre of dust and grime ran along the window sill. My bed was old and busted – no mattress, just a stainless steel slab, like something you'd find in a morgue. I had entered a war zone – low on facilities, staff, and everything else required to run a hospital. *Fuck this.* I got Cain onto the job of relocating me to a private hospital.

That was good, because I needed time to think. There was a lot of time in the hospital, and a lot of time to consider my other problem, namely working out who was behind the bomb. I was later told the bomb had been detonated remotely, which meant that someone was watching and waiting, and had pressed the button to set off the blast.

It occurred to me on reflection that the weird noise I'd heard my car's engine make that morning on the school run may well have been the killer trying to activate the bomb in the school car park with the kids still inside with me. Was that possible?

It had been an empty car park, which meant limited extended casualties, but I did have three young children in the vehicle. What kind of a low dog would kill three children? I must have really pissed someone off if that was the intention. Unless I was dealing with a stone-cold psychopath. They're out there. Believe me, I've met plenty of them.

Some cunts just want to be infamous. Known for fucked-up shit that will instil fear in everyone around them. Killing innocent children would certainly do that. But as history shows, when killers get too dangerous, they get knocked. Look at Chris Flannery, for example: 'Mr Rent-a-Kill'. That bloke was out of control, started killing for entertainment, made the underworld paranoid and uncomfortable, and ultimately disappeared. They say he was knocked and buried in the foundation of a city building.

Since the day of the explosion, my phone was blowing up with theories. The bomb had made international news, and all my friends and colleagues from across the world each had their own opinion on who'd tried to kill me.

Cain continued to keep guard in the hospital room and answer my calls – the relevant people got a hold of Cain's phone number, so his mobile was going off. There were a million maybes and what-ifs. Everybody had a theory.

At the time I was blown up, I had been in Greece for well over two years, doing my thing. With my international experience it was normal for me to regularly meet with people from all over the world, including from Russia, Middle-Eastern and Emirate countries, Turkey, South Africa, and many others – too many to mention.

It was not unusual to be asked an opinion or for my thoughts on political developments in matters of the underworld. I didn't specifically get involved, but I suppose I inadvertently did, to a degree, given that opinions and thoughts could be rewritten and shared until they made an enemy of me.

I really can't think of a single thing I did in Greece that would motivate someone to come after me. The local guys had made it clear they had a problem with Australians and tourists coming in and operating in their territory, but I wasn't doing anything to put a target on my back. I kept my head down, operated in the shadows. There was nothing of substance.

I couldn't think of anyone who had a problem with me. No-one.

That said, in this world you don't know you've got a problem until it's too late, do you? While I'd been very careful to keep my head down and lead a quiet life for the good of my kids . . . well, I'd lived a whole lifetime before I was blessed with children. A few lifetimes, really. In one of those lifetimes, I may have done one or two things that upset a couple of villains along the way.

Who knows? You meet the wrong person, say the wrong thing, they take it the wrong way. People hold grudges for a long, long time. Perhaps one of those grudges had inspired an old enemy to finally make a move? And that enemy tried to eliminate me. Unsuccessfully. Who was that? Who can say?

I had a lot of time to think about it. The more I did, the more people I came up with who, due to one misunderstanding or another, might have taken it upon themselves to blow me up. I'll tell you about a few of them. There are some good stories.

If I were looking for an answer, I'd have to go back. Way back, more than fifty years and 15,000 kilometres, back to Melbourne, when I first started putting noses out of joint.

2

THE ALTAR BOY

I WAS AN ALTAR boy. As a child, I was originally destined for the priesthood under the guidance of Father Paul El-Khoury at the Maronite Christian Church, Our Lady of Lebanon, in Carlton.

Communication was an issue. Father Paul spoke only Lebanese Arabic and a little broken English, and I barely understood either language.

When we immigrated, my dad, Antonious, didn't speak English, and I wasn't much better with my Arabic. He only spoke Arabic at home, so I had no idea what he was saying most of the time. Despite the language barrier, I grew up with a really good relationship with my father. Maybe we got along so well *because of* the limited vocabulary we shared; neither of us could tell what the other was saying, but we both understood each other and managed to communicate with limited vocabulary.

Father Paul was not a patient man. I would often be yelled at for my mistakes because I had no clue what he was instructing me to do. To keep up, I would watch what the other altar boy did and try my best to mirror him.

I would keep an eye out for any sign that he would plan to move this way or that, or to swing the chalice in a particular direction. I got very good at it – the act of prayer became part of my muscle memory, and in this way the physical rites of prayer became part of my connection to God, which was powerful. Even though I had no idea what Father Paul was talking about, his sermons made me feel good, and I didn't need Arabic to speak to God in my head. I still don't.

My parents were very devout Christians. We had an icon of Jesus over our mantelpiece all through childhood – an image I had tattooed onto my arm later in life, so it would always be with me. My father would stand in front of that picture, praying for two hours every morning and two hours every night, with his beads in hand. With one hand holding the beads, he would run his thumb over each bead in turn, until the circle was complete, when he would start again.

We'd go to church literally religiously. Weekends and weekdays. That was an absolutely vital part of our culture. It was probably the main social activity for the Lebanese community back in the 70s. On Sundays we'd get dressed up in our best clothes and drive to the Maronite Christian Church on Rathdowne Street. The cars would be double and triple parked on every street around the church.

It wouldn't have occurred to my parents' generation to do any different. These days, the younger generations, including me, aren't as good at fulfilling our obligations to our religion.

When I was three or four years old, Dad set up an altar for us in the boys' bedroom and would pray with us for an hour every night. He'd lead us in the ceremonial prayer, which I didn't understand a word of because it was all in Lebanese Arabic. But I'd stand there each evening and participate, with my hands by my side, because I understood it was important. I picked up on the clues.

Like how if I got bored and leaned against the bed my father would give me a whack, and only go back to prayer once we were all standing up straight.

I grew up in this environment, so this type of discipline and level of dedication to God was normal for us. So, it wasn't unusual for me to have conversations with God while I said my prayers. It seemed perfectly natural to me – if I had a problem, or had something to think about, big or small, then I'd talk it over in my head with God. Where was I going to get better advice than that?

My parents wanted me to be a priest. I considered it for a minute, but you know why I turned it down? The food. I don't eat fruit or vegetables. Tomatoes, bananas, they make me sick.

I remember being eight or nine, having the conversation in the car with my mum about going into the priesthood. Asking questions about dedicating your life to God, wearing the robes, living in a monastery, all of that.

'What do priests eat?' I asked.

'You have to eat what they give you.' Mum explained all about fasting and that priests basically avoided meat and dairy and survived mainly on vegetables.

'Nah,' I said. 'Not going.'

If I liked vegetables, would I have become a priest? I don't think so. Wouldn't have lasted. Because while my connection with God was strong, my calling wasn't to the cloth. It was to fight. Because where I came up, everything was a fight. You fought for everything you had, because if you didn't you had nothing.

Mum was a Palestinian Christian and Dad was a Lebanese Maronite Christian. They had an arranged wedding in Lebanon and six children. I was the fifth.

My parents were introduced, and their marriage arranged, by their own parents. My father was a welder by trade, a skill he had learned from his own father. Together they would walk 20 kilometres across the mountain from Barsa, our small town in the north of Lebanon, to the city of Byblos on the coast, where the work was. A full day's hike. They would leave on Sunday and return on Saturday, spending only one night with the family. During the week they would camp on site and work twelve-hour shifts.

My mother was hard as nails. When they married, they moved into a small flat in Barsa and quickly had my two eldest brothers, George and Joe. Mum was pregnant with the third, Elie, and expecting to go into labour soon when visitors for the neighbours in the flat above knocked on her door. The neighbours were out for the afternoon.

As is the Lebanese way, she invited the visitors in for coffee and to sit and wait for her neighbours to return home. There was no running hot water back then, and all water was boiled over a fire. So, my mother put the coffee on to boil, and while she had the fire going, put on the hot water for her bath in a tin tub.

Eventually the neighbours arrived, and the visitors joined them for a few hours' visit upstairs, leaving Mum to her bath. As the visitors left, they returned to Mum's to thank her for her hospitality and discovered that in that short time she had gone into labour and delivered her third son, all on her own, in the tin bathtub. Tough as nails.

Years later I was fooling around, talking with my mother at our family farm one Sunday, when I mentioned that I had a tight abdominal area – the gap between my ribs and hips is barely a centimetre, when it should have been four or five. 'You and Dad must have been distracted when you conceived me,' I joked.

'Oh yes, that's probably from the pills I took to abort you,' she said, real matter of fact. 'We could not afford another child and your father was highly stressed, so I tried to abort you. But you were a fighter and refused to die. I tried for a month to stop the pregnancy, but you just hung on and so here we are.'

No wonder I grew up to be a fighter, right? It's not like I had a choice. I've had multiple hits out on me over the years – in Europe, in prison, and, it turns out, while still in the womb. I wasn't even born yet, and people wanted me dead. Can't get a break, honestly! Back in the day that was common practice, but I'm not kidding about my mother. Hard. As. Nails. She was a survivor. Had to be.

In those years, Lebanon was a hard place to raise a family. A civil war had just finished, the United States had sent in the Marines, and the risk of further conflict was constant.

When I was very young, around 1965, we immigrated to Melbourne, as the Australian government needed labour and was opening the borders to skilled immigrants. My dad's welding skills were enough to get us a ticket to a new life. It was a way out of poverty and the threat of war back home.

Dad immigrated to Australia in March 1966 on a ship called the *Angie Koro*. When he arrived he lived with his uncle and family in the Melbourne suburb of Brunswick. Dad secured work and saved to purchase our tickets to Australia and find us a home to rent.

Nine months later he'd saved enough money to purchase the five tickets to Australia on board a ship called *The Australis*. The ship left from a port in Egypt, so we first had to catch a boat south to Egypt, a voyage of four days across the Mediterranean, from where we caught a train to Port Said, then waited five days to board the ship and begin our final leg to Australia.

Problem was, Dad had bought the tickets but we didn't get them confirmed in time, so the ship left without us. My mother, God bless her, she was tenacious. She realised the ship's route took it through the Suez Canal through to Alexandria. So she decided to cut it off.

Mum arranged a driver and gathered all our belongings together, and off we went for a seven-hour drive to the coast, where we stayed overnight and waited for the ship. In the morning she managed to convince a small boat operator to chase *The Australis*, and we boarded one at a time while the ship was still moving. On instructions over two-way radio the captain would turn off the engines for sixty seconds while one of us jumped onto the ship's ramp as it heaved on the open water. The small boat quickly circled away before the engines started again and risked pulling us under the propellers. This was repeated until we all got on and all of our belongings were on board. Big effort for a mum with five kids, but this was our only way on. We finally arrived in Melbourne on 17 December 1966, a few days before Christmas.

We lived in a small housing commission house in Reservoir. Over time, my parents bought the red-brick house off the government and built a huge extension, adding three bedrooms and a new kitchen. Mum and Dad worked nonstop to make the payments. Dad found construction and welding work, and Mum did whatever work she could pick up. Back in Lebanon, she'd been a full-time mum, but that wasn't an option in Melbourne. All of us had to work. Even us boys contributed the minute we were old enough. My first job at fifteen was as a brickie's labourer. Sometimes I'll be driving around the north of Melbourne and I'll see a brick wall that looks familiar, and then I'll realise that I helped build it half a century ago. Hard work, but I liked it. I was proud to be able to contribute with my small wage to our family.

I was young, but I was driven. What little money I had, I spent wisely. The first thing I ever bought for myself, for about $50, was a horse. It was a busted-up old breeder horse, destined for the knackery, but I wasn't about to let that happen. Instead,

I bought it, looked after it, gave it a new life in a field nearby. Back then, the area had open land everywhere. Long before I could drive, I'd ride a horse around. Me and my mates would take horses to the drive-in cinema – just ride them in through a big hole in the fence and watch movies from horseback.

Mum expressed her appreciation often with compliments and special dinners of our favourite dishes. We watched our parents work hard, usually two jobs each, and save and do their best for us. Sure, we grew up poor, but we had everything we needed. None of us was scared of hard work and all pitched in however we could.

My parents sacrificed every moment and every penny and did the best they could for their children. They enrolled us in the local school and although we all had issues with the local language, we did our best. We boys always struggled at school; we weren't stupid, we just didn't get the right support.

I was stuck in the middle of two cultures; I was two-and-a-half years old when I arrived in Australia, and when I began school at five, I could not speak English at all.

I went to school when I was five speaking only Arabic – and only barely. Although it was my first language, my vocabulary was very limited. English, however, was worse. On my first day at school, I couldn't understand a word anyone was saying to me. When I was asked to write anything down, I just copied what the kid next to me was doing. As it turned out, the first thing our teacher asked us to do was write our name in the right-hand corner of the large piece of paper we'd been given. I copied him to the best of my capacity and got in trouble for writing the kid's name on my paper instead of my own.

I was really behind the other kids and never had an opportunity to catch up. When my report card came in, I failed at everything. Literally everything, except for physical education and sports, where I got an A. I got maybe D in geography because I could look at a map and figure stuff out, but nobody really ever taught me to read, so I was completely lost with the rest of it. But I still showed up to class every day and did my best. My English did get better. My Arabic didn't. It's safe to say I struggled. But struggling was normal for us, just a fact of life.

Where I grew up, there was a lot of poverty, a lot of government housing. Irish, English, Italians, Arabs – we were all there and we were all struggling. In an environment like that you had people from all over the world, a lot of them carrying serious trauma and other problems.

Refugees who'd just escaped a war. Or people from tiny villages that had been dirt-poor for hundreds of years. There were some Aussie families as well. Not many, and they had troubles of their own – drug or alcohol abuse. A lot of problems, all crammed into one neighbourhood.

There were a lot of gangs in my neighbourhood. There were three gangs in my street alone. We were the first Arab ethnics in the street: George, Joe, Elie, myself and our sisters, Helen and later Janet. We boys fought all the time with the Irish, English, Greek and Italian boys.

They fought among themselves, one ethnic against the other, but we Malkoun brothers were the only ethnic Arab kids, and everybody wanted to have a crack. Back then, guys with Arabic features and brown skin were rare enough that people would stare at us as we walked down the street. If there were two of us walking, that was enough to provoke them. It was like clockwork – I'd be walking with my brothers, minding our own business, there'd be some Aussie kids coming the other way, and they'd yell out, 'What the fuck are you looking at, wog?' and it'd be on. That was the environment I grew up in. It was pretty innocent, just kids playing up, but the aggression set a certain tone to how I learned the world worked.

Everyone was struggling, so there wasn't really envy between groups just because some people had more or less than others. Everybody had less. Everybody's parents worked, most of them at least two jobs, to put food on the table, which meant that kids were left to their own devices. Not out of neglect, but out of necessity.

I made friends with an Australian kid, Jason, who was very, very smart. Spoke perfect English, didn't seem to struggle the way I did at school. I thought he was a genius. His life should have been easy, but his parents divorced, and they ended up hating each other, and he was stuck in the middle. We drifted apart, and when I saw him again years later, he was a drug addict, addicted to speed, the go-to drug back then. I was really alarmed by what happened to him – a bit of culture shock, I guess. The concept of a family not sticking together was really disturbing to me.

My mum and dad were built different. They only ever had each other, and they did their best for us kids. Dad would never eat dinner without Mum; he would feed the kids and wait for Mum to get home from her work. It didn't matter what time she arrived, he would wait for her. Our culture held family in a different respect – we were in it for the long haul. Loyalty is everything to us. Literally in our DNA.

Both my parents had a very, very strong sense of right and wrong, good and bad. Absolutely unshakable. They raised their sons to be good, in the true sense of the word, and to make sure we behaved they ruled with an iron fist. If we fucked up, we were punished. And I got punished often because I was always playing up.

Ours was a background where we had to fight for everything we had, and we fought to keep it. My father used to stand just inside the front gate of our house, holding his belt in his hands, waiting for us to come home to see if there was any evidence of us fighting, like a torn shirt or fat lip. If we came home bloody and bruised, then he'd give us another whack. Dad hit a lot harder than the local gangs. Basically, if I lost the fights out on the street, I was fucked when I got home. So, I learned to win. Always. That was the mentality.

As a kid growing up in a housing commission suburb, I was always in combat/survival mode. We had to fight to get home some days. There were six blocks between my house and my school, and in that short distance there was at least two gangs and one mad family of thirteen kids. If you were lucky you breezed by unnoticed, sometimes even greeted by a familiar face, but mostly up until the age of twelve, maybe thirteen, I would have to navigate around or go through the crazy kids in gangs.

My method was basic: I was super-fast on my feet. No-one could catch me; I would literally sprint past anyone who wanted to take a swing. It was a foolproof technique, unless I was with one of my mates, especially not a particularly fast runner, as then I'd have a problem.

One evening I was walking home from football training with John, a kid from around the corner. We were twelve years old. We got to the third block, about halfway home, and out of nowhere the local gang of kids appeared and surrounded us. It was already dark, and the street was not well-lit, so our prospects didn't look good.

My instincts kicked in and I took off like a rocket and swerved around the boys in front of me as I sprinted to safety. I got a block up the road and turned to see the situation, only to realise that John was still surrounded and getting pushed around by probably six kids. I couldn't leave John to cop a beating.

Back in those days the council planted trees in front of every house and supported the trees with timber stakes. There was one laying on the footpath right in front of me, so before I could overthink it, I grabbed the timber post and charged at the kids attacking John like a madman, swinging at anything and everything.

I fully expected to get the shit kicked out of me, but they took off. All of them ran. I was so surprised to get that reaction. That particular gang was so menacing and aggressive. I'd had run-ins with them before and thought they were a crazy, dangerous bunch. Turns out it was all a front.

That was a lesson for me: to not hesitate to get on the front foot and take the fight to them and watch them crumble. After that I stopped running from bullies or taking the long way around and started soldiering through with aggression and purpose. Game changer. Kids started to treat me better. I became the kid other kids went to when there was going to be a fight after school. I'd thought the neighbourhood bullies were people I should be afraid of. Turns out it was the other way around.

Looking back, we grew up in an era where every TV show and movie was about war. The fear of war breaking out was always being discussed. The country was at war with Vietnam, and it was all you ever heard about on the news – the television would be on in the background and there'd be this constant low-level hum of war. This was way before social media, but it was the first war that was brought into living rooms by the media. Every night there was footage of kids being killed in a jungle, photos of kids getting napalmed. As a kid myself, it made an impression.

But not as big of an impression as Bruce Lee. I discovered Bruce Lee when I was five, and through him the world of martial arts. The guys on the screen were so cool, so tough. They'd just touch the bad guy and knock them straight out. Sometimes they didn't even touch them. You'd see their punch miss and the other guy would still go flying. As a kid, I thought that was the coolest thing in the world.

The minute I saw my first kung fu film, that was it for me. I wanted to be Bruce Lee. But in our neighbourhood in those days everybody wanted to be Bruce Lee.

My brothers and I all started martial arts training – taekwondo classes every Tuesday and Thursday at an academy.

I loved it, but it wasn't all-consuming. Not until a couple of years later, when I realised what strength and violence actually meant in the real world.

Gangs were organised by your ethnicity back then. Simple. If you were Irish, you were with the Irish. We Arabs were with the Lebanese Tigers. Weekends we'd get dressed up, go and hang out at City Square in the CBD, play up, drink some beer, punch on with other boys and meet some girls – rich girls who caught the train looking for trouble, or homeless girls who lived on the street. There were some really beautiful girls sleeping rough back then. I don't know how they did it, but they were stunning, and they liked the Lebs. We used to run amok. And we looked after each other.

One night, we heard that one of our guys had been bashed at the Moreland Hotel, up the top end of Sydney Road. We all jumped in a car, and I went along for the ride. At the pub there was some pushing and shoving, and in all the commotion one of the Lebs pulled out a gun. This guy was a bit off tap and was always finding trouble – I could tell things were about to end badly. I put my arm around his shoulder and whispered into his ear, in Arabic, 'It's all in God's hands,' then snatched the gun from him.

He piped up but understood this was not the time and place for guns. I put the gun in the boot of the car and told Joe, the driver, to wait down the end of the street and not let anyone into the boot. The head of security saw this exchange.

Back then, the Lebanese were becoming a problem in that part of Brunswick, and having seen me create a solution to this situation, the security manager, Sammy, introduced me to the owner, Ronnie, who offered me my first real job on the spot.

'What's your name?' Ronnie went.

'Amad.'

'What?'

'Amad.'

'*What?*'

'I said my name is Amad.'

'Alright.' Ronnie shrugged. 'I'm just going to call you Jay.' Then we went around to introduce me to everyone: 'This is our new bouncer, Jay.' That was that. Afterwards everyone called me Jay. Everyone still does.

So I got my first job as a pub bouncer, aged barely eighteen years old, and started having real, proper street fights. It was such a rush. I couldn't believe that this was my job; that someone would square up to me, and I was contractually required to knock them out. And I was being paid money for it. Not great money, but not bad. Twelve bucks an hour. I'd work a whole night and make maybe $50. But when you've got nothing, $50 seems like an infinite amount of money.

On one of my first nights working the door, Ronnie was doing the rounds while me and Sam were on the door. Ronnie had spotted these five guys smoking weed in the club and told them to put it out.

'Make us,' they said.

Ronnie came back to the door and said, 'Let's go. We have to throw these guys out.'

This was probably an hour into my first night, so I was a bit green. I followed Ronnie and as we approached the five guys started towards us to punch on. I don't know what I did exactly – instincts kicked in and it just happened. Before I knew what I was doing I had dropped two of them, and Ronnie and Sam punched the fuck out of the other three. Later, Sam would tell me that as the first guy came at me I threw a front kick straight into his face and knocked him out, then repeatedly punched the other guy in the head until he dropped.

This was my first real fight – one that was for real, not training, not just mucking around with other boys. There's a big difference between training and street-fighting. I was so green I didn't know that. If I'd had a better idea of reality, I probably wouldn't have been so quick to start. I was a skinny teen – six feet tall and maybe seventy kilograms – up against grown men. It could have gone either way, but thanks to my training and speed, the fight was over before I had time to think it through.

There's dignity in being paid a fair wage for what you are good at, and I was good at the job. Nearly everyone I fought was bigger than me back then, but I was trained and motivated. And fast. Really fast.

Hit that spot – move the chin just enough that it blocks the circulation for the briefest second – and it's instantly lights out. You don't even need to smack them hard, just fast and clean and they go straight to sleep. That was all it took.

I learned early that every fight is a race to the finish line. Whoever crossed that line first, who hit the chin just right, they were the one left standing. That's how it was, so I didn't give my opponents an opportunity. I was always quicker because I didn't hesitate. Couldn't hesitate, because to hesitate meant escalation and blood being spilled. Perhaps I moved a bit too soon on some occasions, but I needed reasonable safety margins.

We used to play up in the City Square, and one time, a friend of mine saw me fighting and told me that I had to meet a martial artist who was visiting Melbourne to scout talent – Sifu David Lacey.

David Lacey and his twin brother Vince were old-school martial artists. They were born in Hong Kong during the Japanese invasion of China. Their Irish father was killed while the boys were still very young, leaving their mother to raise them in Kowloon, one of the toughest parts of Hong Kong at the time. They were legendary martial artists. They'd literally gone to school with Bruce Lee and had trained with him on the rooftops of Hong Kong in the wing chun system of kung fu. To me, a young martial artist, that was about the coolest fucking thing imaginable.

They'd emigrated to Australia and started a kung fu academy in Perth, and now they were in Melbourne looking to start a new school in Victoria. We met and had a training session, and I showed them what I could do. Must have done something right, because they asked me to join them so they could train me up to my full potential as a martial artist. They wanted to train me in choy li fut – Sifu's style of kung fu. It was very aggressive and known for its effectiveness against multiple attackers – a style that fit me well. The Laceys wanted me to represent the style in the the Sixth International Martial Arts Tournament in Macau and Hong Kong.

Those fights were legendary – sort of a cross between the Olympics and a street fight. Five-ounce gloves, all disciplines welcome, and no rules. You couldn't gouge eyes or kick someone in the nuts, but otherwise, anything went. A bit like UFC now, but not in a cage and with fewer rules. Free-range combat, big challenges, big rewards. I liked the sound of that. When the cards were on the table, that's what I wanted out of fighting. I didn't want to hurt people – but I wanted to be the guy on the TV, in the movies, doing flying kicks, kicking arse, getting girls.

So, they started training me towards the goal of fighting in international tournaments held in Hong Kong.

I'd just turned eighteen and I'd been training in the park six days a week for six months. I was determined not to miss my shot. But by the time the competition came around, I was physically ready to fight but couldn't afford to go. We just didn't have the money, and I wasn't making enough as a bouncer to drop everything and chase that dream.

That whole time Sifu Dave would visit and assist with my training, shaping the direction I was taking as a fighter. He taught me that no defence was ever as effective as offence. The philosophy was to attack fast and strong. Smash through your opponent's guard, destroy their defences and blocks, then take victory in the fight.

It's possible there was more to the philosophy than that, but if Sifu tried to impart it to me, then I wasn't listening. Chances are my eyes glazed over when he did, and I went back to stretching and practising high kicks.

But Sifu didn't mind – his priority was finding fighters with potential and teaching them how to unleash it. His goal was to win the prestigious mixed martial arts tournaments in Asia, and he invested his training in the fighters who he thought could achieve it.

All my brothers started working in security, and we loved it. Although we weren't making big money, all of us were happy and well adjusted. We all lived at home with our parents, and all of us gave most of our wages to Mum. After a couple of years working the doors and expanding our social network, we became known in our area as the Malkoun brothers. We had the usual amount of dust-ups in the pubs and clubs, and mostly did alright, and developed a bit of a reputation as formidable, maybe even hard to beat. We were one-in all-in. You fight one you take on all of us.

Old-school that way, but not the only family in the neighbourhood who backed their own. If you took on some of the big tribes, such as the Smiths or the Lays, then your prospects wouldn't look good: brothers, cousins, dads, uncles – the whole fucking family tree would drop on you and you'd hit every branch on the way.

That is how it was back then – most families had six to twelve children, most of them boys. I can only remember two families that had more than three daughters, so the rest were male, and all of us were cheeky little cunts that bridged up to anybody and everybody.

This was how we rolled, and it was ingrained into us from an early age, and it worked well for us in the pubs and clubs. On reflection, George, Joe, Elie and me had the upper hand when bouncing. We were always sober, whereas our opponents were definitely not. Most fights were a result of drunken behaviour – one or two blokes who'd drunk too much and started some shit. We ended it quickly because we fought together. If I was at it, my brothers were with me or at least close by.

I usually took the initiative and kicked it off in order to take the advantage. My point is that under different circumstances, maybe some of those fights would have ended badly for us. Sifu Dave had ingrained in me that the first one to the finish line wins, so why would I wait to cop a big hit from a reckless drunk when I could smash his chin and draw events to a conclusion? I would be sizing the person up while he or they were giving a bit of verbal resistance.

We all knew when to have a crack. When we were working, we stood in an elevated position in the club and watched everybody. As soon as we saw two patrons start to argue or size each other up or do anything not consistent with dancing and having a good time, we swept in, gave the old, 'What's doin'?'

If their response came back negative, we'd escort them out. Any resistance then they got knocked out. It was easy to deal with drunk men.

Fuck me, though, what about the drunk women? Nothing worse than an aggressive drunk woman who's just had her bloke knocked out. They'd attack armed with shoes and handbags. Fucking deadly, and there's fuck-all you can do except run to the manager and get him to deal with it.

One of the doormen we worked with, Bimbo, had a beautiful, petite girlfriend Tina, an Italian glamour, who popped out of her dress in all the right places. Bimbo and Elie were working the door one night when the club was filled with Iraqis.

One of them stupidly grabbed Tina's perky arse. Big mistake. Bimbo was not the sort of bloke to let that go. It kicked off quickly and the numbers were on the side of the Iraqis. He looked around, did the maths and ran for the doors. Bimbo wasn't running away, though. He was escalating.

The doors had a metal crossbar you pushed down to secure them when locked. However, if you needed it to, this metal bar also slid out of its brace and became a weapon.

Bimbo pulled the bar off, and he and Elie went up against a lot of angry men. At this point, my brother Joe (another local psycho) arrived, so it was three against a lot of sick cunts. Stools, bottles, anything and everything was thrown and used as a weapon.

They managed to get most of the Iraqis out the door, lock themselves in and put in a call out for backup. I got there way too late. The place was a mess – we're talking a few split heads, some broken knuckles plus smashed furniture every-where. Management was not happy. Not only was the place trashed, but with all the chaos, people weren't sticking around to pay their bar tabs. The takings for that night reflected a loss of spending of a few hundred patrons. Needless to say, Elie and Bimbo were fired and Bimbo's pretty, petite girlfriend was banned.

Relatively harmless brawls like this one got rarer as the years passed. I can still remember the night I heard of the first murder in the entertainment industry in Melbourne. It was 1984, and after years of fights being just fists and feet and nobody really getting hurt, suddenly there'd been a shooting at a club called Bombay Rock up in Brunswick.

Suddenly people were getting shot or stabbed on their nights out and it was getting out of control. I remember hearing this news and realising that it was only going to escalate from there. It really bothered me that now you didn't have to train and learn to fight to be a sick cunt anymore. You just needed enough stupid to stab someone.

Before too long, I was training and working in Perth and staying with Dave Lacey. I slept in his spare room at night and trained in his academy every day. At that point the priority was training with the Lacey brothers and getting ready to fight in Hong Kong. I had an upcoming trip where I would stay with Sifu's own master, my grand master, train, and fight in the tournaments. It was to be my perfect month in Hong Kong, training and fighting.

I felt invincible. But nobody is invincible, and I was a dumb kid, out partying and fighting all night in a shirt in the middle of winter. No big deal – except that I caught a cold and it esca-lated with the altitude on the flight to Hong Kong, so that by the time we landed I had full flu symptoms. As we left Hong Kong airport, I was very ill, shivering and shaking and out of it. I didn't know it, but these were all the symptoms suffered by heroin addicts going through withdrawal.

The local Chinese master I was staying with always had a bunch of guys hanging around, looking after things. One of them saw me suffering what he thought was withdrawal and offered to go out and get some heroin for me. I guess he saw a lot of guys fly in from the west looking for smack. I said no thank you, and explained I just had the flu and needed a doctor.

I was so crook I had to return to Melbourne after only a week, and had to explain to my mates what had happened, the reason I'd come back early, and how the Chinese thought I was a junkie. The way I told it, it was just a funny story, but a mate of ours – I'll call him Demon – was present when I was relaying this story. He listened with great interest and pulled me to the side and asked if I could get some of that heroin.

'Sure,' I said. 'I don't know, but I'll ask.' I was that fucking naive. I didn't even know what heroin was, really. So, when I was in Hong Kong for another tournament later that year, I asked if I could obtain some for a friend in Australia.

Grand master was a powerful member of the Triads – the Chinese organised crime syndicate. Once I understood his standing, Hong Kong began to open up to me in new ways. I loved that city from the first time I set foot in it, but this proximity to such an influential figure changed the game for me.

I became fascinated with the excitement of Hong Kong, and especially the neighbourhood where my grand master lived. At night, the streets were blocked off and turned into markets. There were incredible things that I'd never seen back in Australia and can still remember vividly after all these years, such as two little boys, maybe aged six and nine, with a basket full of live snakes on the street. They had a pot of boiling water and were selling snakes – they looked like cobras – to eat. One of the boys would lift the lid, the snakes would poke their heads up, and people would pick one.

The younger boy would whip a snake out of the basket and with a pair of scissors cut its head off, make an incision along its belly, pull off its skin, throw it in the boiling water for a few minutes, and then present it to the customer to eat. Chinatown was full-on. I started hanging out there and I loved everything about it.

One day, my grand master set up a meeting with the Hong Kong commissioner of police. He needed to have a meeting to talk about issues in Australia. I was told that there was a problem back in Sydney with Vietnamese thugs standing over Chinese businesses and taking over territories traditionally protected by the Triads. Until recently, the Triads had controlled Sydney's Chinatown using a three-part process, which they described to me as one organisation with three heads.

The first head would be in control of the 'mediation', to arbitrate the deal. For example, if a business in Sydney's Chinatown was being menaced by another criminal organisation, the mediator would calmly and firmly negotiate the terms of the deal and have the rival gang step away.

The second head would be in control of 'collection' and send his guys in to collect what had been agreed as part of the deal.

Naturally enough, the third head would be in control of 'protection and violence' and whatever else was necessary to bring the deal to a satisfactory conclusion.

The Vietnamese groups back then were an emerging major threat to the Triads. Kids who were forged by the war with the USA and who were aggressive, organised and sometimes violent were settling in Australia's cities and making a life for themselves. Machetes were the weapon of choice. The Sydney Triads felt they had to escalate to take back their territory.

The police commissioner in Hong Kong, who wanted to see the balance of power restored in Sydney, believed it was necessary to use guns to be effective in Australia.

I was easily drawn into what, looking back, was my first Triad connection. They needed my help and I felt compelled to do it. I was already in – and I felt I couldn't back out. They needed guns, lots of guns, so I obliged them. I went and asked Demon if he could get his hands on some weapons. He was the closest link I had to the underworld and had just the right kind of connections. He was dealing in anything and everything, and true to form he delivered – got me an assortment of pistols, machine guns and some rifles, twenty-three in total. Some really nice bits among them, as well as a couple of ugly rifles that would do the job. Most of these I gave to the Chinese, some of them I kept for myself. But I made sure the Chinese were happy.

At the time, the Triads were powerful underworld players. They probably still are, but are undoubtedly more sophisticated given that technology and markets always evolve. Back then, things were done a little more traditionally. A little more analogue.

The Sydney-based Triad wanted to meet me in person and issued an invitation to dinner in a Chinese restaurant in Haymarket. I was the only outsider around the table – just me and seven Chinese men who introduced every single one of themselves as 'Peter'.

A lot of Peters for one dinner. It's not unusual for Chinese expats to take western names, and I guess they felt the need to hide their identities. It made an impression, and these guys were turning it on for me in order to make a strong one. They ordered lobster, a classic power move in the underworld, just like the corporate world.

I was a Lebanese kid from government housing – I hadn't been around a lot of lobsters and had no idea what to do in this situation. So, just like in school, I watched 'Peter' next to me to see what he did.

He and the other Peters were tearing into their lobsters. The top of the tail had been removed and ice placed onto the exposed meat. As I picked up a fork, my lobster turned its head and looked directly at me. I don't think I'd ever flinched at anything in my life up to that point.

'It's moving,' I said to one Peter. 'My lobster, it's moving. It's not dead.'

'Yes, we eat the tail live,' the Peter replied. 'Then it goes back to the kitchen where they cook the rest.'

It was a window into a world I didn't understand. Barely out of my teens, I just wanted to train, to fight and to live well. So when that opportunity was offered, I grabbed it.

The grand master was clearly someone who made things happen. With the respect his association afforded me, I was soon taking calls from some of the Chinese Peters. One of them had a pound of heroin to deliver. We arranged to meet the following day in the city. I let Demon know that he was coming and to get the money ready for the Chinese.

Peter and I met in Melbourne's Chinatown in front of a

restaurant. We had a little chat and agreed that I would meet him in a few hours with the cash, then he handed me a pound of heroin. Straight away, I threw it into the glove box and drove to Demon's house.

I was excited. Demon was excited. This deal had been a year in the making. A full year after he started asking, he finally got some gear. He paid, probably a lot less than usual, but I didn't know any better, so it was fine by me.

I returned to Peter as arranged and handed him his bag of cash. I took out my share first, of course. I went home and thought, *Wow, that was easy.* So crazy a small amount of white powder could be worth so much money.

Months went by before I received another call from a Peter with a package. During that time I had a lot of visits from Demon. He was relentless. Don't get me wrong, I also wanted the transaction, but I had no control over when it would take place, no phone number, nothing. I only had the call when I got the call.

Demon was up to his neck in everything: drugs, guns, more drugs. Once I was around his house banging on his door and waiting an unusual amount of time for him to open up when he finally appeared at the door holding a bag of powder and a knife.

I followed him to his bathroom where he proceeded to cut open bags of what was shit speed and flush it down the toilet. After a few minutes I was ready to leave, but Demon said, 'Can you do me a favour and dump the rest of this shit in a bin?' It was about thirty-six 1-ounce packets of speed that had been cut with other substances to bulk it out and was not good quality.

'Sure,' I said, and threw them onto the back seat of my car, forgot about them and drove home. Later that day, not knowing what to do with all this shit speed, I decided to bury the bags under a mound of dirt over in the creek near my place. I got a shovel, walked up to the mound, dug a hole and buried them.

About a year later there was a drought in Melbourne – no speed supply anywhere. I went and exhumed those 36 ounces, put them into one bag and sold them back to Demon for a small profit. I was starting to learn the ways of making a little money for myself but was still pretty stupid and naive and had no idea of the consequences of my actions. (Later with maturity and understanding from my journey, things changed.) All I understood at the time was that heroin was a product that was relatively cheap in Hong Kong, and Aussies couldn't get enough of it. You could move small quantities without ever opening it and make thousands and thousands of dollars. The Triads helped me out with this and in return, they wanted certain favours.

Next thing you know, things started happening. Didn't happen often. Didn't need to. The Triads would bring in a package that I'd pay a few grand for. I'd sell it to Demon, and he'd hand it off to someone else for three times the price. Just like passing off a footy to the next guy on the team.

I didn't know it at the time but Demon had been informing to the police. I started noticing increased police presence around me. I was ambitious but certainly not stupid. Maybe a little stupid.

One time I was doing a transaction in Carlton and met the

Peter upstairs at a billiards parlour. At one point we looked out the window and noticed undercover police everywhere. This was tricky: I had two guys with me and Peter had one of his guys with him. We sent them out all together to walk quickly down Lygon Street like they were up to no good. Peter and I watched from the window as the police collectively followed.

While the police were distracted, me and Peter went out the back door, Peter got in his car and I jumped on my ride, a Yamaha YZ 1000 sports bike. We met not too far up the road, I pulled up next to him at the lights, he passed me the package and off I went, floored it, got away with the product. Solo, I took it straight to Demon, grabbed the cash and met Peter 50 ks out of the city in Wallan to make the exchange. Then I went home and waited for the police to run through in the morning.

I decided then that this was getting too real, so I gave it up – I didn't need that type of drama in my life. After this incident it became too dangerous. I wasn't greedy, I didn't need all the money in the world. I was just a kid, and back then I could live on the smell of money.

I didn't make big money from working with the Triads, but enough to get a bit ahead in the rat-race. Of the small amount of money I made, I didn't spend a cent. I planned to put it to work.

When I'd fulfilled my last obligations to the Triads, I peacefully made my exit. The guns that had been used in the conflict with the Vietnamese in Sydney went back to the Triads. Except for two of them. There were a couple of machine guns I kept as souvenirs.

Don't forget, I was barely in my twenties at this point – a young, cocky kid, and I'd seen *Rambo*, just like everybody. I wasn't going to just give up the chance to own machine guns. Besides, you never know what the future holds. So I buried them out in the state forest in Wallen and made plans to start life again from a position of advantage. That meant moving forward into legitimate business. And that meant going back to Perth.

3

PERTH

I WAS OUT OF the game. As far as I was concerned, I was done playing up. I'd made a tidy sum through my connections with the Chinese, had lived modestly and now had a nest egg, which I put to work as capital to build a new life for myself.

I wasn't too worried about the future. Australia is a country with endless possibilities. If you know how to work hard, if you can be creative, can take a risk – then this is the country for it. There are opportunities everywhere, you've just got to find them. Back in the 80s, as a kid with a few bucks in my pocket and big ambitions, I saw opportunities everywhere.

I wanted to buy some land and had my eye on a town called Wandong, 50 kilometres out of Melbourne. Thirty acres of beautiful undulating land, ready for a home and some horses. With no real assets to my name, borrowing from the bank was not an option, but I struck it lucky, as the seller was happy to sell on vendor terms, meaning you don't borrow from the bank and instead pay back the seller over ten years with an interest rate of 10 per cent. Perfect for me. I was twenty-one years old, ambitious and driven.

I bought the land for $60,000 and paid the first instalment of $6000 plus the 10 per cent interest on the remaining $54,000. Total for first payment: $11,400. Too easy! I couldn't have achieved that on the dole. The second year I paid $5400 plus 10 per cent interest on the remaining $48,600 ($4860), so a total of $10,260 and so on – as the years progressed the payments reduced.

I engaged a military architect to design a house. He had lots of interesting ideas, probably more suited to the military. He designed me a huge home with a secret tunnel to exit in an emergency. The tunnel was a novel idea, couldn't hurt and connected to an internal secret corridor at the end of the garage. It was a simple idea. The main bedroom above the garage had a manhole ladder in the wardrobe that led down to a secret corridor behind a false wall in the garage that then proceeded into a small tunnel from where you'd emerge in a garden bed. I loved the idea of sneaking off while being raided or attacked. Looked good on paper but the house was never built.

I met with Bess Martin, a local landowner who had 30 acres for sale that were already approved for development. Plans were drawn up for sixteen individual 1.5-acre blocks. Her asking price was $200,000. The acreage had potential for sixteen subdivisions worth $40,000 each. I did the calculations quickly in my head: 16 x $40,000 = $640,000. I was ambitious. I wanted more.

I did a bit of homework and discovered it would cost between $120K and $160K to develop the whole site. Worst-case scenario, I would still make $300K profit.

Bess and I developed a friendship over a year of many lunches. We got out pen and paper and came up with a plan to work together. I looked up to Bess, admired and respected her. She answered my questions and was happy for me to pick her brain about property and development opportunities. I realised quite quickly that she was a lady I could learn a lot from.

I offered to buy the 30 acres with a $40K deposit and settle the balance in a year. She agreed, on the condition she could buy one block back off me for $40K – because she needed access to the land behind and was looking for an understanding buyer.

Now my buying price was down to $160K, easy-peasy. Now it was a question of maths: from a $40K deposit, I had a year to pay the balance of $120K. I spent a lot of time thinking about how I could make this work. I on-sold seven blocks to friends for $28K deposits, with a balance of $1 on completion of the development and a promise the titles would be available within a year.

Now I had $192K in working capital for the seven presales, but I was under the pump. I only had a year from the time of purchase to develop the land, pay Bess the remaining $120K and hand over the seven titles to my buyers. Very quickly, I put the development out for tender. I had four applicants ranging from $96K to $180K. I had a good feeling about one builder in particular who priced it at $102K, chose him, bought the land, developed it and had the titles within ten months.

True to my word, everyone got sorted within the year. Not bad for twenty-one.

The next opportunity I saw took me back to Perth. I'd loved living in Perth when I was training with Sifu and found myself missing the beaches, the weather. There were blue skies and beautiful women as far as the eye could see. The clubs and restaurants were amazing – I particularly loved Italian food, and Northbridge was renowned for its Italian restaurants. That sounded pretty good to me and I started thinking of ways to build a life over there.

I decided to invest in a nightclub with my family, which would be called Zuzu's. We found a small club for sale on William Street in Perth for eighty grand. Not a huge initial investment, but we ended up putting in another $50K to renovate it. All my brothers chipped in, but it paid off. The club could only hold 200 people, but those 200 spent well every night.

The city was flooded with fast money from the resources boom, and people had a thirst for partying that made even the party capitals like Melbourne and Sydney look tame.

The opportunities were endless for a fledgling entrepreneur like myself. The thing about having money is it attracts more money; I was soon offered a second nightclub in Rockingham, right around the time I turned twenty-four.

Rockingham is about thirty minutes out of Perth, past Fremantle. It was a cheap entry, so we jumped in with this shady accountant. We got it up and running a couple of nights a week and making money.

Perth quickly proved to be an amazing place to live. I missed my mum and dad, but we saw each other when we could.

Mum worried I wasn't getting decent Lebanese food in Perth, so she flew over to interview a housekeeper for me. She interviewed this lady for three hours to make sure she was the right one for the job, then spent hours training her to cook and clean to exactly my mum's standards.

And I had family with me all the time. I was living my best life. I was fit, young, cashed-up and making moves. So far that meant two nightclubs, living in a mad penthouse and renovating two properties I'd bought. One was a warehouse I was converting into a huge off-tap five-bedroom home in a residential area less than a kilometre from the Perth CBD. The other was a nice three-bedroom home that backed onto the river. Both were secured with bank loans. Then I had some pretty nice vehicles – a BMW 5 Series for my daily ride, and a Harley Softail that I tricked up with nitrous boosters. I also owned two cigarette boats, one 32-footer and one 40-foot ocean racer. The 40-footer was designed by Ben Lexcen as a chase boat for the America's Cup. It could do 70 knots on the water and be completely airborne if the swell was over 1 metre. We could get to Rottnest Island in nine minutes.

Good times, great people. My brother Joe and me running amok in Perth, and we made the most of it. His mates, as well as my mates, all came from Melbourne to stay with us. All in all, life could not have been any better.

After a lifetime of being broke, we spent big on looking sharp. At the time, that meant *Miami Vice* fashions – Italian tailored suit jackets over T-shirts, designer jeans, sunglasses. Joe and I thought we were sophisticated from the big city of

Melbourne, but Perth people outsmarted us a lot of the time. It was a steep learning curve but we worked it out in the end.

Perth had a six-to-one ratio back then, more girls than blokes. One night my door girl, who we knew as Maria, was standing on the footpath out front of my club with me and Joe when the doors of the pub across the road went flying open and a crowd spilled out onto the street.

In the middle, two men were going at it, smacking each other in the head. Quite a crowd had come out of the pub and formed a circle to watch. Your typical Saturday night in Perth. A lot of young men's idea of a good time was a great fight.

This was a good one. A good match-up – both doing well, both getting some decent hits. Then a third guy king-hit one of the fighters from behind. Suddenly it was two against one. They quickly put him on the ground and proceeded to kick the shit out of him.

Eventually a stranger in the crowd piped up, 'He's had enough,' and went and stood in between them, hands out to break it up. The two guys turned onto *him* and dropped him, then began to kick the shit out of him as well. By this stage Joe had walked across to get a better look. I was more focused on Maria. Figured this was a good chance to chat her up, now that everyone was distracted, and we had some privacy.

Anyway, the fight. A third guy then intervened. 'Leave him alone!' the new guy yelled. 'You're going to kill him.' Third guy put his hand on the first guy's back and restrained him, and again the two guys turned their attention to the interloper and began to punch the shit out of him. By now there was quite a pile of knocked-out drunks on the ground, and all the while, Joe was quietly inching closer.

As Maria and I chatted, I was watching, wondering what Joe was up to when I saw him subtly positioning himself closer to the fight. Just as the two aggro cunts were attacking the third guy, I saw Joe position himself in between them then unleash two cracker hooks – one left and one right – that dropped them both out cold. The crowd loved it – they fucking cheered for Joe.

It was beautiful to watch. This was the way Joe rolled. He was a smart fighter as well as a tough one, and that was the advantage. The others declared themselves and got smashed, Joe snipered both of them and got the result.

Maria, by the way, ended up leaving us, but not because of the rowdiness. Later that year when the world-famous band Dire Straits was touring, she met one of the members and married him. I believe a year later they had twins.

There were some incidents at our venues where people played up, but we just dealt with it – normal shit we could take in our stride. I got a call early on a Saturday night from our partner in the Rockingham club, Kevin. It had been run through by some bikies. They did a proper number on the joint, smashed the security guys and did a lot of damage to the club. Kevin was hiding in the refrigerator behind the alcohol. Apparently, he had refused the barmaid entry to his hiding spot out of fear she may attract the bad guys. Too funny. Not exactly a gentleman, our guy Kevin. Truthfully, he had a rep for being a bit of a perv, so there's every chance someone had a good reason to smash up his club. Still, we had to go sort it out.

Elie was visiting from Melbourne and was with me when I got the call. True to form he got the .38 calibre revolver out of the safe and we drove well over the speed limit to the club. Got there in seventeen minutes. Fuck, the club was a mess. What had we done to provoke fucking bikies?

Apparently, local bikies had been bashed by a doorman at one of the clubs, so the bikies hit every bar and club that the doorman's security firm worked for. Impressive really.

I sat there in the ruins of my club, really honestly impressed that they'd organised the logistics required to attack certain venues. They must have had it all locked and loaded before they went in – the entry points, exits, road strategies for police etc. You can imagine a lot of thought went into these attacks, right? Actually, nope. Turns out these were just random seat-of-their-pants, 'Let's fuck those cunts up' sorts of players and they managed to pull it off.

'Fuck these dogs,' Elie said. 'I'll go get the machine guns from Melbourne and we will stand in front of their clubhouse and let loose like *Scarface*. Take the roof off. With four clips of 9-millimetre bullets it'll all be over in seconds. See how they like that one.'

It was tempting. Our two machine guns were totally silenced. The whole barrel worked as a silencer. You fired off a clip and all you heard was the hammer going off like a piston.

'Easy, brother,' I said. 'Who knows what Kevin the perv got up to. Let the security teams work it out and if the bikies keep going then we can have a crack back.' Meanwhile, there were police everywhere and I was carrying a piece. 'Let's get the fuck out of here. This bikie shit is not our problem,' I told Elie.

There were some memorable players around town back then. One of the more memorable ones was John Kizon, a local boxer who was all style. They called him 'Ponytail' due to his slicked black haircut and signature look, dressed all in black. He used to come to Zuzu's now and again, which is where I first saw him in action.

I was sitting on the couch at the back of the club when I saw a random guy and his friends trying to pick a fight with John. They picked the wrong man to have a crack at. What they didn't know was that on top of being a sharp dresser, he was a champion boxer who trained all day, every day. I could see John was getting agitated. He turned to face the guy who was provoking him, then out of nowhere John threw a big punch that sent that poor cunt flying, out cold before he hit the ground.

John ended up becoming a lifelong mate and a key feature of some very memorable nights out in Perth.

There were no drugs around me. I had no interest in them and didn't really even drink – just worked, kept fit and kept on the grind building legitimate wealth. Being a nightclub owner in Perth back then was a licence to print money.

Some of our old social circle from Melbourne had overflowed into the nightclub world out west, and figures in the Perth underworld became aware of my reputation. In all honesty, that reputation didn't hurt when it came to influencing people in legitimate business. It did give you an edge when it came to negotiating. The downside was that those from the more illegitimate side of things were slow to get the memo.

Old circles from Melbourne were linking in with the Italians in Perth. They knew I'd previously had access to the product through the Triads and wanted me to resume operations. There were a couple of crews in Perth who were hassling me to start moving product to Perth, but I wasn't interested. As I recall, I politely declined. My brother told them to fuck off in no uncertain terms. We were 3400 kilometres across Australia having a good crack at a new life. Now and again though, the old life would have a crack at me.

I started getting calls one Saturday from Buck; one of my mates I used to hang out with in Melbourne and ten years my senior. I picked up and he told me: 'I ran into Jason Moran. He's looking for you. Keeps telling everyone he's gonna put a bullet in you.'

'What? Who the fuck is Jason Moran?' I asked. I'd never heard the name before. 'And why does he want to put a bullet in me?'

'I don't know, but he's after you, mate.'

This happened again – a random phone call about this guy Moran – and by the third time I'd been warned Jason Moran was hunting me, I'd decided I'd had enough. I told Buck I was coming to Melbourne for a Friday night out. If we saw this Jason guy, Buck could point him out and we could get on with it.

The next Friday I flew to Melbourne. Buck and I met up at Bombay Rock, a nightclub in Brunswick where apparently Moran hung out all the time. Me, Buck and a few guys got to the club and waited. And waited and waited.

'Where is this guy?' I asked, getting impatient.

'Don't worry, he'll be here, and I guarantee you, he doesn't even know who you are. When he gets here, you watch, he will come straight up to me, start shooting his mouth and start bagging you, not knowing you're right here.'

Right on cue, Buck spotted Moran across the bar and pointed him out.

'There he is. Wait a minute, he'll come over.'

So, I waited about a minute, but that was enough for me. I marched up to him and confronted him. 'Hey, cunt, you know who I am?'

'No, should I?'

'I'm the one you reckon you're going to put a hole in. What's the fucking problem?'

'Ah.' He arced up then. 'I'll show you the fucking problem.' He hesitated for a second then repeated, 'I'll fucking show you,' and started marching towards the exit.

I looked over at Buck and shrugged in a 'dunno where the fuck he is going' sort of gesture. Buck shrugged back. *Fuck it*, I thought, and I ran after him, got him at the bottom of the stairs. We punched on for a second or two before his entourage all jumped in between us.

Turns out he was heading to his car to get his piece. There was a bit of ruckus and a lot of pushback from me. My mate Buck, the guy that brought me to this fight, was nowhere to be found. True to form, Buck took off, the weak cunt.

As it was about to kick off with the possibility of gunfire, the bouncer, Horty Mokbel, got his shotty out of the boot of his car and put it behind the reception for me to use if needed. That was nice of him, but unnecessary. Nothing happened:

it was mostly theatre. Moran and I settled it amicably – some misunderstanding that had gotten out of hand and was easy to settle once we stopped swinging and started talking.

Over the years we got to know each other better and towards his end we caught up a few times. *Good bloke*, I thought, *respected in the underworld, and could hold his own.*

This was before the underworld wars in the 90s when crews from Carlton and Essendon were offing each other by the dozen over drug money. He wasn't a killer then. A shooter, for sure – he would shoot you in the leg without blinking – but then things changed, and he was suspected of a couple of murders.

Still, I liked him, but things caught up with him and they got him. Jason was gunned down in public at a kids' football game. He thought he'd be safe in public. Sometimes, killers don't kill you – arrogance kills you. He left himself wide open. Once you've lived the gangster life, the minute you get too comfortable, it'll all come crashing down.

Back in Perth, I felt I'd fulfilled my obligations to the Triads and had them in the rear-view mirror. They obviously felt differently and kept trying to contact me.

We'd previously had a code for when there was any hint of police interest, and that code meant 'stay away'.

Whenever they reached out to me, I sent out the code. In fact, there wasn't any police attention (ironically enough, considering what happened next); I just didn't want anything to do with that world once I'd gotten my leg up. I knew that now I was on my feet, I had the capacity to make larger amounts of money, and legitimately. But some days it seemed like half the population of two cities were trying to drag me back to my old life.

When I'd first moved away to Perth, Demon, the Melbourne drug dealer, had been very upset. When I'd been the middle-man between him and the Triads, he'd had a pipeline to Hong Kong-grade heroin. Which meant huge profit.

For a while he hassled me to get back into the business and pick up from the Triads. When I ignored him, he started harassing my brother Elie. It transpired that Demon had been pestering him, telling him whatever lies he could think of to get Elie to connect him with the Triads.

He'd told Elie I owed him money – which was utter bullshit – and that by getting gear from the Triads, Elie would be helping me out of a tricky situation. And Elie, who wanted to be a good big brother, agreed. That was his reasoning.

Unfortunately for everyone involved, until that point Elie had nothing to do with anything. No clue whatsoever. That was until I stopped answering calls from the Sydney Triads, who would ring my mum's house because that was the only number they had for me.

I knew none of this until I flew back to Melbourne for Christmas that year and Elie had some news for me. He told me he'd answered a phone call from Peter, and one thing led to another and he'd taken a package from the Chinese. That's when things became real messy, real fast.

He'd picked up maybe a pound of product from the Triads, then stepped on it and turned one into three. To 'step on' a drug means to mix it with another powder – baking powder, sugar, bodybuilder's glycogen powder – to bulk it out and make it weigh more. You make more money for the drug, but the quality declines dramatically.

Unfortunately, Elie had stepped on his product. Heavily. Not so much stepped on it as jumped on it. Dropped a Bruce Lee-quality axe kick onto it. The usual buyers in Melbourne had one taste and could tell it was a terrible product and wouldn't touch it. I don't know what he was thinking, or who taught him that shit – I'd never stepped on a product the whole time, and I never got any grief.

While I was in Western Australia, I knew none of this – this was before encrypted phones and apps and all that, so the only way to talk about crime without the police listening in was in person. I was ignorant – just living my best life in Perth, until that Christmas when Elie took me aside and told me what was going on.

I was pretty fucking baffled. He'd managed not only to become involved in the first place but also to get in so deep so quickly. One minute he was blissfully ignorant of that whole criminal world, the next he owed money to the Triads in Sydney.

'Can you talk to Demon?' Elie asked me. 'Sort it out for me?'

'What? No! What can I possibly do?'

'Just talk to him. He wants to speak with you.'

To be honest, I didn't respect Demon and I didn't care too much about the mess of the situation, so I refused: 'Just find the money however you can, pay everyone back. As for Demon, fuck him off and tell him never to talk to us again.'

The problem was, Demon didn't want the product. Or even really want the money. He wanted to throw us under the bus. The important detail that was missing from all this is that Demon was working for the police.

What we didn't know was that he'd recently been arrested for selling an ounce of heroin to an undercover cop and was staring down two years in jail. That was hardly a life-changing sentence, nothing at all really, but apparently too much for him. He'd decided to make a deal to escape his conviction.

It's important to understand what a low act this was considered. In the criminal world, where morals can be loose and the rules are always changing, there's a hard and fast rule: you don't dog. If you commit the crime and you're caught, you face the consequences. In my experience, setting up someone else to take the fall just wasn't done. I wasn't even a real crook, and I understood that.

When I did take a package, I took on the risk. I knew that if the police caught me, I wouldn't say, 'Oh well, can I hand you someone so as to escape my conviction?' If I got caught, I got caught. That's how it is, and how we were brought up. It's the honourable thing to do.

Given that Demon was the one funding the buy and agitating for it all to happen, I never suspected that he would be setting me up. But that's exactly what he was trying to do. Hence his insistence on me coming out of retirement. He was trying to amass evidence on other people playing up so that he could serve them to the police on a plate.

But this wasn't the half of it – he was doing it on his own initiative. Rolling over and incriminating your associates when the police have intelligence on them is one thing, but before he started volunteering information, the cops didn't even believe him. When Demon informed them I'd done some business, they didn't believe him. They judged him, accurately enough, to be of extremely low credibility and didn't buy any of his nonsense.

In order to convince them, Demon had to buy his own recording device and went about recording his conversations with others to prove they were active. Because I hadn't given him a minute of my time, he'd started trying to trap Elie instead. He convinced Elie that I owed him money and kept at him until he manipulated Elie into saying something on tape that proved to the police that I was active in that world.

That got their attention, and the police began taking Demon more seriously. They involved the National Crime Authority (NCA), who started a taskforce and called it Operation Lucky. The NCA was a specialist law enforcement agency set up in 1984 in response to tax evasion and organised crime – basically an Australian answer to the FBI, with cops who could work across different states and jurisdictions to bring gangsters to justice. The problem was, to date it hadn't been great at its job. It went in gunning for the Italians and organised crime, and basically failed. As a result, the NCA was desperate for a scalp.

I guess a couple of Lebanese brothers living the good life, smashing out a few pounds of smack a year for a short while, was a huge scalp for them at the time. The NCA wanted to make us look like terrorists and international drug lords, perhaps not a hard sell: two Lebs with no education living large, who clearly had bank and had been known to run around with machine guns with silencers. This was the 80s – you went to the movies and if you saw a young Arab guy on the screen, 99 per cent of the time they were a terrorist. Perhaps that's why the NCA had decided they were going to fuck with us. They put a lot of resources into bringing us down.

The police – working through Demon – funded the package that Elie picked up from the Triads. For their investment, they'd obtained recordings of the two of them conducting business – all the dialogue between Demon and my brother was on tape: proof of multiple transactions, records of product moving back and forth, shop talk – discussions of chopping methods and how to step on the product. It was all there, ready to be transcribed in black and white for the warrants.

What it comes down to is Elie took a call he never should have and, while being manipulated by Demon, made one mistake after another. Whether his intentions were good or bad didn't matter – the police had evidence of him actively breaking the law. The NCA had everything it needed to get Elie over a barrel. But they wanted more than one Malkoun brother. They weren't happy with just one of us: they wanted a bigger prize.

Once the police had enough material to incriminate Elie, they started working on me. This meant that from the minute I landed in Melbourne that Christmas, Demon started hassling me for a meeting. I ignored him but he persisted and finally tracked me down. He found me in the middle of a nap on the couch at Mum and Dad's house, sleeping off the Christmas meal.

Elie came in, shook me awake, said that Demon had come over and that he wanted to talk to me. I told Elie I wasn't interested in seeing him, but he insisted, so I went and had a word with Demon.

'What's on your mind, cuz?' I asked, giving him my hand.

'Jay,' he said. 'Mind if we go for a walk?'

We took off in the direction of the nearby creek, and straight away my instincts told me something was wrong. Demon was acting very strangely. Normally a cocky little fuck, he seemed a bit jittery, talking a mile a minute. He was speaking nonsense, just random stuff that didn't make a whole lot of sense, but then suddenly he locked down and got to business. Abruptly, he led the conversation around to the commerce he and Elie had been conducting, talking very precisely. Dates and times. Specific transactions. He told me Elie was in over his head and asked me to help them move the product that had been adulterated and Demon couldn't find a buyer for.

Oh, here we go, I thought, and told Demon the conversation was over.

'I don't know what goes on between you and Elie, but it's between you guys,' I said firmly.

He grew a bit nervous then, and started rambling again, accusing me of lying to him. I cut him off.

'Are you on drugs? You're not making any sense. You've lost the plot, champ.'

We argued a little, called each other a cunt and a liar, and in the end, I walked off. 'I have no idea what you are on about, cuz. Deal me out of whatever you're doing.'

I left Melbourne, went back to Perth and didn't give it any more thought. As far as I was concerned I was done with that world. But that world wasn't done with me.

I didn't know that throughout that whole conversation, Demon was wired for sound. He was wearing a voice recording device, and as backup there were police officers across the park photographing us through long lenses and recording with their own radio mics. Even if I didn't say anything specifically incriminating, it marked the start of them building a case against the Malkoun brothers.

It was dumb of me to even give the guy the time of day. Later on, when I reflected on it – and I would have a lot of time to reflect over the next few years – I'd been foolish in giving him a minute of my attention. He'd been trying to drum up any kind of evidence he could on me for some time, and I just hadn't seen it coming. The guy had a charmed life – the kind of luck you only seem to have when you turn police informant.

Like the guns, for example. There were a few firearms left over from the war between the Vietnamese and the Triads. I'd given most of them back to the Triads but kept a few pistols for myself and sent them over to Perth, and buried those two machine guns in the state forest in Wallen.

Later on, I travelled up to dig them up and do a bit of shooting for fun, but I couldn't for the life of me find them again. I'd forgotten to mark the location, just made a mental note that I'd buried them under a tall tree. Turns out a main feature of state forests is lots of tall trees, so when I went up to look for the machine guns, I couldn't find them.

But then, Demon contacted me one day and asked if he could borrow the guns. 'Oh, mate, there's a bit of activity going on. There is a gang running through houses robbing drug dealers. Can I have a lend of your machine gun until things quieten down?'

'I can't find them.' I laughed him off. 'They're in the state forest, under a tall tree.'

He was a wily cunt and invited me to go hunt for them in his off-road vehicle. He had this little dune buggy that went like an absolute weapon, and I thought that sounded fun, hooning around in the bush in a buggy. So, off we went to Wallen.

It was fun. That day at least, we were mates. We zoomed around a bit, and when I was ready to go home, I pointed at a random tree. 'You see this tree here? I buried them maybe a metre away, under a tree that looked just like this.' Then I went off, laughing. When I returned after barely twenty minutes I couldn't believe it: *He found them under the tall tree, just like I said.*

I'd returned to the forest a half dozen times myself to search and never come close. But Demon found them. They'd been buried for so long that one had rusted up but could be cleaned up and repaired without too much hassle.

I gave that one to Demon and took the good one home to oil and clean. Of course, all of this information went straight to the NCA and gave them cause to use lethal aggression when they eventually planned to arrest me and Elie.

That day was getting closer. After I returned to Perth, it weighed on my mind that Elie was in trouble because he'd leveraged my Chinese connections. But at the end of the day, we were family, and the fact was, Elie had a problem that needed sorting out. As brothers, we were between a rock and a hard place. Couldn't move the product in Melbourne, couldn't give it back to the Triads. The only way out was through Perth.

Because Perth is so isolated it offered particular opportunities. It was off the map for most people who could get a decent shipment of drugs across the state border, but still a big party town. People would pay a premium over there. You could get three or four times the price people would pay for the same product in Melbourne, and it didn't matter if the quality was shit. Anything was better than nothing to that crowd.

Right on time, one of the crews out west who'd been hassling me reached out. Until now, I would always jam it and tell them to fuck off. But then one thing led to another, and right when Elie had this problem in Melbourne, this group in Perth put their hand up to buy the product, no matter how rubbish.

That's when I became involved. I shouldn't have, for many reasons, but I did. I'm the one who told Elie to move the package to Perth. That was all me. I gave instructions for the product to be hidden in the door of a car and driven across the entire continent by a couple of boys from Melbourne acting as couriers.

When the couriers drove across the country with the product, the police followed them the whole way. The police had better eyes on them than we did.

The cops were so eager to grab us that they fucked up the arrest. They were premature. If they'd waited a couple of hours until we actually took possession of the product, they would have had us red-handed, fair and square.

As it was, they raided us in the middle of the day. I didn't even know the courier had made it. The boys arrived, parked near the club and then wandered off to get a juice and a sandwich. They gave everyone the slip, and somehow both the cops and my guys hadn't noticed. The police spotted the car, assumed they were in the club with the product, and when I came out, started the raid.

I'd left the club early that morning because I'd planned to go out on my boat for the day with some mates. I ran back into the club for a few minutes to help my staff do the tills, a tiny little administrative job, then ran out again. As I was running out, the police ran in.

As I exited my club, two of them jumped on me and wrestled me to the ground. Didn't even have time to break my fall. One minute I was thinking about how I was going to get to the marina through traffic, the next I was wearing bracelets with a cop's knee pushing my head into the surface of the road.

That wasn't very much fun, I've got to say. I had big plans out on the water that day, but they didn't work out. That's life, I guess. Wake up in a penthouse, go to bed in a prison cell. In the blink of an eye, I went from eating filet mignon to filling up a tray of the shit they feed you in prison.

At that same time, the police sent raids to arrest Elie at his home in Melbourne. The Melbourne cops were even more gung-ho than the Perth ones. Using the mistaken intel Demon had provided of Elie possessing guns, they sent in the Victoria Police Special Operations Group (SOG) to arrest my brother with assault weapons, live ammo and the safeties off. I truly believe they intended to knock Elie in the process of raiding him, but somehow, they managed to fuck that up too.

When the SOGs arrived, they ran into the wrong house. The NCA had our house under surveillance, and when the SOGs burst into the property next door, they found nothing to shoot. They rushed next door, but by then the regular police had my brother in custody so they couldn't shoot him. They settled for knocking him out with a rifle butt. He didn't even have the gun – I had it with me in Perth. But if we were being honest, they weren't really there for the gun, just like they weren't there to ask questions.

In Perth, the cops didn't bang me up too badly, to their credit. If their intel had been better and they'd known we had guns in the nightclub, they might have been more aggressive. I'm sure they were delighted to find the guns to strengthen their case. As it was, they moved a pound of the product from the couriers' car to the Zuzu's safe, to make sure they could throw the book at us.

I was guilty, no question, but at the end of the day it's a game. Who has more evidence? And where there's a lack of evidence, who has the better story? In time, with age and a bit of wisdom, I understood that what I'd done was not only illegal but also unethical. Nevertheless, we weren't the only unethical side that day in Perth. The police and the NCA had their prize, and they weren't above a little bit of sleight of hand and evidence tampering if it meant they got their convictions. After all, the arrest is only act one of the play for the police. After that is when the fun and games begin.

4

TRIAL AND ERROR

IT'S FUNNY. I'D HEARD the saying that the media never let the truth get in the way of a good story, but you really gain a new understanding when you're on the front page of the papers.

The headlines screaming 'Lebanese Brothers, Heroin Dealers' must have sold some papers. I can't deny that it was a sexy story – two ethnic Arab brothers who were living large finally get their comeuppance. Pictures of our nightclubs, cars, Harleys, and penthouse and houses were splashed over the papers.

They weren't afraid to editorialise. Lebanese, terrorists, gangsters, drug dealers – they called us every name under the sun. The media did their best to beat the story up until we looked like the most full-on, ruthless criminals on the planet. In reality, we were amateurs. Not sophisticated or even organised to be honest, with limited potential in that world.

They thought they had the 'Mr Bigs of the drug world' that the NCA had promised they were going to bring down – not realising that we were just a couple of dumb brothers who fell into a bit of small-time trafficking and fell out of it again. Stumbled into it and then tripped over. We were not moving large amounts of drugs, didn't even have consistency, but I guess back in the day we were significant.

The NCA was very happy with the newspaper version of events. It hadn't been exactly masters of strategy when it came to catching gangsters, but it was when it came to controlling the narrative. The police media units worked with the press to full effect. I'm not denying the allegations of breaking the law and drug trafficking, that's a shoo-in; I'm just saying I don't think we were the sophisticated operation with terrorist intentions they were suggesting.

At our first day in court in Melbourne, we were arraigned in courtroom number three, specially set up for highly dangerous prisoners. There was a tunnel that led from the holding cells to the courthouse, its walls lined on both sides with police officers armed with rifles. Is that overkill or what? I mean seriously, I was impressed with the effort and theatre that was going on around me, but I didn't like the tone it set for mine and Elie's trial. They even had snipers on the roof of the courthouse, ready for an imminent attack or perhaps an attempted jail break. There was a picture on the front page of *The Age* of the sniper kitted out in full tactical gear, laying on the courthouse roof on guard, protecting the city of Melbourne.

No doubt the police and courthouse security had the full

support of the SOG ready for action, whom I'm sure would have loved an excuse to put a couple of bullets in me.

Multiple snipers, just in case the shotguns couldn't get us, I suppose. We were in handcuffs – how much damage could we do? How were we supposed to take out a battalion of armed cops in a tunnel? Did they think we had fucking magical powers? Hang on, wait a sec – what had we actually done to suggest we posed a physical threat? Nothing. I guess we did have machine guns, but not on us, and besides, I don't know how well I'd handle the recoil wearing cuffs.

Seriously – it was all theatre. The multiple cops and the snipers were there for the photographers, not for their service to the community. They weren't there to subdue me and Elie, but to control the story. It was all optics, to paint us as terrorists because that's how the prosecution wanted to portray us.

That was pretty much how it went from day one, and it was only the start of a long, long process. A year after the arrest we had the committal hearing, when the court weighs up the evidence on the seriousness of the charges that'll be pinned on you. Sometimes this stage can go quite quickly, but ours didn't. All up, we were at the committal hearing for eight weeks.

While we were held for committal, Elie and I were housed in remand cells at Pentridge. That's where they locked up temporary prisoners who were waiting for sentencing or release. Every morning we'd travel to court, and each time we didn't know what our legal position would be when we came back that night.

On the first day we were marched to the meat wagon, this big steel bus for prisoner transport. There were fifty prisoners on the bus, and forty-eight of them were smoking. The bus was airtight – it could have been a spaceship. Limited ventilation and it's at least a thirty-minute ride from Pentridge in Coburg to the courts in Melbourne's CBD.

By the time we arrived and the guards opened up the meat wagon, this big toxic cloud of smoke plumed out. It must have looked like a cartoon, with dozens of prisoners stumbling out, blinking and coughing. Elie was suffering badly from the smoke. He is a fit guy, treats his body like a temple, so the smoke was making him feel really sick. Not what you need when you're about to do a full day of court and are doing the walk in front of cameras every morning.

The next day, I thought, *Here we go*, and before I got on the bus, I did a quick round of, 'How you going? Please don't smoke on the bus today, it makes me sick.'

Remarkably I had no pushback. I was expecting a bit of resistance from the desperate-for-a-smoke-stressed-out-can't-deal types, but surprisingly it was all good. The hardened crims and serious offenders were fine with it. Every few days you'd get a new kid or a junkie who had a bit of a problem, but it was sorted out quickly. After that, nobody smoked for eight weeks.

When committal finally ended, we learned that the prosecutors were going in hard with the charges. They wanted us on trafficking, conspiracy and possession of a commercial, traffickable amount of heroin. Because the product had been stepped on so heavily, they initially charged us for having way more heroin than we actually did. The cops are like butchers – they charge you by the gram. It didn't matter to them that the product in the packages was more like two-thirds glucose. It was so cut with glucose that it was probably the only smack in the world you could gain weight on – but that's not how prosecution works.

The media reported the drugs as having a street value of $5.5M. Good luck to anyone trying to get that price for a few pounds of poor-grade heroin in the 90s!

On top of that, the prosecutors were going for a raft of weapons charges because of the guns I had lying around. From the court's point of view, there was no reason for a Lebanese guy to own a gun except for terrorism, I surmised. They were going in hard, trying to imply that we were linked to Middle-Eastern terrorism. Seriously?

I was a nightclub owner in Perth – I surrounded myself with booze, girls, good times – not exactly the MO of an Islamic extremist. Pretty sure I wasn't on the Christmas card list of the mujahedin back then. But the journos were going to write what they would write. Couldn't do much about it from inside a cell.

The one upside of doing jail in the Coburg prison was that it was close to my parents' house so they could visit me easily. But visits were limited to an hour a week.

We had one sixty-minute contact visit – where you can sit in an open area on chairs and tables that are bolted to the floor – and one thirty-minute box visit – where you're separated by a Perspex barrier, and you talk through a phone – per week.

On top of that we got two ten-minute phone calls a week. That was it. There was very limited communication with the outside world, which made things extremely difficult from a legal point of view. How are you supposed to defend yourself from a massive court case under those conditions?

We had to shut down the nightclubs. They were seized, along with every other asset I had to my name. I had to apply to the courts to have money released from my asset pool to defend myself.

Each time I walked out of the cell, I didn't know where I'd be sleeping that night. Cells were reallocated every evening because prisoners on remand usually have a high turnover. You go to court, and depending on how the day pans out you are either set free or sent to a more permanent place to do your jail time.

Practically speaking, you couldn't own anything. No personal possessions, except for what you could carry with you in one green duffle bag you were issued. It wasn't even big enough to carry my court documents, let alone any belongings. My deposition files were kept in big cardboard archive boxes – one, and then two as the case dragged on and on.

I was determined to fight the charges. The method of the Perth arrest and the way the drugs had been discovered were questionable. On top of that, the cops had done a bit of a dodgy magic trick with the evidence. The police alleged they'd found a pound of heroin in a safe in my nightclub, Zuzu's, which was impossible. The couriers from Melbourne had only just arrived and all three pounds were still concealed in the car when the cops raided. If the cops had been less eager, if they'd been smarter about the arrest, things might have been different. The police had fucked up by loading me with a pound of heroin in the safe of the nightclub. During the committal cross-examination, one of the police officers did not corroborate the story that a pound was found in the safe, instead telling it as it was – that the heroin was all located in the door of the car.

All it took was one officer to tell the truth to cast doubt on the integrity of the police case. The only solid link they'd had between me and the drugs was the police testimony that I was in the nightclub at the same time as a pound of heroin.

They had nothing on me except for a brief conversation with their informant Demon and some long-range photos of me meeting with him. And long-range audio recordings of the informer calling each other liars. If neither of us believed each other and said so on tape, then what was a jury meant to believe? The case against me was weak at best. I was walking for sure.

Elie was a different story. Demon had been quietly collecting evidence for the police for long enough that they could go in hard on Elie.

As it was, they had made significant errors in their efforts to entrap us. There were heaps of dodgy little details and examples of evidence tampering in the prosecution case. I knew that it would be easy to demonstrate that the police were lying if we went to trial and I got them cross-examined.

Months passed while I went over the details of my case, readying myself to fight it. We went into court to pick a jury, but we never managed to secure one. My barrister, who I'll call

Helga and is long since dead, rejected jury after jury until two days had gone by and the judge was becoming really impatient. I didn't understand what was going on, which was that Helga was deliberately sabotaging attempts to get a jury together because she wanted to avoid a trial, didn't want me to fight the case.

My council stalled selecting a jury for three days. The prosecution was ready; it was all my barristers who were fucking around. The trial judge was losing his shit and directing his frustrations at me and Elie. This was a very intimidating situation for us, facing these angry white people with so much power and the capacity to throw away the key, who were clearly getting less and less patient with the defence side of things.

Helga would not select a jury. She just wouldn't agree to any jury members. Helga was talking about a plea bargain. Her view was that to plead was a safer bet than going to trial. She insisted that with a plea we could get eight years on the bottom, and she wasn't having anything else. She said whatever it took to get us over the line and plead guilty, there was no case against me, certainly not a solid one. I could have gone either way.

The pressure was applied, my barrister setting the scene: angry judge, great deal on the table, all you have to do is plead guilty and you will be out in three to five years.

'I'm not pleading,' I told her. 'The cops don't have much on me. Are you crazy?'

I believed that the prosecution's case would not hold up in court and refused to back down. I've got this part of my mindset that means I can't deal with injustice. With me, if things aren't fair and equal, it does my head in. When I perceive something to be corrupt, I have to find a way to rationalise it if I'm going to be at peace with it.

The whole time I was playing up during the early years, it was really cat and mouse back then. You really had to trip over and land into an investigation before anyone knew anything. These days, good luck being a crim. The next generation have a lifespan of two years if you're lucky.

The tools and techniques applied by the police now are so sophisticated that ultimately, they will pinch you. I don't know any crook that's got away with being a career criminal. A few have migrated overseas to escape an arrest, but even a foreign country is not safe anymore.

Despite Demon trying to serve me to them on a platter, they still couldn't get it right. As court proceedings continued, the police revealed that they'd managed to fumble obtaining legitimate evidence on me time and time again.

I remember a particular time when I was on my motorbike in Melbourne, carrying a bag with a hundred grand of Demon's NCA money, and the cops put a tail on me.

Their plan was to pull me over and catch me red-handed handing the money to the Chinese. Should have been game over for me, but somehow, they lost me. Not even because of something I did to escape; I had no idea they were tailing me. I was just heading up the road and not even riding hard – just having a bit of fun with the throttle here and there. How they could lose a Harley in a few minutes' ride, I don't know – it's not exactly a discreet vehicle; you can hear it from miles away. When I heard that story, my response wasn't relief, but 'For real? They lost me *and* the money?'

I maybe wasn't the smartest guy back then, but it did make me reflect on how much I could have got away with in those days if I'd been dedicated to it. And made me realise why the police were motivated to manipulate events until I was drawn back into the game.

But I could not accept it enough to plead guilty to a charge I could beat. Helga kept insisting that I take a plea bargain. I felt she clearly didn't want to go to trial and be seen defending this high-profile case. I could tell she had a moral obligation to the community. In her worldview, she had the higher moral ground, and when she saw me, I was just some heroin-dealing Lebanese thug moving these drugs that did immense damage to society.

It didn't help that I was so cocky, with little respect for authority or the judicial system – institutions that the lawyer worked for. I didn't give a fuck. In my early twenties I was an alpha with a bit of money and too much testosterone and no experience of losing a battle. I would have never backed down from a confrontation – that just wasn't *my* worldview. At the time I had so much ego, so much attitude. If the man I am today met the kid I was then, I definitely would not have liked me either. So in Helga's defence, I did make it easy to dislike me.

One day we were in court when the judge adjourned for lunch. Standard procedure would be for all the lawyers and staff of the court to go out for an hour or so; me and Elie would be escorted back to our holding cells by the screws (the prison guards), which meant walking past our family and out back to the cells.

The courtroom was divided into three rows: the far right was where the police sat, the middle had lawyers and media, and to the left sat family and friends.

Normally in this situation, we would slow our pace and have a quick word to Mum as we passed. This day she looked quite upset, so I stopped moving entirely to check on her.

The guard reached around and gave me a shove. 'Malkoun, keep walking.' I ignored him and continued my conversation with Mum, then walked on to the cells.

As soon as we got out to the back, the screw who'd been acting tough became very friendly and charming. I'd been ready to punch on, but his change in demeanour caught me by surprise.

'If that guard touches me again,' I told Elie, 'I'm going to attack him. You can't disrespect or humiliate us in front of our mother. I will fuck him up.'

You wouldn't believe what happened later in the day. It was like déjà vu. That afternoon, when we adjourned again and as we were walking out, I stopped to check on Mum again, and the same guard again reached around Elie and gave me a shove and told us to keep walking. Clearly, he hadn't got the memo.

I took one step to the side and turned to smash him, but Elie beat me to it, hitting him so hard he went flying over the prosecutor's desk, scattering their shit everywhere.

The dog buckled and lay there bleeding, too scared to move while the courthouse filled with police. None of them took a step towards us. The lawyers tended to the guard while Elie and I turned to our family and had a quick chat. I told Mum, 'Don't worry about that clown, he will be fine.'

Elie was chilled out on the day-to-day, but he fought with passion whenever the situation called for it. He was all-in. If I was at it – and it was usually me that started – he would go all-in. His punches would start in Tasmania and finish in Darwin – and when they landed it was like getting hit by a freight train. His philosophy was simple: 'Don't fuck with my brothers.'

So, there we were, standing in the courtroom with our mum and our friends, looking down at this screw who was cowering on the floor, blood pouring from his nose and mouth.

Safe to say the court security officers were going to have some opinions about us knocking out one of their own. They were expected to deal with situations like this with maximum violence. Anticipating mayhem, Elie and I bade a quick good-night to Mum and walked ourselves out the back so she wouldn't have to witness the consequences. We took our ties off and waited to punch on. And waited. And waited.

The overwhelming show of force we were expecting from the screws never came. In the end, they sort of apologetically came into the holding cell behind the courtroom and watched as we walked down the tunnel on our own, closed the door and locked ourselves back into the holding cells, because none of the guards were game to touch us.

There were consequences, though. We were separated for the first time since our incarceration. Elie was sent to H Division, a special 23-hour lock-up unit known as Hell

Division to its inmates that housed the seriously fucked-up, out of control prisoners. He nevertheless had a great time while he was there. Made a lot of friends, including Mark 'Chopper' Read. Elie's reputation preceded him, and he enjoyed the attention given for smashing a screw.

They were cautious of us, as we were considered dangerous and capable of retaliating on the outside, as well as inside prison. How much truth there was to that, I can't say. But I can say I was supremely confident of my ability to defend myself. I thought I was invincible. Very little scared me back then. I can only think of one notable person I had absolute respect for.

One day during a court recess, I was talking to my legal team and enjoying a smoke. As I was talking to my lawyer, I noticed out of the corner of my eye that my mum was walking into the courtroom.

'Quick,' I said to the lawyer, passing them the cigarette. 'You've got to grab this.'

The lawyer took the cigarette and looked bemused. 'What's happening?' he asked me.

'Mum doesn't know I smoke.'

'Jay, you're in the middle of one of the biggest drug cases in Australian history and you're worried about your mum seeing you smoke?'

'Mate,' I said, looking over to the family section nervously, 'have you met my mum?"

My dear mum, a typical Lebanese mother, couldn't believe her boys would ever do anything wrong. When Mum first found out we'd been arrested she could not believe it. From her point of view she'd produced a savvy entrepreneur son who was good at maths and made all this money in property development and legitimate business. I'd made her so proud.

She was in court to support us every possible moment. When she couldn't be in the same room as us, she was out in the real world leaving no stone unturned in her efforts to bring her boys home. She said every possible prayer, did her own investigations, and even went to an imam in Sydney who was supposed to have supernatural powers and was able to conjure up spirits. She bailed up all the best barristers in Australia one by one in order to get us the best help.

But it was never going to work out. The Crown prosecutor had staked his whole reputation on this case, and he needed to win it at all costs. My own lawyer wasn't interested in that fight and pushed me to plead guilty and accept a plea bargain.

'The prosecution has agreed to drop the weapons charges in exchange for a guilty plea for the drugs.' Helga explained that the guarantee would be in the Terms of Agreement, a contract of sorts written between the prosecutor and the defence, outlining the sentencing recommendations. Discounts would be given in exchange for the guilty plea as it saved taxpayer money that would otherwise be used to fight the case and as an expression of remorse for accepting the charge and pleading guilty. 'If you and Elie plead guilty as a pair, you'll get sentenced at the judge's discretion. Worst-case scenario is you get eight years. Five with remissions. You've already done two, so with good behaviour you'll be out in three.'

'That's a good deal for Elie,' I argued. 'But it's not for me. The cops don't have anything to get me on.'

'That's not the offer, though, Jay. They want both of you.'

Helga explained that the offer was only on the table if we both copped the same plea. Without us both, there would be no bargain. If only Elie pled guilty, they'd convict him of every possible charge.

'If you don't both plead guilty, you might walk,' my lawyer said. 'But Elie will get sixteen years, minimum.'

It didn't make sense to me. We had the report from the drug lab that had come back as 1.6 kilos of heroin. Just a hundred grams over the 1.5-kilo limit for a basic trafficking charge, tipping it over into a charge of trafficking a commercial quantity. Trafficking alone would mean ten years jail. Commercial trafficking up to twenty-five. That hundred grams could mean an extra decade and a half in jail. Fifty-four days in prison for every single gram.

'If we are doing a pre-deal, then why can't we negotiate that figure down below 1.5, take a trafficking charge and be guaranteed a reasonable sentence?' I asked Helga.

'The judge will take that into account and be lenient,' she assured me. 'It's all good. You've got to think of it like drink driving. The limit is .08. If you're caught driving at .09 you will get a more lenient sentence than being caught for driving drunk at 2.1, for example, although on paper it's the same crime.'

She went on to say that we were only just over the threshold of 1.5 kilos and that the maximum sentence was reserved for the worst-case scenario. 'Trust me,' she said. Which I did. In my mind, it sort of made sense, although my instinct told me otherwise.

My gut was telling me to fuck off all of my legal advice, fire my lawyers and start again, but the clock was ticking. Elie was fucked if I didn't plead guilty. So there was nothing to think about, really. Of course I would plead guilty to get my brother a reduced sentence.

Helga went back to the prosecution and the deal was made. Guarantees were given, a statement of facts was written. Then we fronted up to court for our official sentencing. On 18 October 1989 we were sentenced by Judge House in the County Court of Victoria. As I dressed for that day, combed my hair and straightened my tie, I stared myself down in the mirror and decided I was ready. I was okay with doing five years with my brother, if it meant giving him his life back.

When the judge started giving his remarks, it became clear to me that the future I'd seen in the mirror that morning wasn't going to happen. He gave a speech about the heroin trade, describing it as an evil and vicious business that was destroying society. 'This disease represents a frightening degree of saturation of the Australian community with drugs,' he said. 'If it is not stopped, it will eventually destroy our community and our culture.'

That was around the time the penny dropped for me. Elie and I weren't getting the sweetheart deal we'd been promised. The judge was going to nail us with the maximum sentence.

We each got eighteen years, with sixteen on the bottom. That meant at least ten years behind bars. The next time Elie or I would taste freedom, we would be in our mid-thirties.

★

It turns out that I wasn't invincible. I learned a tough, valuable lesson that day. It didn't matter if I was the hardest guy in the room, the most dauntless gangster in the world: there would always be someone out there who was scheming harder and would find a way to stab me in the back.

In hindsight – you get a lot of time to think in prison – I believe that Helga was working with the police, because she knew they couldn't convict me, and although she was employed to defend me, she wanted me off the street. I had my suspicions Helga rationalised that putting me away would be better for the community. I had a lot of time to reflect over those years – a decade and change in jail – and now have a fuller understanding of the consequences of my damaging actions back then.

I'm not the kind of person who carries around a lot of regrets. But I regret the heroin. It's not even that I regret the ten years I spent in jail cells after I was pinched. I regret the damage that the heroin I moved would have done to the community. At the age of twenty-two, I didn't appreciate the consequences of my actions, nor the devastation the drug could have on users and the ripple-effect on their families. After all, I'd never met a heroin addict, I'd never used myself and didn't understand the hold it could have over people. I didn't understand the fallout effects of my trade, the scale of the financial and emotional burden of addiction.

Ignorance is no excuse, but I was ignorant. If I'd been better educated, if I understood the consequences of what I was doing, I would have thought a lot more about it. Education is the only solution. I believe that we're still not properly educating young people to understand the risks of using drugs.

But such clarity came with hindsight. That day, as the screws escorted me out of the dock, I passed my sobbing, devastated mum. Elie and I stopped to talk to her, as always, and exchanged some words of comfort about an appeal, then suddenly I was in the meat wagon with the sound of incarceration ringing in my ears: the door slamming shut, the locks clicking into place, the engine starting up to take me back to prison for a long, long, long time.

But that's life. You just keep punching. You can't stop thinking about it for too long otherwise you'd go fucking mad. There's always another obstacle coming around the corner, so you're better off getting ready for that one than stressing about what's already gone wrong. Because for the next little while, my new home would be HM Prison Pentridge, one of the harshest and most brutal jails in Australia. And trust me, jail's a place where a lot can go wrong.

5

WAR

THE WORST PART IMMEDIATELY after sentencing was that they took away our civilian clothes, unlike on remand where you wear your own. Once sentenced, the convicted must wear the prison greens. They symbolise the loss of freedom, as they take away your individuality.

Putting on the prison greens, I looked in the mirror and thought, *I'm one of them now, just another prisoner.* That pissed me off. It took away any semblance of hope that Elie and I would be free any time soon; we were being submerged into the system. The reality of doing jail set in. However, we were determined to take it like any other challenge and make the best of it.

The days were structured, which I enjoyed after two years of wasting time on remand. It meant I could actually use my days productively. As productive as you can be in a cage, that is. We were locked away for quiet time from 4 pm to 7 am. I would be up, dressed and ready to run to the gym as soon as the door opened. I'd hit the gym, train, focus, and watch everything and be ready for anything. Because *anything* could happen inside. I was constantly in war mode. In my mind, everything was a weapon, and everyone was a potential enemy.

Our first day in real prison was very different from our experiences in remand. Everyone had a different attitude; all hope of escaping conviction was lost. Unlike the remand prisoners, these guys had no bounce. Miserable cunts surviving one day at a time. All of the men I met through my two years in remand had been mentally beaten into submission, until they were robots doing what they needed to get through the days. This was a different ecosystem. Here, villains didn't survive so much as thrive. Here there were gangs, serious people who enjoyed the power of intimidation. Intimidation in prison is earned, not given. Everyone was tooled up and most willing to plunge a shiv deep into your heart.

The weaker prisoners paid up for protection; some paid cash, some sucked dicks. The long-term psychopaths usually kept a couple of the younger pretty boys around for sexual pleasure. Not condoned by most, but discretion earned a pass.

Rape was not acceptable in prison. That's not to say it didn't happen. Now and then you would hear the cries for help of a prisoner being raped or made to suck dick against his will. Not much you can do about it when everyone is locked up at night. Screws didn't get involved. When a man was raped at night it usually sorted itself out the next day if the victim had survived.

There was one ruthless rapist who preyed on the weak. One of the victims was at the end of his sentence – only had a day to go and wanted revenge – so we tooled him up with a shiv and a vest, and in he ran on the cunt who'd raped him. He stabbed his rapist twenty-eight times while we kept watch at the cell door. As he pushed the door open to exit, the dog rapist was on the floor of the cell in shock, bleeding out, too terrified to move. Beautiful to see.

But it goes to show, you want good people on your team. Jail is cliquey. There are a few crews, as most prisoners team up, and only a handful of people run solo. Elie, who was very friendly and had been the star of the show in H Division after smashing that screw, had plenty of mates. I was more wary but had my trusted offsider, Wally Jeka, an Albanian machine, who I'd met on remand, and we clicked from day one.

Wally kept me level, as now and then I'd forget who I was housed with and treat people the way I would want to be treated. That's okay in civilian life, but not in prison. The difference between life outside versus inside jail is that once you've pissed someone off, you've set inevitable events in motion. There is nowhere to run, nowhere to hide. You are in a fishbowl, and if someone has a problem, you see them every day, just circling each other, eyes open.

When you've made an enemy, they go to a lot of trouble to crush you. I saw prisoners arrive in our unit, be greeted by a crew and given a care bag (with coffee, tea, treats etc.), and be smothered with love while settling-in during the first hours. Then a day or two later, when the new arrival was in his cell making a coffee for his new friends, out came the shivs and

he'd be stabbed to death. The whole time he was a target –
had been from hour one. They just needed him to drop his
guard so they could gain the advantage. Best way to get
someone is from within, and they got in. Keep your friends
close and your enemies with their back to you, not suspecting
a thing until you've got a blade in them.

Mostly I kept my bad head on, constantly had that 'fuck
off' expression on my face, a get-out-of-my-way-before-I-
hurt-you look, and it worked well for me, as generally others
were terrified of me.

Later, towards the end of my sentence, the authorities tried
to house me in other jails, but it didn't work out too well for
them. As soon as word got out that I was to be heading to
another prison, inmates there who I had never met would drop
a note on themselves (basically tell the screws they needed to
be transferred to a new part of the prison) in fear for their
safety, terrified the Malkoun brothers were coming. I really
didn't get it. But then again, I could sort of see their point.
The newspapers ran a PR campaign that ultimately worked
for us. We were on the front page of most papers for a long
time and the shit they wrote made us out to be wealthy and
dangerous.

One Malkoun can be hard for a villain to deal with, but
for the first few years there were three of us. Our brother Joe
got prison despite having nothing to do with mine and Elie's
case. He'd been arrested along with me back when the cops
raided Zuzu's, but they had to let him go. We were all extra-
dited back to Melbourne, where our lawyer told us we had the
opportunity for one bail application. Elie and I told Joe to go

for bail – he had kids and we didn't. He had to get back to his family. No question. So he went for bail and got it.

He was out for two months, and went to the Supreme Court to have his bail conditions changed so he could travel overseas. He was running late, so parked illegally out the front of the court in Collins Street, rushing to make his court appearance. An old man watched him park and scolded him for parking there.

'Fuck off,' Joe told the old man as he hurried to his hearing. 'Mind your own fucking business.'

Of course, it turned out this guy's business was Joe's business too. The old man he'd told to fuck off was the judge who was to hear his case. Neither could believe their luck. The judge took great pleasure in revoking Joe's bail on the spot and sent him to jail.

While he was in there, the police put together a case on him, based on some bullshit evidence dreamed up by one of their informers who said they saw him with a suspicious paper bag that held heroin. Did they ever see inside the bag? No. Did the police have any evidence beyond a fucking fairytale? Again, no. But that was enough for the cops to get Joe three years. The worst luck in the world, Joe had, but at least he was an excellent fighter, and the three of us made up a formidable force. Something we would need plenty of.

Pentridge was hectic. A very, very dangerous place. From the outside, it looked quite nice, a bit like a medieval fortress. High bluestone walls and watchtowers loomed over everything.

The sort of building you would see a horror movie shot in. And fair enough, as lots of people have died there over the years.

People got beaten, burned, maimed and killed. There were multiple divisions to house different sorts of prisoners, 3000 in total, all in a walled community: short-time stays, high-risk prisoners, irredeemable psychos, high-risk inmates like informers and paedophiles, all served by a single hospital on the prison grounds and its very own ambulance.

The hospital was used every single day, and weekends were hectic. As soon as one patient was picked up from being bashed or stabbed, another was shivved. You'd hear the ambulance going into the hospital and then turning back around straight away to pick up another inmate.

Have you heard the saying, 'The way to survive prison is to go up to the biggest guy you see and smack him in the face'? That's bad advice, bro. Size isn't the deciding factor. It's how fucking crazy you are. Even the smaller skinny people could be really dangerous; anyone with a knife and a pair of balls could do the job.

Try and imagine what it's like in a closed society where violence is the standard currency. If you're reading this, chances are you're in civilian society right now. Somewhere in your city or town, there are more than likely some very, very dangerous people living among you. But the likelihood of you crossing paths with them is quite small.

However, put those people in an incubator – a place such as Pentridge where a huge percentage of the population are fucking psychopaths and the remainder are shitting themselves in fear because they are potential victims used to normality – and suddenly they're isolated with the worst of the worst. Shit is going to happen.

Stabbings and murders happened a lot, over money, over insults, over a packet of cigarettes. Sometimes over nothing at all. For example, one time two prisoners from J Division – supposedly the kindergarten wing; the place for young offenders and old-timers with good behaviour – stole shit from another guy's cell. Nothing of real value, just some smokes and a few magazines from the prison commissary. But the two thieves grew worried they'd been seen, so they decided that to kill the guy they'd robbed would be a better option than being labelled petty thieves, which was a big no-no in jail.

Idiotically, they made disguises. No joke, they put pillow-cases over their heads with holes cut out for the eyes, like a kid dressing up as a ghost for Halloween, and ran through J Division with their blades out.

Because they couldn't see properly through the pillowcases, they were running into walls and falling over, not so discreet, until they finally reached their victim's cell. They grabbed him, pinned him down, pulled his head back by his hair and started to saw his head off with a blunt jail-made shiv. They did a horrible job, managed to cut him deep from ear to ear and left a thick, jagged scar. The guy was terrified, froze, and had no idea what was going on but survived; the would-be killers attracted too much attention getting to and from the victim to properly finish the job.

The kicker is that they were surprised they were caught. They really thought they'd come up with the plan for the perfect murder. What were they thinking? It would be hilarious if it wasn't so crazy.

Another pair were always giggling and laughing, having a great time while banged up. They were doing a big whack for killing a homeless guy. These two were fucking weird; they had long arms with big hands, knuckles almost dragging on the floor. They honestly looked more like apes than humans – big protruding foreheads and all. I would have believed you if you'd told me they were the missing link in human evolution. Perhaps they should have been in a lab being studied, instead of in jail.

Over several months they had befriended and developed trust with a female prison officer, and one day they lured her to their cell. They dragged her in, beat and repeatedly raped her for twenty minutes. When she was discovered by her colleagues, she was battered, bleeding and unconscious, her clothes ripped off. It didn't end well for the two crims.

Point is, you can't trust people in that environment. Too many were two-faced and couldn't be treated with the basic rules of humanity. They would pretend – put on a human face and lure you into a false sense of security – then fuck you over. Or kill you. Or both. Not necessarily in that order.

Pentridge is famous for the legendary criminals who have done time there: Ned Kelly, Chopper Read (a good bloke, by the way; very funny, though fucking crazy) – the list goes on. But they weren't the only hectic ones. Most of my compatriots were capable of very serious violence. More than capable. They were ready, and willing. How likely you were to be a victim of that violence depended on what kind of person you were when you walked in on day one, your mindset, or who you turned into as you served your sentence.

The danger wasn't just from the other prisoners, or the screws' brutality, but also from the mental risk of becoming institutionalised. The penal system is designed to break your spirit and make you docile and easily manageable. If you don't have a strong sense of yourself, the screws will break you down in no time, and then you have to rebuild yourself however you can. Some people would walk into jail and not even make it through eighteen months. They would become dependent on the system, and when they got out, they couldn't survive in the community for long. They couldn't cope without the prison feeding them and making all decisions for them. Besides the gangs and the screws, there were hierarchies in prison that were ready and waiting to take advantage of the weak-minded.

If you could handle yourself, if you could stand your ground, you would be okay. However, if you were vulnerable, you had a problem. If you were a drug addict, or you owed money, or you had a big mouth – but not the muscle to back it up – you wouldn't last long. If you showed any sign of weakness, the predators would never leave you alone.

I went into prison with a bit of an advantage. Perception was everything. As much as I hated the media coverage of our trial, it actually worked in my and Elie's favour. We already had this outsized reputation as kickboxers, street fighters, heroin dealers, and multimillionaires with fast boats and the full penthouse lifestyle. Having snipers on the roof and bashing a screw in court added to that reputation. The papers painted an aggressive picture in trying to sell a certain image of us – and we reaped the dividends for years.

Everyone in jail was wary of us before we'd even met them. We didn't even have to bridge up that much. For the first two years, before and during the trial, the newspapers wouldn't stop talking about how we were the hardest, scariest, most ruthless fucking terrorists/gangsters. It was like we'd been given championship belts without ever stepping into the ring. Consequently, we had the respect of the maddest killers in the country, some of whom had the capacity to do very nasty things.

We really didn't deserve it. Nobody is *that* hardcore. The media rolled out the red carpet for us. The Malkoun brothers were prison royalty before we ever walked in the door. But reputation alone doesn't keep you alive. You have to keep your wits about you.

Owing to the way I grew up, I could spot potential issues and resolve them before they became bigger problems. I met a pro surfer once who could stand on any beach in the world and read the waves as easily as if it were a newspaper. While anyone else standing on that beach only saw what was happening on the surface, this guy could see the secret depths, the rip-tides, the reefs and dangers invisible to normal eyes. That's what prison was like for me. I could read the play. If something was about to pop off, I would read the room, anticipate an attack, and take the necessary actions to protect myself.

I knew the crews and their pattern of behaviour. The only daily concern was from the junkies; the sober killers were busy getting on with their sentences, but the junkies had a daily battle to score and that usually meant standing over someone. To stand over them you must be feared, and to be feared you must be unpredictable. You have to hurt people, a lot. There are signs to look out for. If there is less joking around than usual and more of a serious vibe, shit's about to go down. If one hand is concealed, you can be sure it has a shiv in it. If someone who's normally a bit hostile starts chatting to you, real friendly, but you can't see both their hands, you're about to get stabbed. Any time anyone had one hand covered, you'd know they had a tool. At that point, it was just a matter of who could get to their shiv faster.

There were weapons everywhere in Pentridge. If you didn't arm yourself, you were asking to be put in the prison hospital. The classic prison weapon is the makeshift knife affectionately known as a shiv. Simple, elegant, efficient. It's crazy to think back at how easy it was to secure weaponry.

Elie had it sorted. He would get the boys in the metal shop to cut out a 12-inch piece of steel and sharpen it like a samurai sword, heavy and lethal. Did the job. I had probably a dozen shivs hidden all around the division. Elie had so many shivs made for himself we had to bury them in the garden. We'd give a few to the boys in our crew, as it's always handy to make sure your offsiders are armed.

I hid mine in the kitchen, in the mess hall, the garden and the gym. Anywhere that I spent time, I made sure there was one tucked away within reaching distance. I also had a beautiful cutthroat razor that was gifted to me, which I kept in my cell hidden in a cardboard box filled with books. Weapons weren't hard to hang on to despite frequent raids of our cells because the screws weren't exactly winning Nobel prizes for their inquiring minds. This is how dumb the screws were. My cell was raided and searched all the time, so I'd sticky-tape the blade to the top of my book box, then fold the lid inside, covering the shiv, and fill the box with books. They never even thought to check the inside of the lid.

I kept my favourite shiv on me all the time. It was a thin skewer about 25 centimetres long, tape handle at one end and sharp as fuck. It slid perfectly into the side pocket of my overalls and was always accessible.

I was going through the wings to get to the kitchen on one of the days when they stopped to search me – highly unusual, but it happened. They knew I was tooled up and asked for any weapons before I got undressed, so I pulled out my shiv and placed it on the desk. To my surprise they only confiscated the weapon and let me go. Again, unusual.

Two days later I was called up to the chief's office to be told to pack my shit as I was going to the slot (that is, banished to the solitary confinement punishment unit) pending charges of carrying a concealed weapon. No problem, part and parcel.

I let my brother know and true to form he and Keith – our psycho friend – marched into the chief's office and put it on him to also send them to the slot. We were well into a tit-for-tat war with another crew and this was an opportunity to catch up with some old enemies hiding in the slot.

The chief refused. 'You two are not under investigation,' he told Elie.

'I'll jump your fucking desk and create an investigation,' Elie replied. Next thing, I heard my name called over the speakers: 'Malkoun to the chief's office.'

He told me to think myself lucky, that I was no longer going to the slot. The screws fucking buckled, wary of the idea of two Malkouns carving up the dogs in the slot. Or maybe they just couldn't be fucked dealing with Elie. He could cause carnage when he needed to.

If an inmate wanted to cause someone pain in Pentridge, they'd dowse him with wood glue – easily accessible from the woodwork shop – then set him on fire with a cigarette lighter. It happened a few times and was fucking horrific.

Still, the most common injuries were caused by shivs, with throats cut or general stabbings. Prisoners would often try to square up over the weekends when all of the prisoners were available and accessible, and security was more relaxed. There were only ever two guards on weekends, and they always stayed in their box, terrified to wander around the wing.

There were a lot of ways to kill someone inside. The sheer inventiveness of prisoners who were trying to kill each other was like nothing else on Earth. If you could find a way to channel the collected efforts of the psychopaths of Pentridge in a positive direction, you'd have world peace and a cure for the common cold by the end of the week. It was unbelievable the way people could manoeuvre and get things done. Even someone who's under 24/7 surveillance or in the slot, he can still give orders.

All you have to do is get on a personal call with the wife and offhandedly pass on some gossip. Inside that gossip, there'd be an order, which would be passed on to the relevant parties, then distributed back into another wing of the prison by another of the wives or girlfriends.

With any developments in the underworld, the prisoners got wind of them long before the media. By the time a gangland hit was reported in the papers, the factions inside prison were already making their moves. For example, my team needed to take care of this dog who needed to be got. He had to go. He was hiding in H Division, under 23-hour lock-up. Never not under guard. Bit of a challenge, but doable.

I made a plan to get this cunt, and our friend Chopper agreed to help out. He was the H Division billet, which meant he delivered the food to the cells, including a ration of milk. Our plan was to use a needle to inject poison into a carton of milk, mark it, and send it up to H Division for Chopper to hand-deliver breakfast in bed with a side of organ failure to the target. Easy.

The H Division yard and the D Division yard were separated by a chain mesh fence and we would often catch up for chats with Chopper and others through the fence. Chopper was down; he just needed some financial incentive. Our contact had the poison sorted, or at least he said he did.

I organised for the brother of a mate, a dentist on the outside, to get me a vial of poison, which was collected by another inmate's girlfriend. It was wrapped in condoms and she smuggled the vial in and gave it to our guy on a contact visit – 'booted' it, straight up his rectum. Got it back to the division and passed it to me. That was the easy part.

Getting it to Chopper was going to be a bit harder, but doable. We had the kitchen billet good to go, just had to get the poison and needle to him. We decided to test it first so a splash was poured into the milk of a couple of suspected rapists for them to drink it with their coffee. They always huddled in the same cell and drank coffee at the end of the day. So we spiked their jug and the milk, and watched and waited for the ambulance. Nothing happened; the poison was a dud. Not even a sore tummy.

The cunt who was supposed to source the poison had given us a fake product. A lot of effort went into that plan. A lot of people took a risk in order to bring it into Pentridge. It would have worked a treat if we'd received the right poison. In the end, we ran out of time – the target finished his sentence, was released and was never seen again. I heard years later that he'd ended up at the bottom of an abandoned goldmine shaft. His loss. My method probably would have been more humane.

Prison is a closed world, a brutal ecosystem that you can't fully comprehend from the outside-in. But the outside world can reach in. A lot of the violence that happens inside is ordered by someone pulling the strings in the outside world. Maybe you're a rat who turned police informant against your associates to get your sentence reduced. Maybe you've bashed someone inside the prison who has influential friends on the outside. Whatever it is you might have done that would inspire someone to have you knocked, there's a well-established infra-structure of murderers within the prison who were available for outside-in hits.

Some of them would do it for money, or to ensure their families back in society were looked after during their incarceration. Others would be rewarded by prison officers with special rewards – drugs or alcohol. Drugs usually got the job done.

You'd be amazed what you can smuggle into a jail. In Pentridge in the late 80s there was talk of a team in B Division who had a gun. Just a small piece, probably a .22. But it goes to show. Getting contraband into Pentridge wasn't even a challenge. I had electric fry pans, cosmetics, clothes and other essentials smuggled in by guards.

These days it's much harder – prisons have high-tech security cameras with motion-detection that spot and zoom in on anything that moves. Back then it was a piece of cake.

Friends in the free world would stuff tennis balls with whatever contraband you wanted and then position themselves at a precise section of the wall out of view from the watchtowers. They'd then use a tennis racquet to smash the balls way over the wall, hard enough to clear both the iconic bluestone perimeter wall and then a second chain mesh fence topped with barbed wire that stood 10 metres inside.

It would then be up to the individual to grab the ball before anyone else did. Usually this was done only at night. Now and then, a brave or single-minded soul would have a crack on the weekend or during the day, desperate to score their drugs.

Clearly there were other ways of getting shit in. Some guys would 'boot' their drugs on a visit. This was the most common way of scoring. Visitors would pass the drugs heavily wrapped in condoms to the prisoner on a contact visit, and the prisoner would boot them straight into their bottom.

Now and then a prisoner would be caught with a bit of evidence sticking out of his arse during the stripsearch on his way back in. The guards for the most part didn't give too much of a fuck – you'd have to be really unlucky to be discovered with a bag up your backside.

I used to wonder about the laissez-faire attitude the screws had to all the drugs coming into their prison. I guess they were of the view that the more disruption and violence they had to oversee, the more funding the prison would receive. Drugs were always available to whoever could afford them. I did my first line of coke in prison. My offsider got some ripper coke in, so we had a crack, and I have to say it was euphoric. The feeling that it gave me was amazing. The high was so intense I followed it with a Rohypnol at 10 pm to help me sleep. Rohypnol – otherwise known as Rambos – is a killer drug. Literally a drug to kill. If you want someone stabbed to death in prison and you want to outsource the job, you give a couple of willing junkies a few Rohypnol pills each, wind them up and send them off. They become numbed-out killing machines. The job gets done, they get paid, and more often than not the guards don't give much of a shit about one less prisoner to look after.

There are a lot of ways to wind up murdered in prison, and it's not that hard to make it look like a suicide. When someone who'd been making trouble for the screws was found hanging from the roof in their cell after lights-out or seemingly the victim of an overdose, it was most likely a paid hit, or payback at the hands of the screws.

If they hated you, or you were too much of a handful, they would set you up to get bowled. It was easy for the guards to manipulate some prisoners into thinking another one was no good and should be dealt with. Some prisoners would kill specific prisoners for guards to get favours. That wasn't something that Elie and I worried about. The screws hated us, and they could give us a hard time, but they couldn't have us knocked. We were too high profile, and too well connected on the outside.

That power, or that perception of power, gave us a bit of leeway. We were incarcerated, sure, but we demanded certain freedoms. As time went by, we accumulated every possible luxury we could buy or have smuggled in. We were able to buy and wear our own designer clothes and throw out the prison greens. TVs and DVD players. I had a microwave in my cell, electric pans and food supplies that meant Elie and I could make our own meals and not eat the garbage they served in the mess hall.

My brother has a special talent for rorting and he had it all worked out. We acquired our supplies from the kitchen on Saturdays, as he had a thing going on with the head cook who would send boxes of food via the gardener on the tractor. Whatever the kitchen had would be delivered to our units, and our cells were filled with every non-perishable food we could want.

One summer when it was so fucking hot you could barely breathe, Elie decided that we needed our own fridge. At the time we were sharing one refrigerator with 200 other prisoners all trying to freeze a bottle of water to use during the evening.

The screws weren't being accommodating to our perfectly reasonable request for a fridge, so under the cover of daylight,

Elie just marched into the prison guards' break room, picked up their fridge, and brought it back to our wing. He then fixed a lock to the freezer door to keep everyone else out. After that, we had cold drinks day and night. Elie also took their microwave and kept it in his cell for evening cook-ups. They weren't game to get it back from us and had learned quite quickly to not fuck around with him. From then on they preferred to eat their lunch cold than try to get back their microwave oven. The screws were petrified of Elie, and they were right to be.

I can't explain it – he is such a nice bloke. Too nice, too nurturing, to the point where I actually think he has too much oestrogen in his system. But when anyone tries to harm his family, he flies into a rage that's clearly going to take more than a couple of screws to handle.

The screws were shrewd. They knew how far to push a particular prisoner. And with Elie it wasn't far at all, so for the most part they avoided him, let him get away with his rorts.

In prison, he was the same overprotective brother he'd always been. Once when he was in the slot on remand in Pentridge for playing up, I would go to the medication distribution section twice a day so I could walk past his cell and see him. They had him close to the 'circle', what we called the junction where different sections meet. I stopped and opened his trapdoor and began a chat – just to see what he needed and to pass on messages to and from family and his girl. The screws didn't like that, and yelled out, 'Malkoun, keep walking.'

Naturally I ignored them, and naturally, they kept yelling and eventually cracked it. At the end of our quick few minutes' chat, they put me in the slot opposite him. He saw this, and the protective big brother part of him kicked into gear and off he went telling the screws, 'I'll kill you cunts!'

He had a wooden stool in his cell which he used as a battering ram and proceeded to try to knock down his door to get at the screws. Man, I was beside myself.

Fuck, I thought. *What if he actually gets out?*

The banging was heard hundreds of metres away by the governor. He came running down to the circle. I could hear him yelling for an update: 'What the fuck is going on with Elie Malkoun?'

They explained why he was rampaging.

'Put his brother in the slot for disobeying an order.'

They reiterated why he was rampaging.

'Well, let him out of the slot,' he told them. 'And let him see his brother.'

So I wandered back down to the circle and Elie's cell, and opened the trapdoor so we could finish our chat: 'You all good, brother?'

'Yeah,' Elie said. 'They let you out?'

'Yeah. Weak cunts buckled.'

'Good,' Elie said, calming down. 'Fuck those dogs. Slotting my little brother.'

They feared us because we were always hard and serious, plus they perceived us to be wealthy. Money is power. And fortunately, people cared about us and loved us. So, we had a lot of contact with the outside world. We had family visiting us every week, lawyers coming in to help us with our appeals, associates and others to help manage and sell our assets from our old lives. We visibly weren't isolated and alone. If the screws did anything to us, they knew there would be consequences.

What's more, there were two of us, and we were both fully capable of escalating any given situation. The screws knew that if we died there would be an inquiry, and that our family would find ways to retaliate, through the legal system and otherwise. Not everyone inside had that luxury. Most of the prisoners who got knocked in jail had nobody looking out for them. No-one to care about them.

This kid, just a skinny thing, was in the cell next to mine. He was locked up for rape, but he was adamant he didn't do it. From day one, all he would talk about was his innocence, how he'd been railroaded by the prosecutor and falsely imprisoned by the judge. He was obsessed. Every week he made $40 working his prison job, and he spent every penny on stamps – writing to anyone who would listen to his story.

Whenever the media picked up his story, he'd get bashed by the other prisoners. Because in prison, there's a hierarchy, and rapists are the lowest of the low. But every time he got ridiculed on TV and bashed by the other inmates, it only made the kid more desperate and obsessed with proving his innocence. Which only made the media go harder on him. One thing led to another, and I guess at some point he pissed the wrong, powerful person off.

So the letter-writing campaign didn't work out well for the kid, as he ended up getting bowled. A heavy team of five killers ran in on him and carved him up. Apparently the order came from the establishment.

It was a Sunday. Church day. We would go to church for prayer but also to meet up with other prisoners from the other divisions, an hour to catch up to discuss and execute shit. This was not for the mainstream, for those who wanted to hang with their mates. It was only for the alpha men who had influence and power in the prison. I caught up with my allies on Sundays. If I had people coming into the system in the parts of the prison they controlled, I would get my allies to look after them or help them find their feet, and vice versa. Church provided sanctuary. A place for us prisoners to attend to our physical operations, as well as our spiritual needs.

On one particular Sunday, Sister Barbara asked Elie and me to stay back for a catch-up. If she hadn't, I would have walked into the kid's ambush and no doubt got involved, which could have ended badly for me. I believe it was God again protecting me. Elsewhere in the prison that morning, five crazed psychopaths off their heads grabbed their weapons and went into a killing frenzy.

When I returned to my cell block there was an eerie silence in the dorm. It was never silent on a Saturday or Sunday, and things seemed strange in the unit. I saw the blood flowing from outside his cell as I was walking to mine. I pushed his door open and saw the skinny alleged rapist lying under his bed with a towel wrapped around his head. Blood everywhere, but he looked to me like he was still alive. Prison guards were hiding in their boxes, and everyone was pretending nothing had happened.

I went to get help, alerted the guards to call for the ambulance – not the sort of thing you do in prison, but I did it anyway. The ambulance took its time getting there. The kid had no chance of survival. His throat was cut – he was almost decapitated – but to make sure the job was done, he'd been stabbed in the head and body more than seventy times. They made a mess of him. You don't stab someone that many times unless you're sending a clear message, I don't care how fucking crazy you are.

This kid was hit by a crack team of junkie killers, the worst type. These people have no boundaries. If you get in their sights, you are fucked. It's kill or be killed. They were all seasoned killers and at least two of them were feared by all who crossed them.

Elie and I managed for a long time to navigate around these types. Surprisingly it wasn't hard to do. I crossed the path of one killer daily for seven years without acknowledging him, then one day we met, and he turned out to be a champion bloke, also doing a brick. Point is: even though we were in the same prison, it didn't mean we were up in each other's faces. Live and let live. Until there's no other option.

Elie and I came to prison in a position of strength and saw it as our responsibility to look after the weak. We took a lot of prisoners under our wing, especially the new ones. We wouldn't let them be bullied or stood over or raped.

It meant that at times I could be a little aggressive. Sometimes very fucking aggressive. I'm sure a lot of people wanted to try it on with me, but everyone knew it would be a battle. I never let my guard down, not for a second. If you are going to try and get me, you have to run in and catch me when I'm not looking. Not to say that there weren't people who wanted to kill me – there really were. But for the most part, I was too hard to touch.

The closest they came to getting me was after I stuck my nose into their business over a kid they were standing over. Two very serious killers – an older guy who was weary with experience, and a kid who made up for his youth with pure crazy – called out to me, 'Hey, Jay, can we have a word?'

I could see another three of the crew huddled together, fidgety and nervous, and clocked that they were trying to position me.

I walked back over into the open area, where I'd have room to move, and kept my eyes open for signs of when to kick it off. I reached down into the side pocket of my overalls where I had tucked in my skewer shiv, pulled it out and held it menacingly by my side.

I clocked that the younger one had a hand under his jumper, hiding a blade, I suspected. The older one must have been the 'grab guy'. Standard procedure – one guy grabs and the other stabs. I decided the young one would have to go first, as the rest were nothing without him. Instantly, the old instincts turned on, and I was doing the maths on how to survive the situation.

I could see they were confident; we had a bit of a chat over an issue, and I was about to kick it off, but at that minute my offsider Wally appeared. Wally had a mad reputation. He was a born recidivist and constantly in and out of jail. The sort of guy who was more than willing to add a few years to his sentence if it meant winning the fight.

'Everything alright here, boys?' he called out all cheerful. 'You sweet, Jay?'

Suddenly the hidden hand appeared and the psychos were all conversation: 'Yeah, all good. We've just heard a bit of talk that you've got a problem with us.'

'No problem here, bro,' I said. 'You do your jail, I'll do mine.' Then Elie appeared, and all at once there were a lot of men in the yard, curious and supportive, some with them, some with us. The upside was that I recognised a couple of good blokes who usually sat on the fence but in this instance were leaning towards the junkie team.

'Yeah, yeah. Sweet, bro,' came the reply. And that was it. That was the closest someone got to bridging up and taking a crack at me.

It was on, there was no point waiting around to get ambushed, and the next morning as soon as the doors opened the younger of the two got iron barred across the head as he walked out of his cell. The bar was passed to another inmate, who quickly took it to the laundry, gave it a quick wash then hid it behind the washing machine. The kid who did the job got cleaned up and was all good for the morning muster.

The young killer ended up in hospital for the rest of his sentence. He was released, but after two weeks of freedom he was dead, shot in the head.

The team that rolled with the late kid went to water; they bailed that day for good. They dropped notes on themselves – applied to the prison authorities for asylum to be transferred to other jails on the grounds that they were not safe in the same prison as me and Elie.

Unfortunately, others from their crew took a bite out of my brother. They got him one day in the kitchen. He was reading the paper with his back to the door, which is fucking stupid. Two of them, men with shivs, snuck right up on him, jumped on his back and went for his throat, but only managed a deep cut all up his chin and along the side of his face. He was lucky, but it was a dumb mistake to make.

In my whole time in prison, I never sat with my back to the door. Elie wasn't always on the ball the way prison needed you to be. But he had big balls, and when they stabbed him, he got straight back up and attacked his assailants and made a mess of them with a rolling pin.

He was taken to St Vincent's for surgery where the doctors wanted to keep him for a few days, but true to form Elie was back on the muster before 3 pm. No way he was going to stay in hospital and leave his little brother alone to fight the crazies. That's how we were brought up, to love and respect each other first and before even yourself.

Naturally, we had to respond to the attack, and it was on for years and years. We were moved down to Barwon Prison, but that tit-for-tat stuff just drags on and on wherever you go. Because of the little war happening in Pentridge, I already had enemies waiting for me in Barwon, so I had to be ready.

I worked out how to travel with my shiv – shaped like a skewer, long and thin – my favourite, a really handy weapon. I had a foam vegetable box from the kitchen that was used to transport chilled broccoli. I pushed my shiv up the corner of the box then pressed some of the foam to cover the thin hole, then filled the box with my books. When I went through security I put the box on the table, walked through the metal detector then reached around and picked up my box of books and continued through the checkpoint. I did that at both ends, leaving Pentridge and entering Barwon, so I arrived at my new cell to unpack, already tooled up.

I'd barely left when I realised I had to get back to Pentridge briefly to settle a score. I got word that a bloke from the gang that had stabbed Elie was back in the system, so I had to figure out an excuse to return.

Pentridge had an X-ray machine in their hospital, so I faked a back injury. I convinced the doctors to send me back to Pentridge for medical attention. It was empowering to navigate through the system. I arrived on the Thursday, had to keep quiet until Saturday and get access to this cunt before he was any the wiser.

I couldn't believe my luck when, as I entered his unit first thing Saturday morning, I spotted him walking into a cell. I quickly went to grab an old shiv of mine I'd left with another long timer – he had shivs pushed up the legs of his bed. Hidden so well he'd kept them for years. Problem was, he'd hidden them so well they were stuck in the bedposts.

We went to town trying to get them out, but they wouldn't budge. I looked around for a coat hanger to pry out at least one shiv but it wasn't happening. Fuck it, I couldn't risk losing this opportunity, so I ran in on my cunt and his two mates empty-handed.

They froze, didn't get involved as I kicked and punched the shit out of him. I hit him on the chin hard but didn't knock him out. It must have been his adrenaline keeping him awake. I turned to the other two and warned them to keep it dark.

Even though this dog wasn't one of the ones who'd stabbed my brother, he was however part of that crew and was loud about it, bragging how his team stabbed one of the Malkouns. I figured if the fucker wanted the credit for the job, he could get royalties as well.

That war might have gone on indefinitely, but it ended up dying a natural death. The fighters on each side either checked in their chips or were transferred to other prisons out of the war zone. Most of the crew who did my brother are dead now: one was shot in the head, another died in jail, and the rest overdosed on drugs.

I looked after myself, my family and my friends, and concentrated on survival and making the best of the situation. Because that time wasn't all misery and bloodshed. Prison is an incubator for crooks and psychopaths, sure, but you also meet people from all walks of life, and a couple of them really changed the whole way I saw the world.

6

PEACE

ONE OF MY BEST friends and the person I respected most in prison was Greg 'Doc' Roberts, who was doing time for being Australia's most polite and intellectual bank robber as well as for escaping prison previously. After prison, he would go on to become one of the biggest authors in the world with his block-buster novels *Shantaram* and *The Mountain Shadow*.

Doc is a legend. He escaped from Pentridge and was on the run for ten years. People escaped from time to time, but normally they were caught two miles down the road. He commanded a lot of respect. A solid bloke. Extremely intelligent – street smart but book smart as well, which you don't always get at the same time. Loyal as fuck, he would take on the world for you if he loved you.

He used to follow me around tooled up just in case I needed backup. He never mentioned it, just took it as given, because we were mates. He was a deep thinker, spiritual, a man who'd made peace with what he'd done. I mean, if you pushed him, he would kill you. He wouldn't feel good about it, but he'd do it, for sure. That was Pentridge. You had to have a different head on your shoulders, or someone would take it off.

Doc was just a great bloke. Everyone loved him. Prisoners, guards, everyone. Years later he was the best man at my wedding, gave the speech. Nailed it.

He was religious by the time I met him. He'd had an experience when he was living in India as a drug addict. He'd been living the life you read about in *Shantaram*, doing heroin and playing up, and one day he felt a weight push him onto the ground and a voice in his mind told him to correct the course of his life.

That's exactly what Doc did. He read all of the religious books he could get his hands on: the Bible, the Koran, the Torah and the Talmud, as well as many other books on religion and philosophy. He told me about bookshops left over from the British so filled with books that in places you could only crawl through the gaps to discover the most amazing writing. That was a turning point for Doc; he cleaned himself up and dedicated himself to helping less fortunate people in the slums of India. Knowing little more than basic first aid, he educated himself and became the slum doctor who treated the locals with whatever medicines he could get his hands on.

When I met him in Pentridge he was in the yard with an academic white man called John. I bailed them up, and in the course of the conversation I found out John had converted to Islam after being locked up. Me being the ignorant, uneducated kid that I was, I said, 'Please explain why this Aussie Anglo-Saxon has converted to Islam . . . What the fuck is all that about? You can't switch teams halfway through the match!'

The two white guys looked at each other, and Doc said, 'I'll let John explain this.'

'Well, Jay, let me tell you,' began John. 'I've studied lots of religions and philosophies. And if there's a God – and I'm not saying there is or there isn't – but if there is, then I believe Islam, and the way it's practised, is the closest point of contact.'

I thought that was interesting. He had a valid and educated reason for converting; he wasn't pressured by others. That was typical of the sort of conversations that would happen around Doc. In one of the most brutal environments imaginable, he found a way to appreciate the spiritual side of life. Because Doc is fundamentally a good person.

Somehow, somewhere, something had hit a switch on him that turned off the hectic, chaotic part of his personality and made him dedicate his life to peace.

He was already this man when he'd been arrested in Germany after years on the run in India and was deported back to Australia to serve the last five years of his ten-year sentence. He was a good influence on me as we did the last five years of our jail together. Whenever there was a problem that seemed like it needed a blade to solve, he would always find a more civilised way to mediate it. He is one of a kind.

In addition to Doc, I was lucky for my path to cross with a teacher at the prison school who saw something in me and, when she discovered I didn't really know how to read, took me under her wing.

I didn't read my first book until I was incarcerated. The teacher in the prison picked it out for me because she thought I would enjoy it and encouraged me to read. *You Wouldn't Be Dead for Quids* by Robert Barrett is a collection of stories about a bloke who lands a job as a bouncer at a nightclub and gets drawn into the underworld. Let's just say I could relate to some of what I was reading. A good introduction to literature for me. After that, I was addicted. I read a lot of books, from thirty-page paperbacks to *Atlas Shrugged* by Ayn Rand. I wasn't picky, and started to read anything I could get my hands on.

Although plenty of the staff at Pentridge had it in for us prisoners, we were very fortunate that there were people in the system who did their best for us. We'd work in the morning in the industrial prison shops, me in the printing factory and Elie in the metal factory, and then do half a day in school Monday–Friday. The teacher saw something else in us beyond our convictions, and I became her little mission. In the evenings when I read before lights-out, whenever I came across a word I didn't know the meaning of, I'd write it down, and in school the next day she'd explain it to me. As I read more and more, my vocabulary improved. I learned a lot from that teacher over the two years I was with her, and I reckon she made more of a difference in my life than pretty much anyone I'd met to that point. I literally could not read before I met her. Afterwards, I couldn't stop. She would often pass me books she thought I would like, encouraging me to read and to do short courses.

She was an angel, frankly – very kind to me and the other prisoners, much kinder than she had to be. A genuinely good person. You have to be a good person to work in that environment. It's not the sort of job you just turn up to and work pay cheque to pay cheque – you've got to have some greater ideal motivating you, because working in a maximum-security prison is not glamorous.

That said, screws will always be screws. Most people end up screws because they are fuck-ups and bullies or psychopaths who thrive in the prison environment. For some of the screws at Pentridge, the only difference between them and the prisoners was the side of the cell wall they stood on. Most of them. But not all of them. Some of them were pretty good.

But the odd kind-hearted screw was the exception to the rule. Most of them were temperamentally fuckwitted moral degenerates. They didn't have the balls to beat Elie and me, or have us knocked, but they did fuck with us to make prison life harder.

The system was rigged. Take what happened to my brother Joe. He didn't have anything to do with our crime yet he did three years. After serving his time, he found himself a job for a guy whom he considered a friend. Problem was, the friend was a registered police informant. On the payroll for the police, employed to feed them information on who was playing up and how.

The problem for this guy was that he didn't always have news juicy enough for the cops, so he would just make shit up. Usually about the Malkoun brothers. He was the one to give the police statement claiming that I was masterminding all the drug trafficking – not just in my section, or in Pentridge, but the whole state. Pure fucking fantasy. I was in the slot half the time! How the fuck was I meant to be running a syndicate?

But time and time again, he'd make a statement saying I was supplying all of the prisons across Victoria with drugs; the police would then send that information to the prison and I'd be slotted, then after two weeks called in for an interview with the prison board.

They said, all serious and with commitment, 'We have intelligence that you are supplying all the prisons with drugs.'

I couldn't help but smirk at this panel of six of the prison hierarchy, sitting opposite me with their poker faces.

'Are you seriously suggesting that I, in this incubator, with all of my calls being monitored, all my associations and who I talk to being watched, still have the capacity to supply the drugs without you guys noticing? Clearly you have no internal evidence because there is none, or you guys are just fucking stupid!'

That didn't end well. Back to the slot I went for a few more weeks.

No drama – I liked the slot. Gave me time to read and do some push-ups. I'd be let out for an hour a day, just enough time to shower, wash my clothes and grab a new book.

Unfortunately, this informant kept feeding false information to the authorities; he had to keep getting paid, I guess.

When Elie and I were incarcerated in 1987, the system would structure your sentence into thirds. For a sentence like mine, you'd do a third of your sentence in a 'maximum' security prison, a third in a 'medium' and the final third in a 'minimum' facility.

I don't know how I would have coped without my brother in jail. I probably would have turned out bitter and twisted, with hatred for the world. Having his love around me really did soften the blow. Plus, he kept me well fed and pulled every rort imaginable to make life bearable. We had a lot of laughs and enjoyed pushing the boundaries together. I used to think he was fucking mad. We were at HM Prison Dhurringile for a few months before getting tipped – this is a medium/minimum security prison where they did a headcount every hour throughout the day and night in case of a runner.

Elie had arranged for a bloke called Mohammed, who had just recently been released, to regularly leave some goodies on the fence line: a mobile phone, long johns – shit like that. No drugs or alcohol.

Usually around 1 am after the headcount, Elie would sneak out of his cell and jog the mile to the fence line, grab our goods and jog back. Let me tell you, that hour always felt like two. Elie is ballsy. Sometimes once visiting hours were over on Sunday he would sneak out to meet his girlfriend for a quick thirty minutes. Ballsy, right? Fucking oath, mate, who does that? Breaks out of prison for a quick girlfriend visit then breaks back in? Elie does. That's who.

He used to take the piss. Some days he'd go out in the yard where they had these big hay bales that were stored for the cattle. (This prison had a herd of milking cows that were looked after and milked daily by the prisoners.) Elie would find a sunny spot at the top of one where no-one could see him on the phone. He'd just be up there chatting away, not a care in the world, while the screws were asking me who Elie was talking to. Problem for Elie is he only has 17 per cent of his hearing left so naturally he spoke loud, and you could hear him chatting away, not exactly discreet.

We had small Nokia mobile phones that we managed to take with us to our next prison, Fulham Correctional Centre. I pulled it apart, which was really only removing the back and battery, unscrewed the back of my ghetto-blaster and stuffed it inside. I then packed tissues around the pieces so they couldn't move or rattle. Easy-peasy. I smuggled the phone through both security checks without a hitch.

In the final years at minimum, leaves are designed to integrate you back into the community by giving you short periods of time outside of the prison walls to help prepare you for the real world. Periods of leave start at four hours and scale up to being twenty-four hours long. But in the government jails, Elie and I were refused leaves of any length.

It was up to the governor's discretion whether we were granted leave or not. Which meant it relied on advice from screws. So that wasn't going to go our way.

The theory is that leaves were created in order to rehabilitate you slowly into society. Makes sense, right? If you're doing nine years jail, say, then the last three years, instead of losing your mind in your cell, they begin to give you leaves so you can work towards getting a job that might help set you up for life on the outside. If all goes well, you can walk right out of prison into something resembling a normal life.

Except, fuck me, when Elie and I got to our seventh year, they changed the rules. The new policy meant that long-term and serious offenders were only eligible for leaves during their last twelve months.

No worries. All those hours hanging out with Doc Roberts and his Zen mindset must have rubbed off on me. We just got on with it. We entered our final year and applied for our first leave. They fucking denied it. The cunts might have hated us, but they couldn't break us or control us – all they could do was annoy us. If they couldn't destroy us, they would keep us in their prison with as few rights as possible for as long as possible. Even when it became clear that Pentridge was no longer sustainable – too primitive and barbaric to survive in a modern world – they hung on to us until the bitter end. We were among the last prisoners at Pentridge before it finally closed in 1997.

We did our own jail and relied on no-one. We hated the screws and the screws hated us right back. We received no favours in prison, which was just how we liked it: no grey, just black and white. The flipside was that any opportunity to fuck us over was taken by the screws in whatever government jail we happened to be guests at.

As our final day in custody approached, we were denied leaves again and again, even while we watched convicted murderers and rapists be granted theirs.

Ultimately, we were granted leaves only during our last seven months, and only because we were transferred to a privately run jail. Through this one, I finally managed a couple of four-hour leaves. Those four hours might seem like a big deal after so long inside, but in reality, it didn't feel that exciting. You're driving from a country jail to the local mall where you may be able to do some window shopping and eat a sandwich, and by then it's time to start driving back. The first few leaves you've got a prison officer with you every step of the way, so it's not exactly romantic.

As my release grew closer, I had a couple of eight-hour leaves, and finally a twelve-hour one, which is enough time to go home, visit family, have a proper meal, and contemplate a life where you don't have to have your guard up against an ambush every minute of the day. The final stage is an unsupervised 24-hour leave, where you go out, enjoy a taste of freedom, then rock up at the prison for them to lock you up again. I had a couple of those towards the end of my sentence, and I enjoyed them immensely. Go out, buy a sharp outfit, freshen up, straight to the strippers, fuck all night, then back in time for breakfast.

That also wasn't as big a deal as it might seem, as it wasn't my first experience with a woman in a decade. In prison, if you play your cards right, there's ample opportunity to get your leg over. There are female security officers, social workers, teachers, nurses – and that's just professionals. There's a certain kind of woman who reads about gangsters in the papers and develops a crush, and they write to you and a relationship develops. I wasn't often lonely during those ten years. Even before I was sentenced, I was caught fucking my lawyer's legal assistant. She was lovely, a very sweet, blonde hottie. Felt bad that she got in trouble. Don't regret it though.

The screws thought they were punishing me by denying my leaves until the very end, but honestly, they were doing me a favour. I would have gone crazy if they'd let me out once a month for three years to smell the fresh air. Much preferred to do my jail in one hit, then walk out forever. If they thought they were punishing me, they'd have to try a bit harder. And try they did.

They even found a way to keep me inside a touch longer, just to twist the knife. I had a little more time added to my sentence over the years. Once you're in the system, if you're accused of a minor offence, you're given a governor's hearing, which depending on the outcome can result in up to four more days being added to your sentence. Any more than that and you're entitled to a court hearing, but if there's a screw who hates your guts – and I had plenty – then they can hand out those extra days in jail like jelly beans at a kid's party.

By the end of my ten years, I had an accumulated twenty days on my sentence, which meant Elie was due to get out twenty days before me. He wrote to the parole board with a special request that he be given twenty extra days as well, because he wouldn't feel right walking out of prison without me. They were happy to give him the extra time. That's just how we are as a family. It was a huge sacrifice for Elie to make, but that's the kind of man he is – always thinking of others. Take this one example, out of hundreds. Years earlier, before we got pinched, we were driving into Northbridge from our home in South Perth. We were on the freeway when Elie spoke up suddenly. 'What's that old lady doing walking on the freeway?'

'What old lady?'

'We just zoomed past her,' Elie said. 'Get off the freeway and go back.'

So I took the next exit, got back on the other side and drove past her again. We repeated the manoeuvre and pulled up behind her so we could jump out and ask her if she needed help.

Turns out she was disoriented and dehydrated and had been walking for hours and had no clue where she was. She must have been in her eighties. We gave her some water and took her to the local police station to assist her.

The poor lady was grateful that someone had finally stopped to help. Unreal, when you think about it, that it took a couple of Leb thugs to stop and take notice of an elderly woman in great danger, lost and walking on the side of the road.

Not saying I'm special, but fuck me, I had some thoughts for all cunts who think they're a do-gooder because they show up for work every day and pay their taxes. Probably don't walk on a red signal. But what about actually noticing a person in need and extending a bit of time and care? Most villains I know would always get involved and assist. They might not love the law, but at least they keep their eyes open to other human beings.

Elie always puts others before himself. He spent the year leading up to the arrest looking after the new priest of our Melbourne parish, Father Joe. Father Joe came from Sydney and was finding his feet, so Elie took him out to dinner most nights. They were like besties. It was very wholesome – the young Leb hotshot and the holy man.

Fuck, that didn't end well, though. The priest wiped him as soon as he was arrested. Not even a character reference. Bit like those cunts mentioned above. I wonder if Father Joe would have stopped to check on that old lady by the side of the road. Same story with do-gooders all over the world. Not much substance, just going through the motions.

Understandably, Elie was devastated, not for the character reference but for the love he had for Father Joe and how quickly he'd dropped him. I mean, it's not like we are talking about an employer – he was the priest, for fuck's sake. That broke Elie's heart, because he is a guy who genuinely sees the best in people. He's a people person and missed every single day he wasn't outside.

I didn't sweat prison as much. Elie suffered more than me, I think, whereas I just got on with it. I can do that. It is the way I live my life. But Elie longed for everything he'd lost.

You could tell he was dreaming of life outside of jail. Torturing himself. He pined for freedom with every part of his body and mind. Me? I was in jail, but my mind was free. It was an opportunity to grow, to work out, to think, to read, to expand my mind. He did his time differently, and he felt every single minute of his incarceration. He didn't roll with it, and he was punished every single day. It was painful to watch.

Everyone does their jail differently. When you're looking at nine years, that's an impossible thing to face head-on, so your mind finds ways to make it work. Some people do their jail by planning escapes. Say they've got ten years, they think,

Well, I've got three years in maximum security, before they move me to a medium-security place and I can escape. So really, I'm only doing three years. When they reach medium, they realise escape isn't feasible, so think, *Well, only three years in medium, then they move me to minimum and I'll escape then.* But when they reach minimum, they've only got three years left on their sentence, and they know they can do three years, because they've just done it – twice.

In my case, I was fighting for most of it. By the time I was tricked into pleading guilty, I'd already done two years. So those years didn't count. Then I was busy with appeals, fighting again and again to get my sentence reduced. I was sure I was going to win, that I was going to walk out any day. In my mind, I wasn't doing ten years, I was doing six months, or a couple of years, or another day. Court cases and appeals and learning the law took up all my time. By the time all my appeals were finished, I was already on the downhill run. So, mentally I didn't have to look at the whole sentence until I was halfway through. Read a few books, have a few laughs, do a few push-ups and go home.

The day I finally walked out of the prison gates forever, I left it all behind. I wasn't going back. I'd learned my lesson and I wasn't interested in prison life anymore. I'd grown a hell of a lot in that period and I didn't think I'd wasted my ten years in jail. I was fitter, stronger and smarter than when I was locked up. In that time I'd evolved and turned into a man who knew how to fight using his mind just as well as his fists. When I came out of that gate, I felt as though I was twelve feet tall. I had my freedom, but more than that, I had plans, ambitions.

In the scheme of things, ten years in prison had only made me hungrier.

I had a girlfriend, a stripper that I'd got to know on my leaves. She picked me up at the front gate of the prison. I jumped in her car and never looked back, too excited about the future to stress about the last ten years too much. I walked out without anything but the clothes on my back. I'd had millions in assets when I went into prison, but most of it had been confiscated under a law called pecuniary penalty, where the state seizes any money and assets it considers gained through crime.

The rest of my money was eaten up in the legal system as I was trying to fight my conviction. Everything I owned, every dollar I'd ever made – they took it all. I had nothing, but I could start again from scratch. On paper, I was broke, but nothing about me was broken.

Our family gave Elie and me a little bit of money, ten grand each, to survive on until we could find a way forward. Going back to our old lives was weird. What stood out for me is that the world hadn't really evolved. Everyone else seemed like they were wearing the same clothes, had the same ideas. Nothing had really changed. I had. Although I walked straight back into the swing of things and in many ways it was like I'd never left, I wasn't going to waste any time in repeating the same mistakes. Our parole period was two years and involved meddling parole officers monitoring our movements, asking silly questions. It was fine and didn't present any problems in readjusting; it's just the system, though it did feel ridiculous and a waste of everybody's time. I didn't need a babysitter!

I wasn't in a hurry to play up, and besides, nothing was going to stop me from getting back on my feet. I refused to fall into any of the old drug-related shit, as I wasn't prepared to risk my freedom again. I understood how harsh the system is and knew it would never cut me a break. Instead, I had to make my own luck.

The minute I got a little money, I invested in a sick car, the kind that I'd been dreaming of getting behind the wheel of for a decade, and ordered custom plates for it: EASY10. A bit of a statement. I'd taken ten years in jail in my stride and shrugged off the system designed to grind me down and break me. An easy ten, but I was never going back. Not in this lifetime.

7

DIRECTING TRAFFIC

W HEN I WAS IN jail I had some good company, but when I got out I left it all behind except for Greg 'Doc' Roberts. That's because I knew he was towing the line. I couldn't trust anyone else to go straight.

The legal term for people destined to end up incarcerated again and again is 'recidivists', and I could spot them from a mile away. Some people I could just tell – from their first taste of freedom, they were already on their way back inside. They would end up back incarcerated trying to support their habit, be that gambling or drugs. Such people, well, they'll drag you down if you let them. It didn't matter what my relationship with them was inside; as soon as I got out, I left that life behind. I wiped them all, except for Doc.

Doc got out six months before me and was one of my first ports of call on release. He'd shacked up with a bird in

St Kilda and was working on his book. His advance payment for his book was keeping him afloat, but that wouldn't last forever so I brought him in on a couple of business opportunities with me – all legitimate, nothing naughty – until he finished his novel, *Shantaram*, and the rest is history. A bestseller and amazing story. People were blown away by his experiences and the manner in which he conducts himself. He was – still is – an extraordinary guy. Puts positivity into the world, and good luck just seems to find him. A little of that luck ricocheted off him to me, and I'll be forever grateful for our friendship.

I received a call from an organisation that found dormant companies – ones that had ceased business and been abandoned but still had cash assets. He found I had a business account left over from Perth with $180K in it. Somehow the law had missed it when they were seizing my assets, and I'd forgotten all about it. I was the sole director of that company, so all I had to do was sign an authority to the finder to recover the money, which I did for a small fee of about 10 per cent. It was literally a gift.

So, quite quickly on release, I had money in the bank and was finding my feet back in society. I was asked to help a mate, Grant, recover his furniture business from his ex-girlfriend. She'd shacked up with another bloke and taken control of Grant's business while he was away sourcing more products in Indonesia. He wanted me to get all of his stock back, and for this he would pay 50 per cent of the sale, which would make for a generous payday. To be clear, everything on the shop floor belonged to Grant. He had the paper trail of orders and payments, source of funds etc. – it was all above board. He'd been robbed by his ex, and he needed a little help.

There was over a million dollars in stock. Grant was from Perth and had no-one in Melbourne. Too easy. I went around to the premises, met the ex-girlfriend and new boyfriend, and gave them a heads-up and asked them to leave; they called the police, and it became a bit of a stand-off for a minute.

After consideration by the police, they said the following: in this circumstance, 'no law has been broken, and this is a matter for the courts to decide who is entitled to what'.

The officers suggested we instruct lawyers and work it out in court. Before leaving they encouraged me to vacate the premises so that everyone could get back to work.

No worries. I went straight to Bunnings, bought bolt cutters and a huge chain and new lock. As soon as Grant's ex and new beau left to go home, I let myself in and went to work. I called Doc, and we started securing the place and conducting a stocktake. We kept the store locked down for a few days and I had a couple of associates stay overnight, never leaving the premises empty, because in this circumstance possession is nine-tenths of the law.

There was a clock on this caper – the lease was about to expire, so we had three weeks to sell everything.

It was fun. We hustled, called everyone we knew and offered huge discounts. But there was so much stock that we had to find another location. I knew a guy who was renovating a building in Fitzroy, perfect location and free rent, so we relocated and started again, running a pop-up furniture shop selling to everyone we knew. Doc and I did well out of that, made a few hundred grand each.

We did a few jobs like this for a bit of side-hustle and entertainment. They were a dime a dozen in those days; people want quick results and are prepared to pay a premium for them. Not all were success stories, as often you would get to the resolution and find out you hadn't been given all the facts. Or the story had been changed to favour the client. In which case it becomes a grey area: are you recovering rightful goods or standing over a business? If it's not kosher, I won't touch it.

It was a fun time of life, me and Doc bouncing from job to gig. Easy money and some good stories. We hustled during the day and Doc wrote his book in the evenings.

My friend Charles Giglia, a film producer and concert promoter, was involved in various businesses from Perth. Charles called me to ask if I would invest in a tour featuring Andrea Bocelli, the blind opera singer; Riccardo Muti, the famous Italian conductor from La Scala; and La Scala's resident classical ballet company. I didn't know anything about opera or the ballet but I would give it a shot. Looking at the maths, I could understand that the number of records the guy was selling in Australia would translate to ticket sales to his target demographic. So I decided to jump in.

Bit of background: Jack Rigal was the lawyer who secured Andrea Bocelli for the tour, and the one handling all the money. We'd connected because Charles was looking for investors to bring Bocelli and his management team to visit Australia and tour the venues and accommodation before committing 100 per cent.

Although it was a risk, I put in $80K, and I transferred the money over to Jack. He was dealing with the Italians, and they were very specific in the way they did business. They didn't want to sign contracts until the eleventh hour, I started to feel a bit impatient, but it all came good. The tour was green lit.

Jack and Charles then did the deal with IMG to take over the tour, fund it, and in return we would get our initial investment back on signing and a third of the profits to share equally between us. That would translate to about $180K to me.

IMG decided to drop Teatro alla Scala and Muti and just run with Bocelli. A good deal, but because of some tricky manoeuvring by the Italians to minimise tax, profits were escrowed for a year until the tax was paid. So I wasn't going to receive my money for another year, and when the money was finally due to be released and it was time for my dividend, Jack took off with all the money. Just took my investment and fucked off to Monaco with it!

Safe to say, I wasn't happy. The minute I heard about this I was on a plane to Europe. Charles sent me Jack's contact details and address in Monte Carlo and let him know I was dropping in to see him. Charles told him a cover story that I had investors looking for opportunities. This triggered his interest.

I called Jack before I arrived and arranged a catch-up at my hotel. He arrived with two bodyguards – for his protection, and possibly to try and intimidate me. They buckled quickly. Pair of flops had no chance. As soon as I bridged up and got in their face they retreated and clearly wanted no part of an issue.

You must understand I was fresh out of jail back then. In 1999 I was not the person telling this story now who's been mellowed out by time and experience. It did not take much for me to accelerate from a standing start to turning it on. Once I had my hands on Jack, he began with promises of a settlement, telling me, 'No problem. I'll get your money, just give me time.'

A couple of days passed and he suggested I go home, and he would transfer the money to me in a few days. I guess he thought I would leave empty-handed. 'Not a chance,' I told him, 'I'm not going anywhere until we are sorted.'

Then he disappeared. Just stopped taking my calls and coming to the hotel. His English bodyguard was with me every day – mostly, I guess, keeping an eye on me for Jack's benefit.

Realising that conventional methods weren't going to succeed, I started to work on plan B. I rented a car then asked the English bodyguard to direct me to Jack's house, where I knocked on the door. More of a compound than a house, it had a high fence around it with a buzzer and camera at the gated entrance. I buzzed a couple of times, no answer, so after some duress, English drew me a map of the front and back doors and a floorplan of the inside of the house, marking the main bedroom and office.

I jumped the fence and had a bit of a look around, peeped through the windows and could see there was no-one home.

I made note of the back and side fences and where I could go for a quick exit. Then we drove to the hardware store and stocked up on gaffer tape, cable ties, a taser gun, plastic bags, various blades and some nasty but effective tools. I now had a map of his house with all the entrances and exits marked and accounted for. Where he slept. Where his wife slept. My plan was in place.

To be honest, I knew the English bodyguard would report to Jack what I was up to, and the risks associated with my reconnaissance mission and shopping spree. Knowing the lay of the land, he would either pay or run. Either way, I was getting to the end point quicker with aggression.

Later that day I received a phone call from The Dentist in New York. Bit of background: The Dentist was one of those classic Italian players – cool guy, operations on both sides of the Atlantic – but his ambitions as a gangster were greater than his abilities. He had a gift for getting himself into situations that he needed a little help getting out of. There are a lot of guys like him running around.

I'd already tried to do a little business with The Dentist, who somehow had in his possession a number of mining tenements in Africa, each with a range of minerals and precious resources – including diamonds.

As a first step I put The Dentist and LK together to broker a deal, and possibly vend in his diamond tenement and add value to a project.

It didn't work out. LK tried hard to reach a mutually beneficial agreement but couldn't get a real result from The Dentist. I thought he was probably another one of those

New York types more focused on the short-term scam than the long-term potential. No stress – sometimes deals don't work out. That's how it goes.

The Dentist requested that I put a hold on my plans with Jack until he had the chance to fly in and see me the following day. We caught up briefly at my hotel as soon as he landed. The problem was, I wasn't the only person Jack owed money to. The Dentist was heavily invested in some scam Jack was running. If Jack disappeared, then The Dentist stood to lose a significant amount of money. So, he wanted to work out an outcome where Jack would live long enough that he would get his investment back.

Effectively he was saying he was sent to tell me that my business with Jack was affecting him and his Italian associates in New York. Everything he told me came with a subtle threat – he was inferring it was Mafia connected. That was a strong possibility, and I was on high alert. After all, we weren't far from Italy and the potential for an Italian plan B to send over a couple of shooters was real.

I arranged to meet The Dentist again in an hour for dinner. I'd been ready to meet the minute he called me, but I strongly suspected he needed to make some phone calls to put safeguards in place.

We sat down for the meeting in the hotel restaurant, and he spelled it out for me. 'Jay, I understand that you're upset, but this is bigger than you can imagine. New York is involved. If you get involved, then they get involved, and if that happens nobody gets a happy ending.' He wanted me to drop off, go home and forget about Jack.

I glared over the table at him. I couldn't believe he was trying to do the old one-two on me. I fucking invented the old one-two. It had usually worked out well for me, but it wasn't going to work out too well for him.

'I don't give a fuck,' I said, loud enough that the couple eating at the next table startled and looked over. I lowered my voice slightly. 'I'm sorted, cuz,' I let him know. 'I have my tools and my exit plan. I don't give a fuck about the money. I'm getting Jack. It's a matter of principle.' I meant it, too. Fuck Jack. I wasn't messing around, that cunt was off.

The Dentist had started looking a bit sick by now. It was a nice restaurant in Monte Carlo – easy-listening music, silverware, candlelight – but you could see the cunt looked sick even in the mood lighting. So pale he matched the heavy linen napkins. He held up his hands for calm and started in with a new proposal.

'What if I pay you the outstanding $180K, would that work? Would you then leave Jack alone?'

Here we go, I thought. *He should have started with that statement.*

'Let me get this straight, you are offering to pay Jack's outstanding bill of $180K, is that correct? I just want to be completely clear with you. Don't answer me before you think about it for a minute, because if you give me your word, then you must pay the debt.' The Dentist insisted I accept his generous offer.

I could see The Dentist doing the maths in his head and realising that $180K was a small investment compared to what he stood to lose if Jack got what he deserved.

We agreed, I flew back to Australia, and a week later I flew to Perth and collected my $180K.

Once The Dentist and his friends properly understood the situation, suddenly the money appeared. Story as old as time – these dudes are all front and chatter, but as soon as shit gets real, they fall apart. You don't even need to lay a hand on them. You just need to terrorise them a little, to make them understand what the likely outcome will be, and they'll come to their senses. That's the beauty of it. Sometimes a bit of theatre is better than a bit of action. If someone is going to rip me off, then what does he think is going to happen? If he doesn't have the imagination to play that scenario out, then you can make him understand it fairly easily.

By this point in my life, I thought I'd seen everything. There isn't much that shocks me out there. But it still boggled the mind how many fucking gronks make a few bucks in business and think they are big enough to mess with the bulls. Jack was just one of them. But those cunts were a dime a dozen.

Long story short: I made my money back on Bocelli, and then some. I went to one show, the opening night at the casino in Perth, and fell asleep halfway through. It turns out that I didn't love opera after all. I couldn't tell you about the quality of the tour, but financially it was a huge success for me and the touring company.

My first apartment after jail was in The Melburnian, right on the edge of the city, overlooking the park and the river. At the time it was one of the most prestigious buildings in Melbourne, and a hard building to get into. Luckily, the real estate agent was a woman, and we hit it off. We started hanging out together, and she sorted me out with a beautiful two-bedroom apartment on the eleventh floor.

Ten months after release I had the apartment, a mad Porsche with my EASY10 number plate, and a healthy growing bank account.

Funny how things work out. The concierge/doorman for my building was a former prison guard. I thought it was pretty funny, and highly ironic, that a screw was still opening the door for me morning and night. In the biggest irony of all, in some ways prison kept opening doors for me, long after I'd gained my freedom.

My reputation had preceded me when I came out of jail. I didn't do much to encourage the rumours about me; I just tried to focus on surviving and building wealth. Nevertheless, the public image that the media had created when I was locked up proved persistent. And lucrative.

It turned out that the skills I had picked up in nightclubs and then refined in prison – people management, an eye for opportunity, the capacity to negotiate political situations, a certain ability to resolve conflict, should it arise – were valuable. Not just in the underworld, but also in the outside world of legitimate business. Before long, I had many acquaintances from both sides of the fence calling me for assistance in solving their problems.

My first real protection job was for a small outfit that owned a nightclub. Billboards Nightclub was part-owned by a

Melbourne gangster. His name was Victor, one of the Carlton crew. He had a couple of major investors in on the business – guys down from Bendigo who wanted to get in on the Melbourne nightlife.

Or they were supposed to, but they got spooked one day when the club was ransacked by a hectic crim. This local character, Steve, who was a real loose unit and recidivist armed robber, had run through the club, chased the manager into the office and battered him over some shit. I don't even know if Steve was trying to rob the place or was just losing his shit.

Either way, it had terrified the investors – two guys from Bendigo, Mark and The Doctor (the latter was actually a doctor and came from old money) – so much that they wanted to pull their money out and run. Victor called me, as he knew I knew Steve, and asked me to sort it.

'Mark and The Doctor never want to come back,' Victor told me. 'But we need them. Can you sort this Steve cunt out, so they feel safe?'

'Yeah, sweet,' I said. 'No problem.' I knew Steve well. Had done time with him and so knew how he operated and where to find him. He avoided me as long as he could – it took ten calls to track him down and explain that I wanted to arrange a sit-down between him and the guys he'd run in on.

I eventually dragged Steve to St Kilda, sat him down, introduced him to Mark and The Doctor, and cut to the chase: 'There's no issue here. You just need to meet these guys, talk with them, and let them know you're sweet, and there'll be no more hecticness. So that they can go back to work.'

I was maybe expecting some pushback, but I didn't expect his reaction, which was to start crying. Really fucking sobbing, bawling his eyes out and apologising. This was a formidable man, a proper fucking villain. I don't know what happened to him that day to make him so emotional. It was a bit embarrassing, really. I didn't know where to look.

Long story short: I got the job done, so Billboards engaged me. From there, I got paid. Got paid well. A shiny new car, a BMW 7 Series, was given to me as part of my income. I provided security from the underworld – not the bouncer work I did as a teenager, knocking out rowdy cunts at the door. This was looking after the shooters and gangsters who gravitated towards nightclubs such as this, which required a more delicate approach.

Billboards' Hard Kandy night opened on Friday at 11 pm and closed at 11 am on Saturday, and in between the most hectic cunts in Melbourne came to cut loose. Everyone was there. Everyone was on it – smashing bags of rack, eating pills by the handful. The dance floor was absolutely rammed with beautiful women.

All of which is to say, it was an environment where young bulls would inevitably grow rowdy. People would find themselves in fights all the time, guns were pulled out often, and it was up to me and my team to handle those situations.

Before long, it was clear to anyone who was anyone that this was now my club, which meant you could turn it on, but I would turn it on too. The difference between us in any conflict, though, was I had the home advantage.

It got a bit loose a few times – guns drawn, that sort of thing – but fortunately I had the capacity in those particular situations and with those particular villains to defuse, de-escalate and encourage all parties to put down the bit, grab a drink and keep partying.

No-one got shot while I was around. But a knifing or two might have got past the goalie.

I kept an apartment above the club, the only one in the building, so I was always on hand if someone was playing up and needed to be dealt with. I was good at it – most of the time, it wasn't a matter of meting out violence but just directing traffic. Reminding people that they were stepping on the wrong toes and should watch their footing. It was closer to old-fashioned diplomacy than anything else. Very rarely did it escalate to proper violence. Fairly rarely.

For the first year out of prison, there was a period of adjustment. I'd spent ten years in an environment where often the only way to solve a problem was with a crude weapon, so the corporate world was a culture shock. Honestly, there were a few incidents; teething issues where I wanted desperately to knock some cunt's teeth out. Doc was the voice of reason for me then. He was absorbed in writing his book and had his religious man-of-peace vibe about him. He somehow always managed to calm me down with a few of his words of wisdom. Just when I was about to go into battle with guns blazing, he would appear and talk me down. It was like magic. Doc was with me from the time I got out of jail for the whole of my first year.

We made some money and had each other's backs. I don't know if I would have been quite so chill when I encountered obstacles outside jail without his influence. But he kept me grounded while I put in the foundations for a new life. We had a lot of fun, and he remained – and remains – one of my best friends as my horizons expanded.

My social circles back then were diverse. I counted some of the underworld players of Melbourne as friends, but also solicitors, corporate executives and other respectable old-money types. They gravitated towards me because I was polite and present-able, but they knew what I'd done and what I was capable of. It's a weird thing common to a lot of upright wealthy people – they all love the vicarious thrill that comes from being near someone they perceive as dangerous.

I would be invited to parties in fancy suburbs like Toorak and Kew, where I would be the token gangster in a crowd of suits and evening gowns. Perhaps I didn't meet the normal expectations of a gangster because I am respectful, polite and easy to be around. When I went to a party, it was to have a good time, not run around hurting or scaring people.

There were certainly times and situations that called for that, however, such as the time I found myself being invited to become part-owner of Spearmint Rhino. Bit of background: In 2002 me and my cuz Eddy Malkoun opened our restaurant Shamiana at 420 Lonsdale Street in Melbourne's CBD. It was a really amazing place to eat – a cross between a fine dining restaurant and a gentlemen's entertainment establishment. We had a classy fit-out. Plush wine-coloured curtains divided the space into a dining room, bar and private dining area. Lots of wood and old-world glamour, beautiful silk tapestries on the walls. We hired Paul Knight, ex Circa, one of Melbourne's best chefs back then.

The real draw was the waitresses. They wore these lovely jumpsuits made of sheer fabric that were barely see-through. Classy, but still very sexy. Great food, beautiful women. What can I say? The reviews were good.

Guys went nuts for it. Whenever operators and businessmen came to town, it was the first place they went. For many high rollers, lunch at Shamiana was non-negotiable. I used to welcome customers flying in on private planes for Friday lunch, doing their best to pick up a waitress. I did lose a few to wealthy suits who would pay them $5K to $10K a week to stay home and be available for that girlfriend experience. No sweat. I didn't begrudge my girls moving on up; everyone's got to make a living – I was happy that both my customers and my waitresses were getting their happy-ever-afters.

Our reputation for stunning waitresses went out into the world, and when Spearmint Rhino – one of the best strip franchises in the world, with seventy bars on multiple continents – came to town to scout out opening a Melbourne venue, they came to see me. It was a principle of the owner to fly around the world looking for potential locations himself and then go about setting them up. He'd jetted over from the USA to set up in Melbourne and hired a club manager, Brad, a local guy.

I was introduced to Brad by the concierge of the high roller VIP area in the Crown Casino. I liked Brad, we caught up a few times and I helped him navigate a couple of potential issues. The Spearmint policy is to take on a local partner to invest and help smooth things out. Brad and I talked about that local partner being me, possibly at a 10 or 20 per cent stake, at a buy-in price to be discussed.

Brad had done a deal to buy an existing strip club on King Street, around the corner from Shamiana, from the former owners – two brothers who'd recently been locked up for an incident with a stripper. They had a couple of years behind bars to deal with so it was decided to sell ownership of the club to Brad and the Spearmint team. The deal was done, deposit given, contracts signed, keys handed over. Only thing left was the final payment of $300K. They set about renovating it to become part of the Spearmint franchise. This club used to be the Hippodrome nightclub, an awesome old club that had a feature wall of illuminated windows behind the bar in the design of a comet racing through the night. About two months into my friendship with Brad, I discovered he had instructed the builder to cover the light feature with plaster.

'Fuck that', I told him. I would swing past with a van and some boys and grab the eight pieces of 2 x 1 m leadlight windows and put them away for safekeeping.

While there supervising the extraction of the light feature, a friend who'd just been released from prison, Gary Lewer, paid me a visit. We did about a year together, champion bloke and a champion body builder. He went up to the office to find me and came down looking a bit out of sorts. I was busy, but still noticed he was acting off. He seemed disturbed after a chat with the club manager, John, and Brad the American owner.

'Are you okay, mate? What's the matter?' I asked him.

'I walked into the office and said I was looking for you . . . It's the way they were speaking about you,' he said. 'I guess I'm just not used to it.'

'What do you mean?'

'Well, they were being very disrespectful.'

'What the fuck did they say?' Now he had my attention.

Bit of background: I met Gary at the beginning of his sentence and towards the end of mine in Pentridge. They were winding Pentridge Prison up – Elie and I were set to be literally on the last bus out – and there were only a few hundred prisoners left, mostly in transit.

I was well into my sentence, nudging nine years completed. I had become a little more tolerant; the sting of incarceration had dissipated, and I was less angry, but I did have the full run of the place. Demanded respect from everyone, prisoners and screws alike, and I got it. Gary witnessed this firsthand, how Elie and I were treated differently to everyone else, took what we wanted without contest, ran our own race.

Nothing spectacular, but enough to notice: you don't fuck with the Malkoun brothers. As you can imagine, Gary was somewhat taken aback when a couple of office workers from a strip club were not offering the same degree of respect towards me as the hard gangsters and bully screws had up the road in Pentridge.

Gary was a gentleman, an honest guy who wouldn't have brought it up if something wasn't very wrong. But I was busy and made a mental note to investigate and sort it out. If someone does the wrong thing to me, rest assured that I'll get to it eventually.

This was the week leading up to the first visit of the Spearmint Rhino global CEO, John Grey. *Hmm,* I thought, *clearly they are mistaking good manners for a weakness. They need a wake-up call.*

I could have walked in with Gary and turned it on, smacked them around a bit, got them to beg for mercy, the usual one-two. But I needed more than that to fill my appetite for respect.

I kept an eye on them over the next couple of days and I did notice they started to get a bit too cute, a bit too comfortable, a bit too tricky. I made a point of arranging a meeting at my restaurant on the day of John Grey's arrival. He was due to land at 10 am and come to meet me for lunch at 1 pm.

When he turned up, he was pretty shaken. That morning, just a couple of hours earlier, a team of guys had run through his new premises. It was still being renovated, and they kicked their way in, carried on a bit, smashed some furniture, pistol-whipped the manager. The same manager who Gary had spoken to that day when he felt they were a bit flippant.

The manager copped it, cried like a little girl, begged for his life. The team smashing the place up had a message: 'Tell the dogs to pay their bill. Next time shots will be fired.'

It was assumed that the former owners – both dangerous guys currently in prison – had sent over their men as a reminder to pay the outstanding bill, as they were still owed $300K.

Now the Americans and the manager were petrified. John had only just landed in the country and his staff were being battered and pistol-whipped in broad daylight. They came to me asking for help: what do we do?

'No worries,' I told him. 'I'll find out who's behind it and defuse the situation.' John, to his credit, insisted he'd come with me to sort out the guys who'd smashed up his club. Ballsy move, good on you, John.

I called my boys and told them we'd all come up for a visit to talk through what had happened. Together we drove out to the Dandenong Ranges, CEO in the passenger seat, a good 25-minute drive, and you could see that Brad – the other big mouth who'd been bagging me that day to Gary – was getting more and more shaken as we drove up into the hills. I let them know that they were dealing with serious people who would not think twice about shooting either of them, so advised them to keep quiet and follow my lead.

We arrived to a reception of bikie-looking dudes with guns and dark glasses. Could have been a scene from a movie. They had a high brick wall around the house with big solid gates that gave the appearance of a compound. Bikies on the outside, bikies on the inside. I drove past once then circled back and pulled up, took all my jewellery off, pulled out my piece, checked the clip, loaded a bullet in the chamber, then slid it into the front of my jeans. Easy access and clear to anyone who knew how to handle themselves that I was carrying. This made the Americans very nervous.

We went in, saw the boys, and it was all hugs and kisses to begin with. 'What's going on, boys? Were you playing up this morning? That was you, right?'

They laughed and I sort of frowned. I introduced the Americans and there were a few words over that $300K.

I made it crystal clear that these Spearmint Rhino guys were with me now. We spoke about the debt for a minute, the cover story, and I got assurances the bill would be paid. I let everyone know that I was now part of Spearmint Rhino and to have a crack at them meant that you were having a crack at me. Any issues in the future must come through me.

'No worries, Jay, we didn't know that,' the leader of the team went, but then thought for a minute and continued, 'But can't we just fuck them up a *little bit*? They don't pay their fucking bills!'

I argued against that, they argued back; the boys turned up the intimidation towards the Americans a notch, just to the point where Brad was shitting himself. It was all theatre though – obviously they weren't going to touch him with me there. But by the time we settled it and got back in the car, Brad needed new underwear.

This whole show was about teaching the Rhino guys a lesson: don't get ahead of yourself; you're only visitors in this country and must respect the rules and the relevant people.

To his credit, John was all over it. He was quiet the whole drive back to the city, whereas Brad was one degree away from a mental breakdown. On arrival at Shamiana, John pulled me aside and offered me 20 per cent of Rhino, but no money would need to change hands. All I'd need to do was keep my arm around Rhino and look after tricky issues that couldn't be resolved at the door. Then the shares in the club would be mine.

Bottom line here is, Brad and the manager created this situation. The cheeky cunts thought they were smarter than everyone else, but this didn't work out too well for them. It's the old one-two again, the oldest play in the book – make someone aware of a problem, then resolve it for them. They'll be so grateful they won't think too hard about it. Back in the early 2000s, niche businesses like Rhino needed protection.

I was involved with Rhino for seven years and had a lot of fun. Owning a strip club on King Street was the perfect sweet spot between the underworld and the overworked. Perfectly at street level. In many ways, at that time I was at a crossroads in my life, still heavily involved in the underworld and still making shit happen. I was the 'go-to guy' and if something needed to be done, and you had enough folding, you could come and see me. If I could, I would make sure it got done.

I had been out of prison for a year or two and made some moves, gained some ground. I was already known, feared and respected by most, but there are always ambitious cunts who will make a move because they want to get famous. And fame-hungry gangsters are always up for gossip. You know, the he-said she-said type of shit to start trouble.

I got a call from the president of a bike club who had on a few occasions invited me to his clubhouse. I always politely declined. Then one day, he became angry with me, insisting, 'We need to catch up. Now.'

Bit pushy, I thought. It was more of a demand than a request. He told me he was waiting in St Kilda. I read the play and anticipated an ambush so I called my trusted offsider Nick Matthew. Nick was a giant Cypriot. He grew up in England and was as tough as they come. Nick did a year in jail with me for assaults, nothing out of the ordinary, just doing his job at the door of a nightclub. We did a lot of work together and he was always my go-to guy when I wanted backup. One call and Nick was en route, twenty minutes away. For good luck, I also called my mate Johnny, who always appreciated a good dust-up.

I was there inside of ten minutes and positioned myself across the road to quietly observe the bikies for a minute. There were eight that I could see in colours, walking around and positioning themselves. To be honest I didn't really rate these guys at combat, however there was always the possibility of a shooter among them stupid enough to pull his weapon. The president was marching up and down the street barking orders at his members, clearly angry and agitated.

He rang me again, asking how long until I'd arrive.

'Are you fucking high, you cunt? I'll get there when I get there,' I said, and hung up. Now I was agitated. *These cunts join a bike club, think they earn respect by wearing a vest and doing little else? Fuck him.* I was so mad that when I got out of the car I was almost running at him.

'What's on your fucking mind, cunt?' I barked at him, clearly angry. He buckled for a second, then rallied.

'Let's go into the laneway,' he said, indicating a narrow alley down a St Kilda side street. Now this is where it could have gone bad. I knew that there was definitely a shooter waiting in the laneway, otherwise what was the point of walking off the street and into the privacy of a laneway. I was not tooled up – no gun, no blade, nothing, not even knuckle dusters. But I couldn't back down now.

'Move then, you cunt! Get in the laneway!' I yelled at the bikie, positioning myself behind him in anticipation. Just as we were walking, Nick's car screeches to a halt and he jumps out armed with his favourite baseball bat.

'Jay! Wait! Don't start without me!' he yelled. Nick is a big man and goes off like a freight train. He was clearly looking forward to a fight. I'm not sure what these bikies thought about me but they were definitely thrown by Nick.

The bikie president looked surprised and was now on the back foot. All he could manage in response was, 'We just want to talk.'

I cracked my crooked smile. 'Are you sure? Looks more like an ambush than a conversation.'

He ushered us to a cafe for a seat and a latte. Turns out that they'd been sold a bunch of gossip that I was talking shit about them. Full transparency: on one occasion, I'd slipped up and mentioned to Steve – the loose unit who I'd put in line and reduced to tears, which landed me the nightclub security gig earlier – that I wouldn't be caught dead in a bikie clubhouse.

Steve clearly did not live down that cry-baby shit because he went back to the bikies and told them a whole story about how I thought they were all weak cunts and that nothing good would ever come from that bike club. This is why they were fired up. Me and Nick put out that fire pretty quick. He buckled for a second, then rallied at the first sign of resistance.

Me and Nick ran our own race. We didn't interfere or get over involved with the underworld and its workings, however we often crossed paths with all sorts. It's hard not to. There was always an issue to be sorted, and Nick just didn't know how to back down – it wasn't in his DNA. In his twenties he lived in Britain, and would walk into the toughest pubs there and turn his beer glass upside down as a sign to fight anyone in the pub. Which often meant he fought everyone. He was the human version of a pit bull terrier: the more you hit him the harder he came at you. But there's no-one you'd rather have on your side in a fight. I surrounded myself with good people, and he is one of the best.

The first time I ever travelled to London I was with another mate of mine, Michael B. Things were heating up in Melbourne with the tit-for-tat underworld war that was seeing cunts getting bowled weekly. I had to hit the road for a minute and decided to join Michael on a trip away for a month. Michael, a lawyer from Melbourne, was having some issues with Gary Burman. Gary owned some venues in Crown Casino and was doing well. As I understood the situation, Gary wanted to get Michael out of the way so he could continue a relationship with some chick Michael was seeing.

The cunt had been seeing Michael during the day as his mate and partner in various deals, then banging his chick in the evening. Shit form. There are too many available women out there to be banging someone else's. I knew them both but favoured Michael, circumstances that didn't work out too well for Gary in the end – cost him a stack, and he got stuck with the chick. Fuck that.

Michael was in the UK because he was involved in the business side of the latest Kylie Minogue tour. We were going to see her London show and then go on to her birthday party at the Sanderson Hotel, before hitting Paris and a few other countries for a bit of a holiday. Before the show, we checked into the Sanderson and Michael asked if I could source any coke for the party. It was my first time in London, I knew no locals, so I rang a friend of mine in Antwerp, gave him my room number. He said, 'Give me an hour or two.'

We went to Kylie's concert and left some Aussie girls, stripper friends of mine, in my room. A couple of hours later there was a knock at the door, and a courier delivered an ounce of coke, a hundred ecstasy pills and a block of hash. A gift from Antwerp.

It was an insane party. It went on for a few days. We couldn't even put a dent in the coke. There's only so much you can use on a trip, and obviously we couldn't travel with it. I called my pal to return it.

'Flush it,' he said. 'Plenty more where that came from.' So that's what we did. It was just another day at the office. The hectic life seemed to follow me everywhere I went. There's every chance I would have kept going down that path, but a random encounter at Rhino would change all of that.

8

THE GENTLEMEN'S CLUB

LK IS A BUSINESSMAN and investor who has a rare combination of extreme wealth and a sense of humour. He is well connected. One day the media reported that he'd been seen out dining with Mick Gatto – the staunch mediator and survivor of the Melbourne underworld war who once shot a hitman dead in self-defence. While others would run from any potential negative press, LK embraced it.

LK had made millions in biotech and mining. Lost millions too, but didn't sweat it. There is always more money to be made. The sort of guy I like to work with.

Although LK was a legitimate businessman, he still conducted a bit of business at strip clubs. It's the type of environment that corporates usually drop their guard in. That's where I met him, when he came to my club. We met and instantly hit it off.

We became friends. He's a man who appreciates a good friend. An entrepreneurial guy, he always had opportunities on the go, but this also meant he often had gangsters and crooks hovering to have a crack at separating him from his wealth.

LK would never let reality stand in the way of his ambitions. If he wants things to be a certain way, he'll find a way to make it happen.

It was fortunate that I met LK at a point in my life where it could have gone either way for me. Though it seemed I was doing really well on the face of it – nice cars, beautiful apartment, beautiful girls on my arm, thriving businesses – there was a really dark side to it all. I was letting myself get swept up in increasingly hectic situations and being carried towards certain actions and inevitable outcomes that would more than likely have seen me back in lock-up before too long.

Even though I was operating at a fairly high level, I was not truly in control of the situation because I wasn't truly in control of myself. I was living large, but something essential was missing. LK saw it before I could.

One day, he confronted me about my behaviour. He'd coaxed me out of the club and the city, far away from the chaotic shit, and convinced me to come on a hike up a track to the top of Mount Macedon. LK was planning to walk the Kokoda Track and wanted a training buddy. At least, that was what he told me.

We were halfway up, and he stopped and said, 'Sit for a moment.'

We sat on a log, and LK turned to me. 'What are you doing, Jay?'

'What are you talking about?'

'What the fuck are you doing with your life? You're out of control.'

He literally stopped me in my tracks. And for some reason, I trusted him enough to stop and hear what he had to say.

'If you keep going the way you are, you are going to fuck it all up. You're going to end up living a shit life. That or you'll be back in jail – or dead.'

I thought about it and could see where he was coming from. I could look at his life and see him living what seemed like a pretty good one, with all the perks that power and money bring but without the commotion. And understood that it was a lifestyle that was within reach for me.

While we were talking, LK made me an offer. There was one road up that mountain, but there were many possible roads down. Some better, some worse. Most would take me back to jail or into an early grave. But there were other roads I could go down, and one of them would mean travelling with LK for a while. He had a job offer for me, something substantial that LK thought could benefit both of us. There were some complications with some people he had invested in.

Always on the hustle, LK had surrounded himself with the right corporate people, including brokers and miners. He ran an office complex in Perth that housed a few different mining concerns, all of whom networked and got things done. Getting everyone together under the one roof was good business and was doing very well for everyone in LK's world.

He was compounding his wealth by seizing legitimate opportunities and throwing money into them. This wasn't a line of business I understood back then. When LK would get excited and start talking to me about IPOs, stock options and franked dividends, it was all Greek to me.

But I was willing to take a chance on LK because he shared my old-school Aussie wog belief that you take on a fight for an old friend, the way we did growing up. We were the same in that way. The main difference was the apprenticeship we'd done in our youth.

LK had cultivated a persona as a corporate hustler and entrepreneur; I'd had different experiences and accomplishments, but they earned me a reputation that seemed to get easy results. It turns out those results translate just as well to the corporate world as the street. Because honestly, the line between those worlds is sometimes as thin as the blade of a shiv.

Perth was the wild west back then. The resources boom was in high gear, money was flowing off tap, the mining guys and brokers were making unbelievable profits. You didn't even need to dig the metal out of the ground – you could make millions trading paper and selling a sexy story to the market.

With financial success, especially the huge amounts made overnight in the mining game, came the gangsters and heavies with hands out looking for a cut. The hustlers that feed off success. It came with the territory – if you earn big and live large, then you're going to attract people who see an opportunity. If you're corporate and you don't keep your wits about you, then those hustlers will make a mark out of you.

I've seen it happen a hundred times. Ostensibly legit people will be caught doing the wrong thing or try to take a shortcut to settle a dispute and reach out to the villains in their orbit. But once they've crossed that line, they're over a barrel. It's not like they can go to the police when things inevitably get hectic with the gangsters. In most cases, they end up on the drip for years, paying for protection from the same people they first turned to for help.

Nine times out of ten, once the corporates are infected by the proper crime, they have no way to fight it, no natural antibodies. You're either corporate or a gangster – you can't be both at once. But if you have to dip into the other world, someone like me receives a call.

LK's problem was a falling out with one of Mick's partners in a mining company – 'The Midget'. His had a real name, of course, but everyone just called him The Midget, for having both a diminutive physique and a brain the size of a fucking peanut.

It all started at the Christmas party in LK's office complex that year, when The Midget had tried it on with the receptionist. She was only a twenty-year-old girl, and a young twenty-year-old at that. Very sweet and naive. The Midget had tried to ply her with booze and cocaine to loosen her up. He'd struck out, and the poor thing had ended up mildly traumatised.

LK saw it as his responsibility to make amends. This incident had happened in his building, on his watch, and he felt an obligation to look after everyone under his roof. It's the Lebanese way.

Take a random example. One night around this time, my brother Elie, who was making his way in the world developing property and flipping houses, was on holiday in Lebanon. He was out with a couple of ladies, had just walked into a nightclub in Lebanon, when a guy at the club asked to borrow his new iPhone to make a call. Elie handed him the phone, and the guy disappeared with it – just jumped in a car and took off.

The girls Elie was with promptly got the owner of the club on the case, who made it his responsibility to retrieve Elie's phone because Elie was in his club and under his care, so to speak.

Long story short: the owner checked his security cameras, identified the thief, went to his house with two guards at 2 am and waited until he got home. Then he bashed him and recovered the phone. He didn't know Elie from a bar of soap at that point – but the Lebanese rules of hospitality applied. Elie was under his roof, and his protection.

Same rules applied to LK and The Midget. LK grabbed him, read him the riot act and fined him $20,000, to be donated to a charity of the receptionist's choice.

It was a slap on the wrist, no money at all when you considered the profits the pair were making, but LK was honour-bound to make it clear that bad behaviour would not be tolerated. Perfectly reasonable, but The Midget didn't see it that way. The Midget's dad went wide to try and get revenge. He engaged some affiliates of his at the Coffin Cheaters and hired them to go after LK and inflict some pain.

The Coffin Cheaters were a one-percenter motorcycle club that started in Perth back in the 70s. They pretty much had the monopoly on bikie violence in Perth at the time.

A few years before this, a bikie club out of New Zealand had tried to expand into Perth, and the Coffin Cheaters had bridged up. They'd made an alliance with other Perth motor-cycle clubs and had banged on with bats and guns until the Kiwi outfit gave up and left town. Since then, the Coffin Cheaters had enjoyed the run of the place.

Although LK was a knockabout bloke and quite willing to throw down, he did not entirely understand these bikies or their capacity. LK got a call from our Perth friend John Kizon and was told he was getting a visit from the Cheaters who intended to break his legs over The Midget incident.

I'd spent enough time in Perth to know exactly what the Cheaters were capable of when shit escalated. You really couldn't win on your own against bikie clubs. You either paid up or ran the ball up and got on with it.

I went to meet LK at his house in Melbourne and told him to call John back and let him know we'd be on the first flight to Perth in the morning to sort it out. This was a ballsy move, as flying over would give them the home ground advantage, but I had a plan.

I also had some hectic friends in Perth whom I could lean on for support if things escalated to a violent situation. John, to his credit, told us not to bother as he would handle it from his end. The Cheaters had their national run on that weekend and wouldn't have time to see anyone.

Honestly, I was a little disappointed. I love Perth; any excuse to go there will do, even confronting a bike club. From my point of view, I was ready to go and work this out. In fact, I was insisting. LK loved that about me, always ready to go on with it, but in this case, he asked me to sit this one out. That problem died a natural death and was never spoken about again.

Soon after that incident LK invited me to join him on tour to Dubai, Lebanon and then London. It was a great trip, a lot of fun and a lot of work. We travelled well – first class – and stayed in great hotels. It was quite an experience travelling with big money. Lots of meetings with corporates and brokers, deals going on day and night. Now and then, LK would yell at me to pay attention and jump on this or that opportunity, but I wasn't that interested; I didn't get it.

First stop was Dubai, where LK and his associates had a villa in Jumeirah, the luxury complex opposite the Burj Khalifa, and two full-time drivers to cruise around with. LK took me for my first visit to the Dubai HSBC, which in time I would become very familiar with. There we entered a private room, with a bank employee and a money-counting machine at our disposal. At LK's insistence, I went to the machine, pressed a button and heard a quick *whirr* as it spat out US$50,000. Very cool.

I carried that $50K withdrawn from LK's account to London, where I met Mick S, the partner of both LK and The Midget. I liked him immediately. He was an overweight drunk who smoked excessively but had a great mind and a huge capacity to earn. Plus, he was generous. Case in point: LK asked me to change the US$50K from Dubai into British pounds and divide it in half for him and Mick. I went to the street exchange and negotiated a good rate, getting around £40,000, £20K each for LK and Mick.

I gave LK his envelope, then handed Mick the other envelope, who handed it straight back.

'Keep it – walking around money,' he said. Safe to say, we hit it off. I appreciated that he appreciated quality people. Clearly, he recognised an asset in me and started with giving before asking. Excellent strategy. We would go on to work together again and again and make each other a lot of money. He invested in me from day dot, and in return I solved a lot of problems for him over the years. Starting with The Midget.

Mick had a headache. He and The Midget had been partners for many years, but they'd fallen out and were dissolving the partnership. Mick was unhappy for a number of reasons, but one in particular was because The Midget had sold a mining lease that Mick had secured many years ago when he was pegging for uranium in the early 80s. The Midget had sold the lease to Rio Tinto, without Mick's consent, and claimed he was paid only $50,000 for the lease.

Impossible. Mick had valued it at hundreds of millions of dollars. The Midget had been on the wrong end of a bad deal, no doubt about that. He'd sold it when nuclear power was a politically poisonous issue and uranium was getting a lot of bad press. He decided he didn't want to be associated with this mineral, so he dumped the company at basically cost. That was his story, anyway. Bit of a stretch given both these guys were not high on scruples.

Between them, Mick and The Midget had a lot of assets and ownership of several companies. As part of the separation, they were splitting assets down the middle. Problem was, both Mick and The Midget wanted one particular company, Ironbark Gold – valued at over $170M at the time – included on their side of the ledger.

It was a sticky point, and neither would budge, so The Midget decided to involve the Cheaters. Good plan, really. The Coffin Cheaters had some formidable soldiers in Perth, where Mick had a lot of interests that they were putting the pressure on. And Mick was feeling it.

LK and I flew into London and into this mess. Mick was really upset. His sense of justice had been dented. He was on the level and just wanted to work it out through the courts, no gangsters or bikies.

He was going on and on about The Midget and the Cheaters and how he had no options left and was going to have to give the company over.

'Why not let Jay sort it for you?' LK suggested. 'He knows his way around Perth and the Cheaters.'

Mick was quite excited about the idea. He knew that if I put my arm around him, so to speak, it would make his businesses in Perth and elsewhere a no-go area for thugs and bikies.

'Nothing makes you a target like making yourself a target,' I reasoned. 'It's best to deal with these matters head-on before they escalate. There's no sense in talking or fighting with anyone in Melbourne if they have orders to bang on. We need to go to their leadership in Perth.'

We hammered out a deal between the three of us. LK and I would receive 16 million shares and 16 million options in Ironbark Gold as a payment. The shares were trading at 72 cents at that time and predicted to go north and possibly reach $2; my share would be equal to $5,760,000. In return, I would do whatever it took to get the Coffin Cheaters to stand down and let Mick and The Midget work things out in court. Easy.

From there, it was just a matter of directing traffic. I called my friend and local gangster John Kizon, who since I'd first met him knocking cunts out in my nightclubs had become something of a kingpin in Perth. Next I was flying straight to Perth, to let the Cheaters know I was coming, and that we wanted to have a chat about The Midget and Mick.

With boots on the ground we caught up with John and the leader of the Coffin Cheaters at a pub for a civilised chat. It was not an aggressive situation, more one built on mutual respect. We all wanted to find a solution we could all live with. There was some back and forth while we hammered it out.

Their side were onto a lucrative income stream from The Midget, who was paying them to be his friend and getting them involved in profitable projects. I suggested that their investment in him wouldn't be worth much if he disappeared.

The Cheaters president saw the wisdom in that. Between us we worked out terms: they would continue to look after The Midget, I would look after Mick, and we would each continue to earn. Meanwhile, Mick and The Midget could sort it out legally in the courts with no interference.

For a two-hour negotiation, I made 8 million shares that were trading at 72 cents, plus 8 million options. I was thrilled. Mick was just as thrilled to be left alone – I could almost feel him crying with joy over the phone when I gave him the good news. Most people would run if they saw a bikie club heading in their direction. I did the opposite and fronted up to them. The results speak for themselves.

The whole experience was a revelation to me. These mega deals were going on all of the time, and any new-money millionaires were vulnerable to being bullied into paying big fines and fees by anyone willing to have a crack. Which meant they all needed someone to keep them safe. LK opened my eyes to that world, and I never looked back.

It was quite a welcome into the next phase of my life. I couldn't believe how much money there was to be made in the corporate world for someone like me who could exert pressure in the right places during a negotiation. It seemed too good to be true. Turns out everyone can use a friendly neighbourhood gangster in their life now and again.

I got a call from a friend about a girl who was being harassed by her ex-boyfriend. He was some drug dealer with a tendency for violence and aggression, to the point that she was scared and asked for help.

'No issue.' I told my mate to get me the ex-boyfriend's number. 'I'll call him.'

I rang the ex-boyfriend and told him that I was seeing the girl now and to stop bothering her. He must have thought I was a gronk because he told me to fuck off and promptly hung up.

Damn. That didn't go the way I thought it would. Time to improvise.

I called my mate back and asked him for an address for the ex-boyfriend. He gave it to me – an apartment in Docklands not far at all from my place in The Melburnian.

I drove straight to his apartment and buzzed to get in.

'Who's this?' he answered through the intercom.

'It's me. Jay Malkoun. You told me to fuck off and hung up on me thirty minutes ago.'

He wasn't so tough now; the cunt shat himself. Wouldn't let me in. Nor come down. He did, however, swear that he would never call her again. Sorted.

The next day, my phone rang again. It's the girl – she wanted to catch up to say thanks.

Her name was Matilda. Good sort, very grateful. Thing about Aussie chicks is that most gravitate towards a bad boy. We started hanging out and had a great time for a couple of years – this was before she started to kick goals in Hollywood. She was amazing. A classic Aussie bombshell blonde, softly spoken, butter wouldn't melt in her mouth. Top sort. Maybe a bit obsessive, could get jealous, but I was surrounded by trim, so it was to be expected. There were always girls around.

I had my gig at Billboards, keeping watch over their infamous Hard Kandy party, and the restaurant Shamiana, as well as Spearmint Rhino. So naturally enough there was some jealousy, and we'd fight about it.

We were fighting in my Mercedes one day when I'd had enough. 'Get out of my car!' I yelled at Matilda.

Quick as a whip, she reached over to my sun visor, pulled it down to reveal the mirror and said, 'Have a look at you and then have a look at me.'

That cracked me up. A brutal finisher from Matilda. Fight over. She was right, though – she was a top sort. And me? Definitely not a pretty boy. We had a good time, but it wasn't going to last forever. A couple of years after we hooked up, we broke up amicably.

About a year after we stopped seeing each other, I got a call from my mate Bruce, who had a friend who was obsessed with Matilda, some businessman type called Aaron. Bruce asked if we could organise a meet.

'Sure, why not?' I said. Both Matilda and I had moved on.

I brought a table to an event where Doc, by now the famous author of *Shantaram*, was speaking. Matilda was already coming, so I instructed Bruce to bring his mate Aaron so we'd all be at the same table.

I gave Matilda the heads-up and she was cool with meeting the guy. I even talked him up a little. So we all connected at the event, and afterwards she and Aaron hung out a bit. Before long, Aaron flew her to Singapore for a shopping spree, under the pretence that he wanted her to be the face of one of his companies.

Matilda called me from Singapore and told me Aaron was bagging me, had nothing nice to say about me.

I wasn't sure exactly what brand of shit he was talking, but it wasn't good. Probably to do with my past and incarceration. I guess he was trying to elevate his self-esteem. That made him the second cunt who bagged me after I'd put him in the driver's seat with chicks. The other was the owner of a Lamborghini. He called me from Spearmint Rhino while I was in London. He was drinking with some of the girls and wanted me to ask them to look after him and put them on the phone. I did.

'I know this guy. He's a good bloke and a mate, so please look after him.'

I returned to Melbourne a week later and was in the club when one of the girls who'd been working that night pulled me aside.

'That Lamborghini guy was bagging you,' she told me. 'He said you are a tyre kicker and time waster.'

'Really, he said that?'

'Yep. That's what he said.'

'Motherfucker.' No worries. I figured I'd run into him eventually, without having to go out of my way. I've got a long memory. Three years later I was driving down Chapel Street, the nightlife heart of the southside of Melbourne, when I saw him standing on the corner of a side street.

I pulled into the street and yelled out, 'Hi, mate!'

He saw me and walked towards me and into the side street, where I landed a big right cross on his chin. He hit the ground but stayed conscious. I'd cracked his jaw.

'Who's the fucking tyre kicker, cunt?' I asked. He knew what I was talking about and pleaded to be left alone.

Anyway, back to Aaron. This was the second time this had happened to me with a rich, insecure cunt. Once is unlucky. Twice is fucking rude.

I shrugged it for a second. Not bothered, but then the more I thought about it the angrier I grew. This bloke came into my world with a request and now he was trying to create a wedge between me and Matilda. Clearly, he didn't know the rules. The thing with entitled types – be they corporate or underworld – is they welcome any opportunity to turn on you, especially if your skin is a darker colour than theirs. I'd only met this guy. He had not worked up enough credit to fuck up with me. I told Matilda to fuck him off and waited for the end of their trip.

When they returned from Singapore, I called Aaron for a quick catch-up. He was in a pub in Port Melbourne on the beach. I grabbed a couple of my boys, and we positioned him outside the pub.

There were people everywhere, so I didn't risk bashing the cunt in public. I settled for expressing myself verbally. He buckled immediately. Bit disappointing. Really, I turned up to slap him around, but he shat himself, so I opted for a fine instead.

I learned this manoeuvre from my Italian mate. This guy was an operator, an impressive earner – worth a few million, easy. A few years back my Italian mate called me and asked if I knew this other bloke – let's call him 'Cash'. I did happen to know this guy Cash – a big earner in the building game and a wannabe gangster – was at that moment very pissed in Bar 20, the CBD strip club, and was telling everyone in the club that my Italian mate wasn't shit and that Cash was the real gangster.

My mate the Italian heard about it and wanted to have a word with Cash. He asked if I could bring him to a meeting in Carlton.

'Sure,' I said. 'But only for a chat, not an ambush.'

I grabbed Cash and took him to Carlton – and assured him that although he'd really fucked up, he had my word nothing untoward would happen at this meeting. The guy was shitting himself. The Italian kept his word but had a very persuasive talk with Cash. Long story short: after a chat, the guy with the big mouth agreed to pay a $100K fine. Which he did. I took that on as a bit of a lesson, and remembered it when a cheeky cunt like Aaron popped up and ran his mouth. A nice, fair way to defend Matilda's honour, is the way I saw it.

After Matilda and I split, I started seeing this English lady, Charlotte from Liverpool. She took my breath away: proper hottie. And the bonus was, not only was she a stunner, but she held it down on the domestic front: great cook, kept an immaculate home. Perfect in nearly every way – except one major one. She didn't want kids.

I had a mate over after a big weekend to pick up his girl who was a friend of Charlotte's. But he wouldn't leave. He was rambling on about a couple of his mates he'd fallen out with over some weed, and apparently, they had given his girl a hard time.

Charlotte piped up. 'That's not on,' she said in her pommy accent. Matt concurred. I just wanted to watch TV, but he wouldn't let it go. In an effort to move him along, I said, 'Let's go see your mates now and sort it out.'

He liked this idea. He was now pumped. We jumped in the car and drove the short distance to Richmond from my apartment in The Melburnian.

As soon as we arrived I banged on the door and got the three of them to come out. 'Stay the fuck away from Matt's girl,' I told them. 'Or this won't end well.'

They were cool, no issue, but for a bit of theatre, I turned to Matt and said, really casual, 'If they fuck around again just shoot them.'

Matt was thrilled I backed him and fronted these boys. I didn't really mean it when I said 'shoot them'. I was just hyped up and still in character, so to speak. Like one of those method actors who can't shake the part between takes.

About a week later I was watching the news and saw that three men had been shot in Richmond. Fuck me. Matt had actually gone over and shot them all, hit them in the legs. I couldn't believe he'd actually done it. That didn't end well for Matt or his mates.

Charlotte was cool with the whole thing. She was great, but she was adamant she didn't want kids, so it was never going to work out in the long run. That was a non-negotiable life goal for me.

I was hitting every goal. Life just kept getting better and better. After brushing up against the law hit the pause button on me building my life, I went at it hard. Hard in the way only a man who knows how quickly life can be snatched away goes. Life is precious, bro. You have to make every moment count. Best believe that I did. I have a lot of happy memories from that time, but my best moment, by a long, long fucking way, was starting a family.

I met Samantha at a party at a friend's apartment after the Melbourne Cup. She had flown in from Sydney to attend the festivities. Fuck, she was so amazing: twenty-two years old, fit body, perfect arse, beautiful face – and an intimidating intellect, too. In conversation, she ran rings around me. She kept talking about really smart stuff like cognitive processes and memory training and shit like that. Needless to say, I left that party without her. However, she did leave quite an impact.

I hit my mate up for her number and we started to have regular chats. At the beginning it was like a long-distance friendship with the potential for more. An intimidating friendship. Nothing worse than a chick half your age correcting your spelling mistakes and grammar. Samantha would send back my texts with the corrections highlighted.

Luckily, I have a thick skin and ignored the condescending tone and criticism. I stayed focused on the prize. We made a plan to meet on the Gold Coast for the Gold Coast 500. She drove up from Byron Bay and I flew in with a couple of mates from Melbourne. Me and my mates checked into our hotel, had a swim then got ready to hit the town. I didn't tell them I was meeting Samantha, so when she walked into the bar and gave me a hug, their reactions were all 'What the fuck? We just got here and you're already with a hot chick?'

We had a lot of fun out drinking that night. She stayed for a few days then that was it, we started a romantic relationship. Maybe a week later she was on a boat day party a bit tipsy and called me, so I invited her over. She called a water taxi to take her from the boat straight to the airport and was with me within a few hours.

These were exciting times. I had swagger, money by the truckload, and now I had the most beautiful woman I'd ever met on my arm. Me and Sam had so much fun together – went to the best clubs, bars and restaurants. Everywhere we went I knew everyone, and everyone knew me, so going out always ended among a group of friends.

Samantha quickly decided, with my encouragement, to move to Melbourne. I really wanted kids and she was definitely a healthy, brilliant candidate for the mother of my children. We were both in tune with our thoughts on parenting. She had a lot of great ideas about early learning and switching on your right brain to nurture a child's creativity, memory and intuition. This was all pizza to me. I loved what I was hearing – I was blown away. Couldn't believe I'd finally met a beautiful, super smart woman who ticked all of the boxes.

We bought some land, a beautiful stretch of property just outside of Melbourne, peaceful and with amazing views. When we started a family, I wanted my kids to have the best both of country life and city life. I'd watch the sun set with Sam and imagine our future children running around playing in the gardens and fields there. In the meantime, I kept horses. A friend of mine gifted me my first thoroughbred Arabian horses – he no longer had space for them on his land – and I got really into breeding horses as a business/hobby/passion. Soon I was breeding champions for racing and for show.

But that wasn't the priority. Sam and I quickly made a plan to have kids.

We were pregnant within a year. We had our first child, Laila, in 2008, our second, Jada, in 2010, and our third, Romeo, in 2013.

There's nothing in the world like the feeling of becoming a parent. Until you hold your own newborn baby in your arms, and you look into their eyes – and you see your own eyes staring back, and your dad's, and your grandfather's – you don't really understand what life is about. I didn't.

You can't anticipate the love you feel at that moment, even if you think you can. I'd always wanted kids. I love kids. I would have ten of them if I could. Family is everything. I live for my kids.

After continuous pressure from my mum, Sam and I decided to get married. We had a mad wedding reception at Crown Casino in 2012. My life was going great. Samantha was looking after the kids and their activities, and I was flat out chasing earns.

Sam is an amazing mother. My kids' first years were amazing. Watching them grow and develop their own personalities and discover new ways of expressing themselves and asserting their individuality – I'd never been so fascinated. They give me grief, but the good kind. Children become their own people, that's part of parenting. But I trust them to make their own choices. Me and their mother both have great intuition, and our children were born with it too. The best choice we ever made as parents was to nurture and encourage their intuition. So they developed good instincts. A child has to be free to make their own decisions and way in the world – good and bad, just like I did.

My own father had given me those instincts, and it was important to me that his legacy carry on in my children. Sadly, he had a stroke, and became extremely sick with a kidney infection, and was taken to hospital.

He declined rapidly there and nearly died. The hospital was not an environment conducive to his recovery. You throw an old man with broken English and no capacity for communication into that environment where they don't understand his language or culture – well, it wasn't going to have a happy outcome. When I went to visit him, he was depressed, confused and highly dehydrated. So I made an executive decision and took him out of there to bring him home. I literally picked him up and carried him out on my shoulder. They tried to stop me. Unsuccessfully.

When he was home, we cleaned him up and put him into his favourite pyjamas, and he started eating, resting and recovering. He lived another ten years. Ten good years. When he passed, I had his favourite image of Jesus from our childhood home – the one he would pray in front of for hours – tattooed on my arm in his honour. Then several more tattoos of Jesus and the saints. There was nobody who loved Jesus more than Dad, so I covered my whole body with holy images to honour my father's memory.

I continued working with LK, here and there, for years. We did a lot of work together – companies both public and private paying me vast amounts just for being present. They write off on their accounts these 'consultant fees'. Since then, I have always been referred to as The Consultant. They never spoke my name on the phone, always preferring to keep it off the wire in case of any future investigations, I assume. I didn't make the title up, my clients did. Even now when they talk about me, they say, 'I've got The Consultant here with me.'

That was just the tip of the spear, though. It was pocket change the amount of money that corporates were willing to pay for a bit of security and comfort, knowing they would be left alone by the villains, and moreover, they would be less likely to have internal issues with their staff and brokers.

I was surprised – happy, but still surprised – how much equity there was to unlock in carrying around a staunch reputation. That becomes even more lucrative when you have the bargaining power of, say, a few hundred soldiers behind you.

A small, heavily armed force of operators is, in corporate terms, good leverage in any negotiation. In years to come, I would find out all about that. But that's a much longer story.

9

THE THREE AMIGOS

GIVEN MOST OF MY experience of outlaw motorcycle clubs involved stand-offs with bikies trying to shake down my mates, I was as surprised as anyone when I became a bikie.

Would have laughed in your face if you'd told me that I would be, a few years earlier. Just didn't see it on the cards. I'd known a few bikies, done some consulting for others, and was mates with a few more. There were some good guys in that world. One of them was an associate of mine called Adam, a Comanchero.

The Comancheros – or Comos, for short – were an outlaw motorcycle gang that started on the New South Wales coast back in the 60s. This was when one-percenter clubs were more like suburban social clubs for dudes to drink beer and wild out rather than serious organised multi-nationals like they are today.

The Comos were a bit more hardcore than your average. The founder, William 'Jock' Ross, was a Scot, ex-military, and as the years passed he grew more and more attracted by the idea of going to war. Through the 70s and 80s, they were considered one of the most violent bikie clubs operating in Australia. He ordered his guys to drill, and train with weapons and tactics, and be ready for battle with other bikies.

They started brawling with other clubs, behaviour that peaked in 1984 at the Milperra Massacre, when members of the Bandidos gang ambushed the Comos at a motorcycle swap meet at a suburban pub. What started as an old-fashioned brawl inside the pub escalated rapidly: shotties and pistols came out, the two sides banged on. Twenty people were hospitalised and four Comos died of gunshot wounds, along with two Bandidos and a fourteen-year-old girl who was caught in the crossfire.

Jock was wounded by shrapnel in the chest and brain. He survived, but was incarcerated for murder, reduced on appeal to manslaughter. He did five years, getting parole in 1989. He remained supreme leader of the Comos, but the club was changing. What had once been an all-white club was bringing in newer members from different backgrounds – Africans, Lebs, Arabs, Pakistanis. Some of them practised Islam and didn't drink, and none of them wanted to sink piss all day and go hang out in the woods and play soldier. As one Como told the media later on: 'If I want to march around in the fucking backyard, I would have joined the fuckin' army.'

★

In 2002, a 22-year-old Leb named Mahmoud 'Mick' Hawi took the leadership from Jock. Mick had only been a Como for three years, but everyone could see he was the real deal. He was huge, physically powerful, fast, smart and capable. Mick knew that the only way the club could achieve its potential was with new leadership, so he and some of the younger Comos went to meet Jock at his house to discuss options.

The discussion was brief and brutal. As simple as that, Mick became national president, and under his leadership the Comos became an entirely new beast of a club.

Hawi's leadership led to some hectic violence, and, in later years, new ways of doing business. The Comos were growing in sophistication and ambition in the way they operated. What started in a clubhouse in Sydney was now a complex organisation looking at becoming international players. That meant expansion.

Around that time, the Comancheros had brokered a deal to expand the club out of New South Wales and open a chapter in Melbourne, and my mate Adam was tapped to be Melbourne president/state commander. He invited me to the ceremony. I declined. At that point, I was not interested in bikies.

Who the fuck likes bikies? I thought. *No-one.*

Outlaw motorcycle clubs had a bit of an image problem back then. Cops didn't like them. Civilians didn't like them. But no-one hated them more than other outlaw clubs with grudges and long memories.

★

On 22 March 2009, twenty NSW Comos flew down from Sydney to swear in three members who would be the start of the Victorian Comanchero chapter. The ceremony was brief. Twenty Comos were present for the swearing-in of the Victorian chapter, they had a small celebration, then the following day they all boarded a flight back to Sydney. National President Mick was with them on the flight. Unfortunately, also on the flight was Hells Angels President Derek Wainohu, along with some of the stauncher Hells Angels.

Before they met in the air, things had been rough on the ground. The atmosphere was hectic and fierce. Tensions between Comos and Angels had been escalating for months.

What began in 2008 as a slight turf war over a tattoo shop in Sydney evolved into full-on tit-for-tat combat between the two gangs. The Angels had opened a tattoo shop in Como territory and refused to shut it down, which didn't end well for them.

Consequently, a car bomb was placed in front of an Angels clubhouse, destroying it and its contents, and members were shot on site. A few days later a Comanchero was shot in the leg by four men allegedly wearing Hells Angels colours. The Comos went to work. They had a dynamic, hungry crew and they feared no-one. It was not a good time to be a Hells Angel. Now the two leaders who'd been circling each other back in Sydney were in the air together.

Worst possible scenario: around thirty testosterone-fuelled, large angry men stuck on an aircraft together. Things escalated soon after take-off, with each side mouthing threats to the other, while on the ground their Sydney crews rushed to the airport with backup and weapons. When the plane touched down, there were bikies all over the terminal ready to turn it on. They started to punch on and to maim each other with whatever they had to hand. One of the Angels had a pair of scissors and was stabbing every Como who came near him. He attacked Hawi and stabbed him a number of times until one of Hawi's boys picked up a security bollard – a big metal pole – and hit him.

This was all captured on CCTV and the eyes of airport security – who were unarmed and didn't get involved. They just stood by and watched the carnage unfold. But unfortunately for both sides, so did many, many witnesses.

All up, more than fifty witnesses watched twelve Comancheros versus five Hells Angels at Domestic Terminal 3 of Sydney Airport. The maths didn't work out well for anyone. One of the Angels' associates died in the combat, bashed with a metal bollard and stabbed in the chest. The Feds arrived too late to do much but put cuffs on everyone. Within twenty-four hours another Hells Angel was shot, and the lawyer representing the Angels was shot multiple times too.

Even if they won the fight, the Comos didn't get off easily. Most of them ended up in jail, including Mick Hawi, who the courts found guilty of affray and murder. The murder rap was overturned on appeal, but he would stay in jail and do at least three-and-a-half years.

The media ran bullshit, sensationalist stories about the Comos nonstop for weeks and years afterwards. So the Melbourne club started off with bad luck: the national president locked up, the media raining shit on them day and night, and with only three members – Justin, Samson and Adam.

A quick background on each: Justin was a car salesman, ambitious but not a cunt. He did his own thing and kept to himself. Samson was his brother-in-law and had no ambition and no job. Unemployed, he just hung around Justin all day and trained in the gym. Type of guy that would have a girl over and watch TV in his Comanchero vest and shorts. Contribution to the club? Zero. Adam was the leader and the most experienced – an ex-Rebel (once the biggest outlaw motorcycle club in Australia) and a nice guy, easy-going but no killer instinct. He was not trying to take over the world. Technically, he had orders from Comanchero leadership to grow the club by patching in new members, but he was moving pretty slow on that front. He seemed happy enough with his day job of being a car mechanic by trade. He'd been our local family mechanic for years. Robbed us blind every time, but we went to him anyway because he was a mate.

I'd known him since I was sixteen, back when I lived just a mile from his workshop. Now and again over the years he'd ask me to come in and join the club, but I had no interest. Still, Adam was one of my oldest mates and would call me almost daily for catch-ups – and when he needed to consult with me about various issues. Nothing too serious. Usually tension with other clubs and mostly because of individuals playing up.

Take Ramsi. Ramsi was another guy Adam kept close. He could fight like a freight train. You didn't want to get hit by Ramsi. A broken jaw would just be the start of proceedings. He was a proper fighter, but no amount of skill will help you in an ambush.

One day, Adam asked me over for coffee – and help with an issue. Apparently, there was a problem between Ramsi and the Bandidos. It had to do with a collect/recovery of some money owed by one operator to another that Ramsi had orchestrated. The players were aligned with the Bandidos, and Adam – in all his wisdom – sent Justin along with Ramsi to the meeting. Muscle, but not enough muscle. He thought that with Justin being a Como, he would be enough of a threat to defuse any ambush.

As it turned out, the reputation the Comos had earned in Sydney didn't make it all the way to this meeting. Ramsi was jumped, and a Bandido enforcer named Toby Mitchell landed a big right cross that dropped him like a sack of potatoes and broke his jaw. I reckon he must have had a knuckle duster on to have broken Ramsi's jaw.

Not sure what Justin did about it, but clearly not enough. Word got back to the Sydney Comos, who waited for a reaction from Adam's crew. When the shit hit the fan, Sydney was available to be called upon, but it was understood that day-to-day you had to stand on your own two feet, to bridge up only when absolutely necessary. Given a Como was involved, the rest of the underworld was watching, and everyone expected a strong response.

A few days passed, and nothing had happened, no retaliation, nothing. It wasn't a good look for the Comos. Adam had been summoned to Sydney by Duax 'Dax' Hohepa Ngakuru – who was acting as national president of the Comancheros while Mick was in jail. That's when a very nervous Adam called me and requested I come along.

'Yeah, okay,' I said. I probably should not have, but since Adam had been a friend since childhood, of course I would accompany him. If Adam was going to get battered and stripped of his colours, which the club was probably within its rights to do, I wanted to be there to stand up for him.

As it turned out, Dax wasn't looking to hand out punishment and didn't even judge Adam on his shit performance to date. He was just offering support, a way to fix the situation. I don't think Mick would have been so passive. I was amazed. And I was impressed.

That was my first real catch-up with the Sydney Comos. I met most of the senior members that day and I have to say I was impressed by their presence, strength and willingness to get the job done. They had so much drive, backed by smarts and strength. If there was an issue, they faced up to it immediately, day or night, and with whatever tactics were necessary.

Even though Mick was already incarcerated when I first got to know the Comancheros, I saw the benefits of his leadership. Under his watch he'd taken a relatively tired old-timer club and injected youth and aggression to drive it hard onto the front pages of every paper in Australia. Mick was loved by all, and the Comos ran the ball up for him, would do anything he ordered them to. The sort of respect you only saw on television – his guys were over-the-top willing and united.

You can't beat that force. The Comos didn't have the millions of dollars other clubs had, or the legacy of a club like the Hells Angels, but they had tenacity and drive. There is no doubt they were Australia's alpha club at that time. Others were wealthy but too focused on bags of cash and good times.

When the Comos got going and started making their presence felt, the other clubs didn't know what to do. The old, international clubs had grown complacent through years of not having to do much to earn respect, then were suddenly facing a relatively small club banging it on and running amok.

When it was time for action, the Como boys brought the fight direct. They came prepared. While other clubs might steal a car when they needed to go to war, the Comos kept hotties stocked in underground car parks – only the best Merc AMG 63s and Audi RS6 Turbos – primed with kits ready to go: overalls, latex gloves and shoe covers, caps for the hair and face, and a jerry can or two with fuel to torch the car and the DNA. This wasn't a preparation for a 'what if' situation: this was being locked and loaded for the next imminent attack. They had it down pat; it was the definition of precision.

Only the best trained shooters would go out on the ride, and only proper, skilled drivers were allowed behind the wheel. Teams that would confidently do a job idling in front of a police car – and enjoy the job, excited to do the drive and getaway. Then, job done, they would torch the car and the weapons, leaving no evidence behind. That might be a couple hundred thousand dollars up in flames on every job – guns aren't cheap – but it was worth it for the safety of the team, and for the terror it struck in the Comos' enemies.

Every single Comanchero was on the same page – literally one in, all in. Solidarity, brotherhood – you can't beat it. These guys were amazing, understanding and supportive. How could you fail with so much love and support? I was impressed by them, and I guess the feeling was mutual. Once I'd met Dax, the Sydney guys began to ask Adam about me, a lot. They wanted me to join the Comos, and Adam went all in trying to recruit me.

'Would you consider coming on as my sergeant-at-arms?' he asked me.

'Not really,' I told him. It wasn't really my scene. The sergeant is basically the 2IC of a bikie club. It's a position of some responsibility, not something you take on lightly. He keeps meetings in order, manages the weapons and bikes, and where necessary, deals out punishment. He is the one who will keep order if someone in the club is acting up – or bring the ruckus when there's a problem outside the club.

All of which was in my wheelhouse, but I'd never considered becoming a bikie. Still, I thought about it for a while. To be clear, I didn't make this decision alone: I discussed the idea with a few close friends, including Simon Main, who by the way responded with, 'Are you kidding? Yes, do it!'

Samantha didn't care either way; she knew how I lived and where my moral compass sat. In fairness, I reckoned she'd enjoy the excitement of being around all of that stuff.

So, I spoke to my wife, I spoke to LK, went to the club shed and had a few laughs.

Even if I'd never given the bikie life much thought, I loved bikes and took my Harley for a spin with the Comos. That way, I got to know the leadership and reconsidered my reluctance to become a proper, patched bikie. These guys were strong, smart and professional. Good people. I decided that – since no-one whose opinion I respected had given me a good reason *not* to join the club – I'd do it.

Me going from an outsider to the club and patching straight in as a sergeant-at-arms was highly unusual. Normally, when you become a bikie, you go through a year-long period of being a nominee. Then there are the stages of getting all your patches, which you wear on the leathers you're given at the patching-in ceremony. The full patch of a one-percenter club involves getting what's known as the 'top rocker' – the gang's name on a curved emboss; then the bottom rocker, a patch with your chapter or country; and finally the colour, which is the gang's insignia. The Comos wear a gold-and-black bird of prey against a red sun. It's a sick insignia, but one that usually takes two years of loyalty to earn. I became sergeant over-night, and I went straight to sergeant-at-arms, which was without precedent.

As second in command, the sergeant's role is to keep members in line, give the orders to attack when needed, and plot and plan in times of war. When the club is at war with another club the sergeant steps up and assumes the role of commander. It's a model of leadership that understands that different times require different leaders. Peacetime requires one kind of leader and one kind of strength. War – well that's a different story.

But in my early days as a bikie, it was peace, and the Sydney crew wanted to celebrate my entry. They threw a party for me at the clubhouse in Sydney. So, we Victorian crew enjoyed a ride to Sydney for the celebration, a few of my guys and the three original members of the Melbourne chapter.

It was a proper, traditional initiation ceremony sort of thing. I was sworn in, which meant that first all the formal proceedings had to happen – the rules were read out, along with the charter and codes of conduct, the responsibilities I was taking on. It was an elaborate, serious formality to enter into a one-percenter club.

While Dax was making his speech, the whole time I was noting the senior members surrounding me. All through the speech, they were inching closer and closer towards me, moving quite suspiciously, and I realised I might be about to cop a beating.

Fuck, these cunts are going to jump me, I thought. That's a tradition in a lot of gangs, going back into ancient history, particularly over in the States. As a rite of passage into the gang, the other members will give you a classic primitive-style beating as initiation.

I braced myself for the first blow, tucked my chin into my shoulder, then as soon as Dax said my name and I expected a big hit, instead the club went up in a roar of cheering. Suddenly all the guys who'd been surrounding me were pouring their beers over me. I was drenched and cold. Yet relieved. I'm not afraid of taking a beating. But given the choice, I'll always take a party.

That party was a lot of fun. We drank and some of the boys did lots of other recreational things. A handful of members preferred to be loved-up on MDMA and did pills, others were flat out doing lines of coke, while most of the old-timers were smoking weed and drinking beer served by beautiful nude waitresses. The entertainment was provided by strippers, along with their associates. You did your best with the girls and if all failed you paid for one of the many escorts who were available.

I stayed relatively sober and kept myself in control, very aware that everything I did reflected on my capacity as a leader. Honestly, I didn't need any sort of substances – I was buzzing with the excitement of the whole experience: the speeches, the rush of initiation, the feeling of brotherhood. All great feelings.

By 1 am, while some of the other guys were just getting started, I was in bed alone ready for a quick sleep of a few hours before the hard ride back south. It's always harder riding after a late night. It's a tough ride from Sydney to Melbourne at the best of times with an open-face helmet and 20-inch ape hangers – those iconic Harley handlebars that get their name because they require the rider to reach up and grab them like an ape hanging from a tree. Nothing looks cooler than the low-slung riding position they give you, and they are more comfortable than your classic cruiser bars, but they also fuck with your circulation on a hard ride. Especially when the blood is pumping because there's business to attend to at the end of the road.

Less than four hours after I went to bed, at 5 am the manager of Spearmint Rhino called me. One of the staff had been bashed. I knew the guy who did it – one of our regulars, named Abdul. Big man, a heavyweight boxer, he'd been hanging around the club over the past six months.

Apparently, Abdul had been doing lines in the toilet and left his bag behind. We employed a full-time janitor in the men's to keep it tidy and clean, a nice bloke, an old man who did his job and did it well. Too well for Abdul, it seemed.

The janitor must have gone into the stall after Abdul and flushed whatever was left down the toilet. When Abdul went back for his bag and couldn't find it, he lost his shit and went to town on my diligent elderly employee. He bashed him hard then dragged him around the club like a trophy. Totally unprovoked and out of line.

Clearly Abdul was off his head, with his pea-brain convinced he was living out the whole *Scarface* experience. Must have thought he was special, if he could go to my club and bash my employee. I called him and calculated that if we rode straight back, I could be at the clubhouse by 5 pm, so I told him to meet me there at 5.30 pm. I arrived at around 6 pm – and would you believe the dumb cunt was actually waiting for me – we had a quick chat, he got bashed, and was home in time for dinner.

It was no big deal. Abdul was a bit battered and bruised but it could have been a lot worse for him. I reckon I was sorer myself – fucking exhausted from a ten-hour ride on those ape hangers, with little sleep.

The next day I was ambushed by a number of unmarked police cars that kept me on the side of the road for ages while they pulled my car apart looking for a gun. I suspect Abdul told them he was pistol-whipped. It was fucking exasperating. Clowns like him want to run around like hard cunts but buckle at the first little bit of pushback. Not bad at dishing out the violence, but go to water after one or two big hits.

The following week Dax was meant to come down to Melbourne to see Adam and check on progress at our chapter of the Comos. It was now more than eighteen months since Adam, Samson and Justin had opened the Melbourne club-house and to date it had not grown. To be honest, it didn't look good for the original Melbourne members.

For a clubhouse they'd rented a small shed next door to a massage parlour in South Melbourne with a specialist sort of clientele – mostly transvestite, a lot of men in skirts coming and going at all hours. This was not a good look for an outlaw motorbike club keen to uphold a particular reputation. Ideally, you want a clubhouse that makes a statement, a show of force. Instead, we had this shed, which was basically an abandoned garage. It sat there, empty and cold through the year, while they paid rent on it and achieved nothing.

A clubhouse is supposed to be the heart of your chapter – a second home where you can work and earn and be a base to expand. It should be a recruitment tool – a new face walking into your clubhouse should be blown away by your hospitality and jealous of what you've earned. There was none of that here. Which meant no new members, no riding in colours and no flying the flag, nothing.

It was a bit of a joke, actually. The three amigos talked a big game to get into the club then hid from all responsibility. If Mick Hawi had still been around, they would have been in a spot of trouble. Speaking of trouble, during my first week I discovered that a rival motorcycle club, the Finks, had leased a shed two blocks away from our pitiful HQ. The Finks were the only club I knew of that had a proper crack at the Comos. These guys – like the Sydney Comos – were proper and very serious bikies.

There was a meeting in Sydney I heard about from one of the guys who'd attended that went something like this: four senior Comos went to a restaurant for a meeting over a dispute with the Finks. At least one non-member was there, also a serious person. Champion bloke, actually, and very willing to bring the ruckus when called for. In this case, it kicked off.

The meeting didn't go well. Tables went flying and punches were thrown. I don't recall if a bit was pulled out at that point or if the shooting started once the boys got back to the car, but shots were definitely fired by each side, and as the boys drove frantically out of there they were being fired at from at least two directions – the Finks had snipers waiting from multiple positions.

The car was cactus – it looked like it had been in Iraq, bullet holes in both sides and the back, a slug lodged in the headrest of the driver's seat. A proper ambush. It's incredible that no-one was hit. My point is that the Finks are serious people and will go on with it, unlike a lot of other clubs.

This could have been a bad beginning for me, one week in and with the Finks moved in up the road. Two clubs in one suburb wouldn't work. Shit always starts. Inevitably, it's not politics, or money, or decisions by the leaders. It's always the upstarts who have bad attitudes that start shit, and usually over a girl.

I knew the Finks' president, a bloke named Richard, so I called him for a quick catch-up. Richard was part of The Terror Team, who were a handful of Finks that were famously hectic. Their motto was 'Violence with Attitude'. Richard was a proper hard cunt who had just recently shot one of his own members. He wasn't scared of a bit of violence to achieve his goal.

A hard man, but a smart one too, and reasonable. In fact, before I'd decided to join the Comos I'd asked Richard his opinion and he said two things: 'Firstly, fuck the Comos, join the Finks. Second, if you do, be prepared to cut all of your friendships and associates in half. Then half again, because they will all run as far away from you as possible.'

Nah, I thought, *my people know me*. I have to say, looking back, that he was right.

I met Richard in Port Melbourne at his tattoo shop on Bay Street. We indulged in some polite back and forth, and I mentioned that the Finks had just leased a shed two blocks from our clubhouse.

'Fuck,' I said, 'that won't work.' In his defence, no-one knew we had a shed in South Melbourne, because they didn't fly the flag, didn't ride in colours, didn't make their presence known. Didn't buy into any businesses or annex any territory for the Victorian Comos. They all but kept the chapter, and its club-house, a secret. What was the fucking point of joining the club if one year on, nothing was accomplished? I arranged to meet Richard again an hour later, this time with Adam, our chapter president, who theoretically should have been having this discussion with the Finks. Adam lived around the corner with his girl, so I grabbed him and explained what was going on.

'Yulla,' I told him. 'Let's go and deal with this, Richard is waiting.'

'Bro, I'm taking my girl grocery shopping. Can you deal with it?'

Are you fucking kidding? I thought. *Shit is about to go down and you want to drive your girl to the shops? Fuck. What a shit leader.*

Five minutes into the discussion and we were at risk of starting a tit-for-tat war with the Finks. When war is on the table, there's usually a better solution. I wanted to find it, but peace would be delicate.

The Finks' national leadership would already know about the new Finks' shed in Victoria. It could go either way, so I caught up with Richard to talk terms. We discussed the fact that since the Comos had held the shed for over a year, we claimed South Melbourne to be ours. And that given his tattoo shop was in Port Melbourne, it made sense that he'd secured that suburb for his club. They were close to each other, but not so close we couldn't co-exist.

He could have dug in, and it would have ended badly for both of us, but ultimately, he was reasonable, so me and him brokered a deal. He had only just signed a lease and paid a deposit on his premises. The Finks were free to move at will, and there were better sheds a few miles up the road. We paid him his deposit and took over the lease, acquiring ourselves a much larger clubhouse than the knocking shop's old garage. This only happened smoothly because of the relationship I'd established with Richard – in any other circumstances, things might have got real bad real fast.

When Dax did come down to see what was going on with the club, he spent the first half of the day with Adam. I assumed Adam told him the news about us getting the Finks' shed, so when Dax called me for a catch-up, I expected him to be thrilled. We chatted and I kept waiting for his verdict on the new clubhouse. And waited. And waited. In the end, I outright asked him what he thought about the clubhouse.

'It's okay, brother. You guys will grow,' he said, in this sort of encouraging way. 'You'll find a bigger base.'

'What do you mean? The new shed is fucking huge.'

'What new shed?'

'Did Adam show you both sheds?'

'No, just the one next to the tranny parlour.'

'Oh shit. What a cunt!' Adam hadn't mentioned my achievement of taking over the Finks' clubhouse. I was so pissed off. I couldn't believe it. Instead of gloating and announcing that we had a mad clubhouse courtesy of the Finks, that dumb cunt Adam kept it a secret. I couldn't work with that kind of stupid.

'Dax,' I said. 'Full respect, bro, but I'm dropping my colours off. I can't be a part of this two-faced shit. I'm out.'

But Dax was a real leader. Once he understood the situation, true to form, he recognised talent and quickly said, 'Brother, I want you to stay. To show you respect I will retire Adam and give you the presidency.'

'Nah,' I said. 'I have known Adam for too long to take his position. This is his thing; I'm just a tourist.'

'He is out either way, bro,' Dax told me. 'Done nothing with the club in eighteen months, not much will change with him driving the club in Victoria. You have, in a short time, turned the Victorian chapter on its head and surged forward. That's the drive we want for the Comancheros.'

Fair enough, I thought, and told him I was in. That was the beginning of the growth of the Comancheros in Melbourne. I was made the president of the Victorian chapter, leaving me second in command of the entire country. This took me a total of two weeks to achieve.

10

NIKE BIKIES

Now I was the Comanchero Victorian president, two weeks after putting on my patches for the first time. A lot can happen in the space of a fortnight. The previous month, I wouldn't have placed money on me being a bikie. Still, here we are.

My first action had to be choosing my team. I couldn't be president and sergeant-at-arms at the same time, so I needed to recruit a sergeant I knew was up to the job. After some thought, I patched in a bloke – let's call him 'Sarge' – to fill the role. I'd met him through a mutual not that long previously, and let me tell you, he certainly looked the part. Sarge seemed like a good bloke, certainly streetwise and a good earner – on a recruitment level and on a financial one. He was smart: before he came into the club, he had his own security company and he was making $20–30K a week through that alone. Plus, he actually looked like a bikie. Didn't have the biggest frame, but every inch of him, from his boots to his bald head, was covered in muscle and tatts.

Our only real experience with bikies to date had been altercations with them in Perth, or when they played up in my nightclubs or at the strippers'. Apart from these characters, the only one-percenters we came across were the proper old-school guys who did traditional bikie stuff that goes back to the 50s.

The very first bikie clubs were started by ex-WWII veterans who missed the brotherhood of the military and didn't know how to fit back into civilian society after what they'd seen in combat. They first made their own little outlaw bands where they could live more freely, which meant lots of sitting around campsites drinking beer, shooting tin cans and not showering for days. Not really my thing, nor Sarge's for that matter.

The Comancheros were different, what we called 'Nike Bikies'. They wore designer clothes, expensive shoes and sharp haircuts. The Sydney Comos took care of themselves, stayed fit, took pride in their appearance. They were exceptionally neat and well groomed. They kept cool, custom motorbikes but rode only on occasion and preferred to drive exotic cars like Lambos and Mercedes G-Wagons. Sydney was another level of coolness.

I recruited eight of my friends and patched them straight away. I couldn't believe how many of my old crew wanted to be bikies. Every one of the guys I asked wanted to be in on it. So in a matter of days, the Victorian Comos had grown to me, plus eight shaved bears, and Samson and Justin, the original two.

My guys weren't conventional bikies. Two of the new members didn't even have bikes. Their names were Danny and Tie, and if they didn't seem like typical bikies, they had talent that was invaluable to the club. Their reputations alone were priceless. Everyone knew Danny and Tie. They had worked together for many years, running a lot of the club and pub security around Melbourne. Physically, they were giants and ridiculously formidable fighters. You wouldn't want to face off against either of them, and they always attacked as a pair.

Danny and Tie came as a pair and had skills and experience – a dangerous combination for the drunks who couldn't help but play up and were dumb enough to do so on their watch. If you were lucky, you'd get escorted out, but if it escalated to hands-on, you were getting knocked the fuck out. You didn't want to be hit by these guys. Danny would fight with a smile on his face and could easily drop a half-dozen blokes without assistance and without breaking a sweat. With Tie watching his back, together they could have taken down a small army.

I remember one time, at one of the nightclubs I looked after, I was having a chat with Tie when across the room a ruckus broke out. Danny dropped three big blokes in seconds, while Tie's only action was to look over with a raised eyebrow and continue his banter without missing a beat.

'Brother, can you clean up this mess?' Danny yelled out to Tie when he was done.

'No chance, bro.' Tie shrugged. 'You dropped them, you drag them out.'

Nothing fazed them. I was glad to have them on the team. But still, bikies need bikes, so they both bought really nice

Harleys and had them customised to suit their individuality. I went out with them for their first ride, along with Samson. We quickly motored to the three-lane freeway, where I opened up the throttle, really powering through the gears, weaving through the cars. There was a lot of traffic. After a while I looked behind me to see all the cars had disappeared.

Ah, shit, there's been an accident, I thought, and I turned around and rode back, the wrong way up the freeway in the service lane. And there it was – the problem that had stopped all the traffic.

The three traffic lanes were taken up by three bikes, and my newly patched members were lined up on the road, Tie, Danny and Samson, all crawling up the road in first gear. Three physically massive blokes on loud bikes, all too scared to go faster than about 30 kph. The traffic was backed up for maybe a mile behind them, none of the drivers being brave enough to try and overtake, too intimidated even to beep their horns.

It was one of the funniest things I'd ever seen. The entire road was terrified of the bikies, and the bikies were absolutely terrified of the road.

I pulled up alongside Danny, who was crawling along, nervous as hell. He was so scared of being distracted he couldn't take his eyes off the road ahead to work out how to stomp the gear lever.

'You okay, bro?' I called out cheerfully. 'We all good here?'

'Get away, get away, don't talk to me,' was all he said. Eyes so wide you could see the white all the way around. It was so funny to me. I knew Danny to be a man who was afraid of absolutely no-one and nothing, except, as it turns out, changing into second gear on his Harley.

I had to lead them off the freeway and onto the back streets so they could start picking up the basics and learn how to ride. It seemed to me that the quickest way to help these guys learn was a long ride to Sydney. To that end, we organised a big run to New South Wales. Sure enough, they worked out what they were doing pretty quickly, and by the time we were on the highway leading into the Central Coast they were hooning along at 120 kph. All it took was a good long run with the other brothers to learn how to ride with confidence.

Confidence is everything. You can be the most physically capable fighter in the room, willing and able to dominate any situation, but if you can't project that strength in a way your opponents can understand, then you've already lost.

A few weeks into my presidency, the Hells Angels rode into Port Melbourne for a walk around and a bite to eat. The Angels walked into the Finks tattoo shop, made some noise then left to go up the road for food and beer.

Richard, the Finks president, wasn't around when the Angels made their move, receiving a call instead about the uninvited guests, and true to form grabbed his sawn-off shotgun and raced down to Bay Street to look for them.

It turned out that the Angels had stopped locally to eat at an Italian restaurant. For the Angels to front up and then chill out at a local restaurant was, if not an outright provocation, a show of strength intended to make a statement. Richard wasn't the sort of leader who would let that slide. He entered the restaurant and confronted the Angels. 'What the fuck are you guys doing here? Do we have a problem?'

One of the senior members spoke up. 'No problem with you, Richard, or the Finks. But the Comancheros moving into Melbourne could be a problem. This Jay Malkoun guy could be a problem.'

'I know Jay,' Richard told them. 'And whatever you've got to say about him, best you say it to his face.'

The senior member of the Angels asked Richard to call me and tell me to come down for a chat. Richard reached into his pocket and pulled out his phone.

I was at home, close by, when I took the call from Richard.

'I'm surrounded by Hells Angels who have some things on their mind,' he told me. 'They want to see you.' I didn't need two invitations.

Shit, I thought. Port and South Melbourne were Finks and Comanchero areas. If Angels were walking around, then we may have had a problem.

Richard was smart enough to say he was surrounded by Hells Angels. Even though it was in a jovial way I got the message: bring a team with you.

I rang around, got a few of my boys tooled up and ready, and instructed them to park across the street where they had a clear line of sight of the premises. Justin would coordinate the men outside. I had Elie and big Danny sit inside at another table in case it kicked off. The only two I knew I could actually rely on to go on with it would be Elie and Danny. Both were tooled up and both would go all the way.

Here we go, I thought. *If one of these guys even raises his voice, Elie will fire up.*

Leadership in these situations is a balancing act. I have to say, it's not always about who's quicker with fists or weapons but a balancing act of personalities. Elie, my beloved psycho brother, doesn't hesitate. I watched him staring down a restaurant full of Angels and thought about the time he'd hit the screw in the County Court during our trial. When the room had been full of police, he hadn't thought twice. A few bikies wouldn't make him blink.

I was given the head of the table, offered food and drink, and then we got down to business.

Joe, an influential Hells Angel whom I knew from before I'd had anything to do with the Comos, spoke for the group. He said a few of the other clubs were complaining about the Comancheros setting up a chapter in Victoria. There had been a rule for many years that no new clubs were allowed to establish in the state.

The Hells Angels had always been the alpha club in Victoria. That was important to the ecosystem – when one club is clearly the most formidable, it helps keep all the others in line. It means that ambitious members of other clubs don't start eyeing off their rivals' territories and business operations. They were the go-to club whenever club-related shit happened in the southern state. All the other clubs leaned on the Angels to sort shit out.

In Sydney, the Comos held the position of alpha club after wrestling it off the Angels in a long, bitter war. There was a standing shoot-on-sight order between the Comos and the

Angels, and while multiple attempts had been made to broker peace between the clubs, there was too much hatred at that time. The Comos in particular wanted to keep going until the natural end. War is always ugly, but it's not easy to choose peace when you're on the winning side. Frankly, the war was going badly for the Angels in Sydney. It was not a good time to be a Hells Angel.

'I understand the problem,' I said. 'However, the fact is we are here. We're not going anywhere, and we're expanding.' I let them know that we were in the process of opening two new chapters in Victoria, and if there was a problem, then the clubs that were complaining to the Angels should swing past our clubhouse, and we could work it out.

We agreed that the issues in Sydney stayed in Sydney and that this should be seen as an opportunity to build bridges between our clubs. The Angels liked what they heard. The Angels' leader had seen hectic action his whole life and knew that all war does is bring unwanted attention and police raids. And no-one wants that. They were happy with the softer option, and we exchanged numbers.

We agreed on peace until something real happened to disturb it. The Comos and the Angels probably weren't going to be friends anytime soon, but we didn't need to bang on at each other. Victoria was big enough for all of us, and the opportunities were endless.

Following our catch-up, the Comos were invited to the first 'all clubs' meeting to be held at the Hells Angels Thomastown chapter. The Angels had called a meeting for all the clubs to have a say on issues affecting outlaw motorcycle clubs in Victoria.

It was partially in response to recent police persecution, as for a long time, the Victorian police had been relatively relaxed about bikies operating in their state. At least compared to other states, where it was illegal to even wear your colours or socialise in certain conditions. But it felt as though that era was coming to an end, and the cops were growing more belligerent. In 2011, a new taskforce, codenamed Echo, was established specifically to smash the bikie clubs. Which was a headache for us all.

The invitation was for me 'plus one' but I decided to bring a few more. We set off in the rain – forty Comancheros on motorbikes, plus five carloads. We even had a police helicopter escort us all of the way there. It was a dramatic entrance, and everyone moved out of our way as we arrived. Our unity was felt far and wide and we purposefully took our time rolling into the meet and getting off our bikes.

Surrounded by my men, I walked into the Hells Angels clubhouse. We moved as one – if I took a step forward, or to the right, so did the boys. It was a visual show of our united front, and with sheer numbers of us we made our presence felt.

All of the clubs present freaked out as we already had so many members, and we were so strong and unified after a very short time. I had turned the club on its head. We were all big, fit, clean, healthy and sober. None of us were drinking or partying as we were not there to make friends or to be social, and we left a huge impression. A lot of members from other clubs were already pretty loose with booze and drugs, standing around in leathers with beers in their hands. Our look was clean and sharp, which was not your typical bike club.

★

The Comos were growing. National leadership in Sydney had directed us to keep recruiting, and the pledges kept coming. I hand-picked the best for my team from the capable operators I'd grown up with or met along the way. Meanwhile, the smarter bikies from smaller clubs saw that the Comos were serious players and switched allegiances. Sometimes whole clubs would patch over at once, immediately bringing their talents, resources and businesses into the club.

Our membership numbers grew, and our supporters grew. It was healthy for some businesses and people to have an alliance with a feared bike club, so we had lots of donations from friends and associates. One donated $50,000, while many others provided smaller amounts of $5–10K. We raised enough funds to turn an empty warehouse space into a really cool club. Upstairs we had the boardroom with a huge table that accommodated sixteen members. This is where all of our meetings took place. Upstairs was all business. Downstairs, though: downstairs was a different story.

At ground level the Comanchero logo was printed into the floor itself in our colours, black and gold. To match that, a custom sculpture was donated by Zaki from the Sydney chapter – the full colours forged out of metal.

We put in a huge bar with a snake tank built into it, where Comos and our guests could enjoy the entertainment of watching snakes writhe around while they had a drink. In the centre of the room was a stage with a pole-dancing pole, surrounded by custom seating where you could watch babes writhe around if you got tired of the snakes. Running night-clubs all those years taught me a few lessons on how to throw a party. It was hands-down one of the best bikie clubhouses in the country at the time.

We'd barely finished our clubhouse when the first national run was scheduled. This was just three months after I took over, and the papers soon got wind of it. The paint was only just dry, and already we were taking shit in the media.

My first big media panic was in the lead-up to our first national party. We were hosting this ride and party to celebrate our new and first Comanchero chapter in Victoria. It would be a big deal as we were definitely going to be judged by our peers and rivals. In essence, a run is a long ride where the whole club will converge, then ride in full colours from one clubhouse to another, and end up back home to finish with a mad party.

For big clubs, this means hundreds of intimidating-looking men riding loud motorcycles. It's a show of force, and lets the world know how many you are and what you stand for. Most bikie clubs will go on a national run at least once a year.

Throughout the year there would be a number of inter-state runs, some to support other chapters and others that were pencilled into the calendar every year as mandatory, such as the memorial run, which everyone must attend as it's in commemoration of the brothers who have passed. We would all meet at a location then ride together to the Palmdale cemetery for speeches and drinks, followed by a party at one of the chapter's clubhouses, usually Milperra in New South Wales – site of the infamous Father's Day massacre between the Comos and Bandidos.

This, though, would be a straightforward run to celebrate the success of our new Victorian chapter. It was going to be a fairly epic undertaking – a run is a complex job to organise and pull off. Getting a few hundred or more bikes from one capital city to another and back again is not easy. You've got to arrange a schedule, calculate how far you'll go every day, where you'll stop and stay over, plus support vehicles for breakdowns or if there's trouble along the way.

There's a special role in every club, the road captain, whose job it is to ensure it all goes smoothly. He's responsible for multiple outlaw bikies to be up and moving at the appointed time, often after a night of entertainment that he's also organised: booze, drugs, strippers, whatever. Not an easy task. He's got to be staunch and have a good head on his shoulders.

But our road captain had everything worked out, and we were looking forward to our first run as a national club. With the rapid growth of the Victorian chapter, there were now 300 patched Comancheros and associates who would be on the ride.

Then, a few days out from the event, the *Herald Sun* published a little article announcing that there were going to be 300 Comancheros rolling into Melbourne to party. Safe to say, this got a reaction from the police.

They sent a response unit to block our street off at both ends. Officers arrived with attitude and reinforcements ready to disrupt our plans and arrest anyone who resisted. The boys didn't love this, obviously, and one of them came running up in a panic. 'There are cops everywhere. What the fuck do we do?'

'What do they want?' I asked.

'They say they want to talk to you.'

'Okay,' I said, eager to finish this shit before it kicked off. 'Tell them to come in.'

The local commander and her chiefs came in through the front, and they were not happy. The commander was a woman. I can't remember her name, but I remember her attitude. She was staunch, with a no-bullshit-don't-fuck-with-me-or-this-won't-end-well attitude about her. I liked her off the bat.

She wanted to know why a few hundred bikers were about to roll into town, and she was hearing about it for the first time in the news. I wasn't looking for trouble, couldn't be fucked playing games, so as soon as she mentioned the number 300, I realised what had gone wrong. The cops weren't communicating among themselves.

I reached for my diary and pointed out that six weeks earlier I'd called the police events liaison number and told them we were planning a run on this date. We had flagged with the cops that we were going to be riding up the Hume and through the city at approximately 4 pm. Strictly by the book.

Then four weeks after I'd first informed Victoria Police about the impending ride, I was advised by phone that there were other events on that day, some competitive running or cycling event. The police asked us to change our route and to avoid certain streets and the city. No problem on our end, I promised. Accordingly, we drew up a different itinerary and had confirmation it was okay to proceed, all done properly. All of which had been noted in my diary.

The four cops standing in front of me were seriously taken aback. They'd come expecting some dumb, belligerent bikie, and here I was showing them the names of the officers I'd spoken with and the dates and times we'd discussed our ride into Melbourne. I also pointed out that we went out of our way not to cause issues for the civilians in the area.

'We only come to the shed after hours, so we don't disrupt or intimidate the locals,' I explained.

I implemented rules that protected us from complaints by the locals. We wouldn't ride around the city during the day in colours. We made a point of not disrupting the status quo or intimidating civilians. Rules that we could both agree on that would give the community less to complain about and still let us enjoy our traditions.

The commander was so cool. Like me, she wasn't interested in playing games. She suggested we exchange numbers and assured me moving forward that if her men wanted to talk to any of my members, they would call me first.

The Melbourne boys rode out to Wallan on the Hume Highway and met all the interstate riders and their support vehicles at a truck stop about 50 kilometres out of the city. It was a sight, hundreds of Comanchero bikies taking up all of the truck and car park. We did our meet and greet, catching up for about an hour before we continued the ride into Melbourne. This was my first big run. I had to navigate to the clubhouse with minimal stops so we didn't break the line-up of bikes that seemed to go forever. Also meeting us was an escort of multiple helicopters – police and news crews that followed us all the way from Wallan to our South Melbourne clubhouse.

Malkoun family photo taken in Lebanon in 1965, without their father. *Clockwise from top left:* George, Joe, Helen, Mum, baby Jay, Elie.

Melbourne birthday party, 2008. *Left:* Jay and his mum, Kerry. *Right:* Jay with brothers Joe and Elie.

The Malkoun lounge room, Melbourne, 1970s. Jay *(top right)* with his father, Antonius, Helen cutting the cake, and sister Janet.

Melbourne, 2020. Nabs *(left)* and Elie *(right)*.

Lebanon, 2006. Jay *(left)* and LK with Lebanese politician and businessman Roger Eddé *(centre)*.

Perth, 2007. Jay and John Kizon at Jay's nightclub, Zuzu's.

London, 2013. Jay with Mick S while working on the recovery of gold bullion.

June 2019. Jay in Heidelberg, Germany, for hospital treatment, with his friend Cain.

Melbourne, 1998. Jay just after leaving jail, with Peter *(right)*.

A meeting for Straits Oil and Gas in Georgia, 2008. FV and associates *(left)*; The Turk and his associates *(right)*.

Cape Town, 2008. At the Indaba Mining Conference in South Africa. Jay, LK and Mike Povey *(left to right)*.

Lebanon, 2009. After the first rounds of a corporate mediation in London. Mick S, Simon Main, Joe Malkoun and LK *(left)*; Bill, The Lebanese Lawyer, Big Frank and Jay *(right)*.

South Melbourne
Chapter, 2011.
Group photo of the
Comancheros. Jay is
fourth from the right.

On the Comancheros'
ride to Sydney in 2012.
Jay is second from
the left.

Williamstown
clubhouse, 2012.
President Tie
and Jay.

Sydney, 2012. Licker, national sergeant of the Comancheros, and Jay.

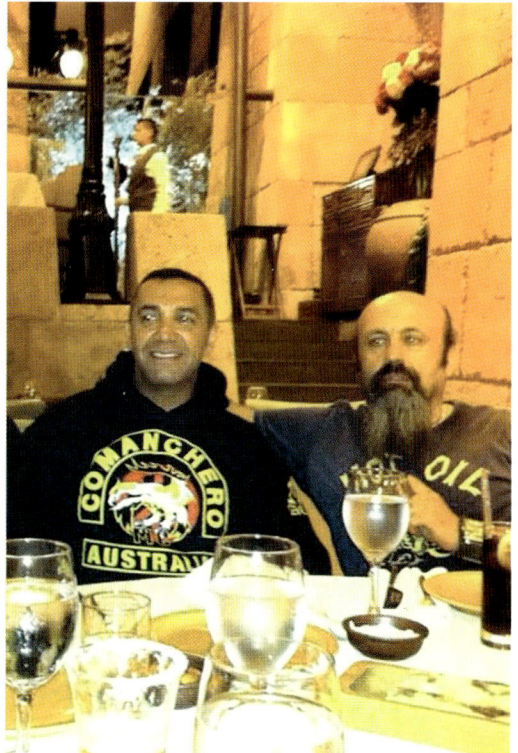

Lebanon, 2011. Jay and LK in a pyramid-shaped restaurant exploring the expansion of the Comancheros into Lebanon.

Madrid, 2012. A group photo taken by Jay of the Spanish Comancheros, celebrating opening a seventh clubhouse.

At the Hallam clubhouse, 2011. *Left to right:* John Kizon, Jay, Nick Matthew and Sunny, an ex-boxer and supporter of the club.

2009. An armoured vehicle during negotiations in Somalia while Jay was there to meet the Minister of Fisheries and Marine Resources.

March 2019. The wreckage of Jay's Mercedes CLK63S AMG post-bombing. It was destroyed in seconds, and a miracle that he survived. © *EPA images*

Athens, 2019. In hospital after the assassination attempt, a doctor inspects Jay's leg.

Jay was on a mission to stay fit, despite severe injuries, and pushed through the pain to train daily. A gym shot from Lebanon six months after the bombing.

There's nothing Jay won't do for his family and closest friends. *Top left:* Pentridge Prison, 1991. The three Malkoun brothers – *(left to right)* Jay, Elie and Joe – with Sister Barbara in the prison chapel. *Middle:* Jay enjoying a holiday in Bali with his kids in 2017. *Top right:* Back feeling mentally and physically fit and strong. Jay recovering at the former consulate home in the Lebanese mountains, May 2019. *Bottom left:* Jay with Greg 'Doc' Roberts at Scarborough Beach, 1999, after their release from jail, and *(bottom right)* London, 2016, in front of the painting for the *Mountain Shadow* book cover, the *Shantaram* sequel.

Thanks to the press we had choppers filming every minute as me and national president Dax led a procession of 300 bikes, accompanied by two black Hummers with the Comanchero logo down the sides as support vehicles.

It was a sight to be seen. The aerial footage the news helicopter got from that day was re-used for years thereafter. If there was any bikie-related news story, all they ever played was a Comanchero clip. It's a shame we didn't get the copyright on that footage, I could have earned well off the royalties. National runs are always an event, but we took it to another level and blew everyone away. Which is what we'd set out to do.

Normally, a chapter clubhouse will put the bar up and charge for booze as a way to raise funds to cover overheads, but we put on the food and piss for the brothers and had an open bar. It was important to me that we were good hosts and didn't want members paying for anything.

To cater properly for our party, I had some local nightclubs and bars donate the alcohol, so when our members rode into the South Melbourne clubhouse to support us, we expressed our appreciation by offering free booze and free food – we had a couple of lambs on spits and beautiful waitresses serving drinks.

We turned the tradition on its head, and everyone had a great time. There were probably some fuzzy memories in the morning, but the party itself is one that will be remembered. There were speeches, some of the boys without patches were promoted, others received more patches, and we had our celebrations. No issues, no drama, just a bunch of men celebrating their brotherhood. All without incident – not a given when you have that many alpha males in one room with free-flowing booze. Just immaculate vibes all around.

A lot of the interstate guys slept at the clubhouse with their bikes, leaving in smaller groups, some riding back as soon as the sun rose. Others preferred to enjoy a sleep-in. I'm proud to say that my Melbourne boys kept it reasonable, as most had to be back to work on Monday.

That was more or less how I liked my club to run. Everyone did their part, and in exchange they reaped the benefits of the brotherhood. My view has always been that it's best to keep everyone at bay and content, without aggravating anyone. If there is a situation to be dealt with, then it's wise to face it head-on.

Sometimes as a leader, you have to assert authority, and sometimes you don't. It's a delicate situation dealing with multiple personalities. Knowing when to take action and when to stay cool is half the job. Men can be real fucking sooks; I learned early on that a little discretion goes a long way. It helps to discuss bad behaviour one-on-one so as not to put anyone on show. If a quiet word failed to get the person to toe the line, then I always had violence to make a point.

In this way, I controlled my environment and solidified my leadership. In time, the Victorian Comos expanded to three chapters, each with their own presidents, but I kept them all under my wing. We held all our meetings in my clubhouse, and I insisted on the final say in everything. It was the only way to ensure unity, and, if it wasn't exactly democratic, it was the only way to run a one-percenter club. In every decision,

I consulted my other presidents and our lieutenants, but at the end of the day, it came down to me. Communication is king. An organisation like the Comancheros still needs a single, strong leader whose orders are the final word.

I had a wealth of experience dealing with both sides of the fence, and I know how creative and manipulative a small team of free thinkers can be. I didn't even let them make small decisions. The way I ran the club, the buck stopped with me. I made all the decisions, and I did everything with regard to the consequences. Part of it was my belief that ultimately, if my boys were acting up, then that was my fault and my responsibility to correct it.

I was of the view that I had to protect my members, predominantly from their own stupidity. I chose alphas to fill our ranks, which made us not only an efficient, fearless club, but also put a lot of heat on us. And meant that the minute I took my foot off the gas, the entire fucking thing went straight off the road.

In some ways, trying to run a bikie chapter is a lot like trying to parent teenagers. Only difference is the children in this scenario are pumped up on steroids and have shotguns buried in their backyards. The same basic rules apply. You need to be fair but firm. I couldn't even travel without one of the boys trying it on.

I was away in Dubai on business a year in and left my second in command Sarge in charge. We had our second national run and party scheduled a week after my return, and it was up to Sarge and the boys to prepare for the event. It's a lot of work to arrange food, beverages, entertainment etc., but Sarge was more than capable, so off I went to look after some foreign affairs for a minute.

On my return, I sat down with him to see how the preparations were going.

'We had the meeting, voted,' Sarge told me. 'And it was decided via a vote that the party would run from 7 pm to 10 pm.'

'Fantastic. That's good leadership, Sarge.'

'Then,' he continued, 'the boys will proceed to King Street to the strippers to kick on.'

'Sarge, cuz, a bit of insight, please. Three hundred plus drunk and high bikies in King Street on a Saturday night. How do you see that ending?'

Violence. Violence and arrests. Honestly, these cunts cracked me up. Could you imagine? The logistics involved in transporting 300 members in colours into the CBD and then doing your best to get them into a club? Then managing them and keeping them safe from trouble or arrest?

Fortunately for my members the only vote that counted was mine. I had to always protect them from their own worst instincts.

Next meeting, which I chaired, I left the discussion of the party till last, then asked all members to vote on the party at the strippers' from 10 pm.

All put their hands up for the yes vote and I took great pleasure in telling them, 'Request denied. The party will begin and end at the clubhouse. No members to go into the city. At all. After the party you members will be busy transporting our guests to their hotels and making sure everyone travelled safe and without incident. We are the host, and it is our responsibility to keep our interstate brothers safe and out of trouble.'

To make this happen, we had multiple noms with cars doing airport runs and hotel runs and available for anything that was required. My boys could go as wild as they liked in the clubhouse, but we weren't going to make it a police issue.

The police made themselves involved, of course. They were on edge that 300 bikies were enjoying themselves in a private clubhouse on the outskirts of their city. The SOGs had blocked both ends of the street, and every car in and out was stopped.

Members were not happy, but at the end of the day we had a mad party and suffered no casualties from basic member stupidity. My word was law because it was the only way to keep the club safe. Not every club ran that way, and some fell apart because of it. Sydney, for example, had many chapters that all ran their own race. This meant that different chapters were competitive and often there was conflict and issues between guys who were meant to all be on the same side.

One of the Sydney Comanchero chapters wasn't towing the line and ended up ambushed by other Comos chapters in their own city and shut down. This conflict could have started with a personality clash and escalated into a proper situation. Licker, the national sergeant-at-arms, had no issue dishing out the punishment required to keep a lot of men in line. He was strong, feared no-one, was absolutely loyal to the club and would not think twice about taking care of business. Members were hospitalised, vests were taken, the chapter was eradicated.

I didn't have such problems because we were one club with one ruler and the same rules across the board. The Sydney Comancheros were happy with the way things were going with us in Victoria and eventually adopted some of our policies. Equally, I had their support, and could call on the strength of the national chapters if push came to shove.

Although valuable, it was an offer I would never take because their support equated to guns and people ending up shot. Sydney is a different animal to Melbourne and extreme violence was absolute up there; in Melbourne violence was the last resort, not the go-to standard. It was a comfort knowing it was available, and they were not unhappy with the way we did things.

We forged our own path, and for a year or so, everything was cool, even with the police. Then the head of Taskforce Echo stepped it up a bit, a guy by the name of Detective Senior Sergeant Wayne Cheesman. I felt that he wanted to prove something to himself and didn't realise that we were playing nice with the cops because we wanted to, not because we had to.

Not long after he took over, the cops started swinging their dicks around. All of a sudden, whenever I went for a ride, there was a roadblock in my way. The Echo cops would pull me over and keep me for an hour asking dumb questions, knowing they had nothing on me but using their powers to waste my time. It was kindergarten tactics – being annoying because you can't do any real harm. But I lost patience after being pulled over and delayed five hours on a short ride to our new and second clubhouse for a pre-opening party.

The police got the date wrong. The real party was the following week, but their intel inspired them to ambush us that day and ruin what they thought was our big party. They had roadblocks and enough police to handle large numbers of bikies. They were expecting hundreds of interstate riders, but only halted me plus five members travelling from A to B. A total waste of police resources. The following Monday, Cheesman called me and introduced himself as head of Taskforce Echo, said he wanted a quick chat to discuss the upcoming ride and party.

'No worries,' I said, 'come to the clubhouse.' I sent out for lattes, gave him a tour, then invited him to sit, along with Sarge and two other Comos with leadership potential, so that they could listen and learn.

I invited Cheesman into our boardroom. 'This is where we hold all our business discussions. This is where you put your listening devices.'

He didn't think that was so funny. He started demanding that we tell him our intended route, from where we planned to meet the interstate riders to the clubhouse for the upcoming weekend's ride.

'You're a funny guy,' I said. 'Your men just fucked us around for five hours for no good reason and now you want me to volunteer our routes? Why is that? So you can continue to harass us? No chance. Best fire up that police helicopter of yours and find us.'

He wasn't happy. He started with threats of raids and roadblocks, to which I responded with a shrug. 'No worries, do your best.'

Cheesman just sort of sighed, and said, 'What will be, will be, Jay.' He stood up and walked out on a fucking quote from *The Sound of Music*. Honestly. Funny guy.

A couple of hours later he called me, trying to get me to cooperate and give the route. I declined again. 'Enjoy the chase, officer.'

Cheesman told me he intended to set up a breathalyser roadblock at the entry of the clubhouse, and to gain entry we'd have to pass through it.

Sure enough, the cops set up four lanes with witches' hats for breath testing and licence checking right at the entry. Was a sight to see, them trying to direct the traffic into four lanes for breath tests. Some of the guys who were not licensed just got off their bikes and walked into the club. We sent out noms to grab their bikes and bring them through. All in all, it wasn't a shitshow: the police did their job quite quickly and without incident, and we got on with the ceremony and partied.

Cheesman didn't give up, though. Not long after the party, I was out for the day and had a call from a member who happened to be driving past the South Melbourne clubhouse as the SOG were preparing a raid.

They were on the verge of cutting through our steel gate with a grinder to gain entry. I asked my member to find the policeman in charge and put them on the phone. I introduced myself and asked if he had a warrant.

'We do.'

'That's fine,' I said. 'Please don't break in. I will be there in ten minutes and will let you in.'

Apparently, a couple of the members had put a couple of guys in the boot of their car – a kidnapping over a personal debt. Police thought this was club business and wanted to search our premises for evidence.

When I arrived, I was told I could leave, but I didn't. Why would I leave? They were in *my* clubhouse. I wasn't doing anything wrong and there was nothing for them to find. So I stayed while they turned the place upside down and looked in hiding spaces I could never even have imagined. They pulled the billiard table apart. I didn't even know you could do that to a billiard table.

All they found in the club were the remains of some old lines of cocaine here and there. Bit of dust, bit of powder – nothing. The trace amounts they found didn't interest them. Didn't even look at them, as they were hoping for something much more incriminating, possibly guns and explosives in secret hiding spots. It was impressive, in a way – they were very thorough, but we had nothing to hide. Certainly, I had nothing to hide.

11

GROWING PAINS

IF I'M HONEST, I don't blame the police for being so uptight. They were playing a losing hand from the start. Back in the day, they just couldn't move as fast as us.

The bikie game was changing. Bikies had evolved. The outlaw one-percenters of the past decades – usually big dudes who liked bikes and brotherhood and didn't have ambitions beyond booze, girls and parties – were being replaced by hungry young blood chasing a different agenda. This new breed was fitter, faster and more aggressive, and had the advantage of sophisticated tools such as encrypted phones. There was money to be made and plenty of ways for bikies to earn – gyms, brothels, protection, security – that were old-school, as well as many other, infinitely more interesting ways.

Being a Comanchero from around 2012 onwards was like a meeting of ambitious minds. An invitation-only concentration of power and opportunity. Think of the Qantas Chairman's Lounge, but with cooler clothes and a better idea of how to have a good time.

As a group, we could leverage our strengths. And maximise our profits. Arbitration and mediation proved to be a healthy business. We often mediated or assisted in recoveries and kept 50 per cent for our efforts in what was a clean way of generating income without crossing the line and risking a police response. Showing up to a corporate meeting in colours was very effective. You don't even have to pull a gun. The inference is that you are there for a specific reason, and it usually guarantees the right result. In most countries it's perfectly legal to attend a meeting with your insignia on show, although I found out firsthand in Germany that it's illegal to wear colours in order to intimidate or threaten. They call this 'predator behaviour', which reminds me of lions hunting their prey.

I was in Germany on a $16M recovery mission. I ended up in the boardroom of the lawyers representing the thief who'd run off with the money and assets. This wasn't my first rodeo, and I had with me five senior bikies I'd brought as a bit of theatre. I was asserting myself and, you know, being a big mouth, making subtle threats – standard stuff. Walked out of the meeting with the desired result, but afterwards the boys told me about this predatory behaviour law in Germany.

Classic Germans. Even the outlaw bikers get off following the rules to the letter! They were the exception to the rule. Elsewhere, if you had the numbers, you could usually make your own rules.

Everyone knows anyone can be got if you put up enough money. That was the risk of doing this type of business. If you are on a team playing in the millions of dollars, you can be sure that team will have millions more that can be deployed to protect their wealth. Certainly, enough for a contracted hit.

There's always a price, depending on the target and the shooter. Sometimes it runs to hundreds of thousands of dollars. Often less. Shit, I've known Albanians in Greece who will do a hit for a nice steak dinner and $20K. But that's a last resort. Always better to reach an amicable solution that keeps everyone almost happy.

There is always strength in numbers, so most clubs were doing everything they could to recruit and consolidate power. Growth had always been one of Mick Hawi's priorities, and even from behind bars he was pushing for us to expand. Every so often I'd fly up to Sydney to visit him in prison and discuss Comancheros business. He would regularly issue orders and chase up prospects from prison through his leadership team.

I got a call from Dax, who was Hawi's right-hand outside of prison and eventually assumed the national presidency. Dax and Hawi grew up together and were very tight, real brothers. The bond these men had, and the apprenticeship they had growing up on the streets of Sydney shaped them into the fearless hard men they became. There was no grey with these guys. Everything was black or white. No ifs, buts or maybes. If they were with you, they were with you.

Dax was a natural leader, but he was also loyal above all else, and in those days he was carrying out Hawi's wishes in the running of the club. Which meant international expansion.

Dax had been following up on a lead about a non-affiliated Comanchero club in Spain. This outfit was fourteen chapters strong, and apparently using the Comanchero name and logo as they rode around Europe.

This was highly unusual because we didn't know a thing about them. So, myself and five members each from Melbourne and Sydney flew over to investigate. We were there to force them to affiliate with us as the official flag-bearers of the Comancheros – or close the club.

Dax was the most senior and was leading the charge. He had organised a translator as our Spanish friends did not speak English, and through the translator they'd agreed to meet at the national president's clubhouse in Barcelona.

We went in ready for anything. If this rebel club was getting a rise out of using our name, they would pledge their loyalty, or we would shut them down.

Dax and some of the other guys were huge units. Naturally tanked and fit. They would have been menacing if not for the polite, respectful manners they carried until they were pushed.

Dax could have led us into any situation and we'd have gone willingly. He had this relaxed but assertive way of issuing orders that made you feel good about being told what to do. We Comos were more than willing to get hectic for Dax, and if it came to it, we were ready. The boys had staked out the Spanish clubhouse for a few days, and worked out plans of attack, extraction and escape if push came to shove. We rolled in ready to assert our will, seven of us in colours and ready to throw down. We did not expect the reception we received.

The Spanish 'Comancheros' were not aggressive or intimidating. But they weren't exactly intimidated either. To our surprise, they seemed highly chilled out. Not the usual reception a squad of Aussie Comos led by Dax received.

The Spanish were not big men – they looked like children standing next to some of our bigger units – but they were generous and accommodating. Their leader was a guy named Pepi – a little guy with a massive smile.

There was some initial confusion about why we were there. It was a very Google Translate type of meeting, where it took a while for either side to understand each other. We'd come in expecting a tense, high-stakes negotiation. They seemed to want to keep giving us beers.

It turns out the Spanish Comancheros were just a social club that liked riding Harleys. They only vaguely understood the concept of a one-percenter motorcycle club. They knew about the Australian Comancheros, but only from following the news, and they got a bit of a rise out of sharing the same name. They told us their history and how they came about. Dax barely blinked at this weird situation. After a lot of smiling and nodding, he managed to explain what the Comos were all about, who we were and how we rolled, and why it wasn't top of the pops for a European social club to go around using our flag as a prop.

Once that was understood, he extended an offer to patch over to us, use our colours and all the benefits that came with it. They were happy with this proposal, and agreed to a second sit-down, after Pepi had taken our offer to a national meeting with all of their members to vote on it.

We felt pretty good about these guys, and the potential for the Comancheros to become an international club overnight was a huge leap forward.

Our hunch played out. Pepi gathered all of his members to vote to continue with us or shut down. They had twelve chapters all over Spain. Five of the clubs declined and chose to throw in the towel. The remaining seven surged forward with us as one-percenter Comancheros. It took around six months from our first sit-down in Barcelona to get everything sorted logistically. All of the Comanchero paraphernalia – vests, patches, colours, worth around $20K – was donated from the Sydney crew.

We gathered as many of the Australians who could afford the time and expense to travel to Spain for a huge patch over ceremony and party. Difference was, we partied Spanish style. No beer kegs and strippers here – the Spanish Comos brought good food and wine and their wives and children. The only thing missing was pony rides.

Despite how it may have appeared from the outside, we were not expanding a criminal organisation, merely growing the club and giving ourselves a feather in our cap. The prospect of enjoying a world run was now achievable, a prospect that excited us.

A major European chapter would also make us an international club. There is value in having people around the world to lean on when needed. Personally, I have people in various countries whom I can tap to assist when needed. Associates from all walks of life, not just the bikie world. This is a powerful tool.

When you have members and contacts in many countries, it gives you a clear advantage in any disagreement. The right ally helps you navigate the language and the culture, steer clear of stepping on metaphorical landmines (or actual landmines in some countries I've mediated in), and open up doors you could only dream of otherwise.

That's the legal side of things. The profit margins are even more lucrative in the underworld. Organised crime in Australia is about a $39B industry. Of that, something like $10–12B a year is just from the drug trade. Compare that to say, agriculture, which tops out at $76B. A lot of Australia is on the gear, and a whole underworld economy runs on it.

A case study in underworld business: once upon a time there were a Big Four who controlled most of the illicit drugs coming into the country. One of them, a bikie from another club, had both the key and the door and was killing it. This individual lived like a proper outlaw king and enjoyed every moment. Unfortunately, that life has a use-by date and his was in his mid-thirties. He held so much power that when he passed away suddenly, there was an actual drought. His networks fell with him, and pretty much overnight the product stopped coming into Australia.

His absence left a huge void in the industry, but there were plenty of willing and capable villains ready to pick up the slack. The new lords of the drug trade had evolved: they were not only interested in the obscene amounts of wealth, but they also wanted power and to achieve that they had to take control.

230

This meant ruling with fear and aggression. They rewrote the playbook. No longer was it about turnover and owning a big house while flying under the radar. This was the dawning of a new era of criminals who didn't give a fuck. If anyone got in their way, they had them killed.

It was clear this new generation was adopting the Mexican way of dealing with conflict. We all know how that went in Mexico. The new lords of the global drug trade had bikies in their ranks, for sure, but they were willing to work with anyone to get the job done. Cosa Nostra, Triads, Mexican cartels, Aussie politicians. Everyone has their price, and ultimately it never ends well for anybody. The money is just too big for most to avoid temptation. I kept my club away from it, but this wasn't always a popular decision, particularly as the Comos got bigger and bigger internationally.

Meanwhile, even as we began to export the Comancheros brotherhood overseas, the push to grow at home continued. We were well-respected in New South Wales and Victoria, yet this wasn't enough. We couldn't just keep riding up and down the Hume highway to party. We needed to have a presence in all of the states and territories. A ride around Australia would be insane and something to look forward to. No other club had the reach, power and ambition of the Comos in those years. No rival could step to us.

We opened chapters across the country, including one in Perth, which had been a Coffin Cheaters stronghold for ages. Month after month, we made big moves like this and picked up promising members where we could, but often that meant absorbing smaller but significant clubs.

There was a recruitment drive by most of the clubs in Australia, all keen to grow in numbers. You would wake up on a Saturday and read about forty members of one club patching over to another club. Bold moves like that were not unusual in Sydney, but we had bigger ambitions than that.

I heard the Ulans were setting up camp in Williamstown, just over the bridge and very close to our South Melbourne chapter. I called Sammy, the leader of the Ulans, who confirmed they had a clubhouse in Williamstown.

Sammy is a good human. We had a civilised discussion.

'You're too close to our South Melbourne chapter. You have to move further away.' I reasoned that any club setting up so close to another would always end badly. I explained that we wouldn't open up within 10 kilometres of another club for the same reason. 'It's best for everyone if we all give each other a wide berth.'

Sammy wasn't thrilled about it but understood the logic and agreed to move way up the road. We did a deal and took over the premises and made it a Como clubhouse. Not even a shot was fired.

Baz phoned me the next day. He told me the National Comos were talking to a team out of Adelaide that we were considering taking on. Apparently, this Adelaide crew – a mid-sized street gang led by a dude named Vince – were also in talks with the Mongols. We didn't want to lose these guys to our rivals, so Baz and I jumped on a plane to help speed up negotiations. In my eyes, the decision had already been made to recruit this lot and we were flying there to get them over the line.

The way Baz sold it to me, the deal was as good as done. In his view this meet and greet was less about negotiating the patch over, and more about gauging their numbers and the quality of their members.

We met with Vince over pizza and discussed what we had to offer each other. We knew that they hated the Hells Angels and had had a bit of a crack at them, so we already had common ground. Vince started off by letting us know the Mongols had reached out to him and they were in talks. The Mongols – one of the five biggest clubs in the world – were on a recruitment drive from Canada and had been reaching out to clubs all over Australia, making promises and gaining ground. Vince wanted to know what we could offer that the Mongols couldn't.

We told him a bit about our operations, what the club did for its members, what it meant to have the Comos' arm around you. I pointed out to Vince he ought to consider that to join the Mongols you had to provide your personal details – home address, licence number etc. – details you don't want to land in the wrong hands. It's a bit of insurance against you turning against the club once you've got access to the inner circle and trade secrets. But risky.

That level of potential liability unnerved Vince and his boys. Our talks went well, we got down to it, and got them over the line. We kept dialogue up with Vince for a few weeks over the phone, then locked in a date for a ceremony in Melbourne for the first four members to be the office-bearers: commander, sergeant-at-arms, road captain and treasurer.

Some of the Adelaide guys were on bail and had curfews so it was going to be tricky to get them to Melbourne, do the ceremony, have a light celebration and get them back to South Australia before anyone noticed. At 7 pm on a Thursday night, the Adelaide office-bearers rolled into town by car with about a dozen of their guys. We greeted them with numbers, because it was a big deal to finally expand into South Australia. Sydney had been in talks with Adelaide factions for quite some time. I was proud that we Victorians rolled out in full force to patch them in, with more than eighty members and supporters in attendance.

As Victorian leader, I was still getting up to speed on who our four new members really were. Without getting into too much detail, we did the speeches and the ceremony, and gave them their patches, followed by the traditional pouring of cold beer over their heads. So far so good – now it was time for a party. That turned out to be the last bit of peace and quiet we had with this foursome.

Our party ended around 1 am. Most of the local guys had to get up the next day and earn, but the South Australian contingent wanted to kick on. That was weird, because I was under the impression they had to hit the road and get back to Adelaide before their parole officers noticed they were AWOL. But they'd come all this way, so why not show them a good time?

I took them to a strip club, bought them a round of drinks and told them not to play up, emphasising how important it was to keep a low profile. 'We're getting hammered in the press, boys. The last thing we want is more negative publicity. So, everyone is on their best behaviour, yeah?'

The new members were all smiles and nods, then one of them pulled out a bag of powder and offered me a line.

'What the fuck is that?' I asked, giving the bag a poke. It was sort of a brownish colour and a really rough consistency.

'It's like coke,' the new guy told me. 'Different, but really similar.'

'No thanks, I've got an early start.' I left a couple of my trusted men with the newbies and went home for some sleep before my 7 am wake-up call. When I left, the new members were busy hoovering up the brown contents of the bag.

I still don't know what was in that bag, but it was *not* similar to coke. Not fucking similar *at all*. If it was similar to coke, then it should have been a little bit of an eye-opener that makes dudes chatty and excitable and maybe want to listen to some bad music. These cunts went *loopy*.

I was sleeping in the new apartment I had recently purchased in Melbourne opposite the casino and two blocks away from the CBD's stretch of strip clubs. It happened to be close to the Hilton Hotel, where the boys from Adelaide were staying. Around 4 am I was woken by sirens and the *chop, chop, chop* sound of a low-flying police helicopter strafing the skyscrapers on the edge of the city. That was annoying but I didn't think anything of it and managed to fall back asleep. At 6 am I was woken again by sirens.

I looked out the window and saw what all the commotion was about. The police had cordoned off the Hilton. There was cop activity everywhere, blue lights flashing, at least two helicopters hovering overhead.

An armed tactical response unit fully kitted out with armour and assault weapons were fanned out on the street. Those guys didn't fuck around. We're not talking about regular coppers – these guys were super fit, totally psyched to do damage and make a point. Not good.

I put the news on and heard some lunatic with a machete had attacked a bloke's car, chasing it down on foot through the city in the middle of the night. Now the tactical response police were going door to door in the Hilton, searching every room to hunt down the machete attacker.

'Fuck me,' I said to no-one in particular. 'Is that the Adelaide boys?' If they were arrested for waving fucking swords around in the red-light district, that was not going to end well. I'd just given them their vests, and now they were about to be arrested with Comanchero colours in their possession? I'd distinctly told these cunts to keep a low profile. And now news helicopters were hovering overhead and beaming footage live on morning TV to every household in Australia eating their fucking cornflakes. They'd been Comos for four hours and they were already getting negative national press.

One of them was arrested, and somehow the rest of them escaped across the border back to South Australia. Luckily, none of them were caught with Comanchero colours, but it wasn't an auspicious start to the Adelaide chapter, and it was only the start of our problems with them.

It soon transpired that these guys were not into the bikie culture and had little respect for rules or traditions, like the national memorial run, where we show up on our loudest bike and ride hard in full colours and full strength as a show of respect to the brothers who have passed on.

These Adelaide guys turned up to the run in a white stretch limo. That didn't go down too well with the older members.

Not a respectful move by the Adelaide boys at all, and on reflection I would say this was probably the straw that broke the
camel's back. Sydney went to work retrieving the colours from
the SA club, and we had to close the chapter on that chapter.

Over a two-and-a-half-year period, the Victorian branch of
the Comos had grown very quickly. We had lots of members
and were on the verge of opening our fourth chapter.

I'd ironed out all of the Victorian issues with reputation
and infighting, and squashed the beef with other clubs. We
took two clubhouses off other clubs, which had never been
done before. Held our ground against the police. For the most
part, we did it without any drama – we were reasonable in our
requests, and people were smart enough to comply.

However, when you run an operation the way I ran my
chapter, there are always going to be dissenters. Especially in
a bikie club, where people guard their individual liberties like
they are their lives. In some ways, they are. It isn't hard to get
someone offside, even if you have the best intentions.

The longer I was a Como, the more I understood that,
although there are some very good people in bikie clubs, for
the most part bikies are fucking parasites.

Blokes like the Comos in Sydney that first drew me into
the club had beliefs – a code and a hierarchy they lived by.
Loyalty was as important to them as getting shit done. I liked
that. They were very cool. But if you look at some of the other
outfits, their priorities are different. They take your membership not for brotherhood but for what they can gain from you.

They gain your bikes, your assets, your income, your loyalty; they put you to work – but you're all fucking pawns. With the exception of the very few high-ranking men giving the orders, you'll do the work, get the blood on your hands, but not enjoy any of the rewards.

If you get pinched doing some hectic shit for someone who gives orders but is too cowardly to do the work themselves, then good luck to you, bro. You're probably going to do some time. Comancheros were not like that, from what I saw. The senior members had their own shit going on and relied on no-one to do their work. Actually, most had their own crews outside of the club. Brothers they had history with and whose capacities they understood. No doubt such relationships had been tested and could be relied upon when shit went down. In my book, this was the right way.

The way the new generation of bikies was shaping up, the trend was to recruit new members only in order to pull a trigger or burn down a building, then rely on them to succeed and keep their mouth shut, merely because they were in the club. That was suicide, I thought. Clubs that ran that way were writing their own obituaries.

Most new members are recruited through existing members. There's a process of judging and testing new recruits before patching them in. We were a brand-new club and relied on good judgement to recruit and were strict about flushing out the flops after they'd demonstrated they couldn't hack it. However, mistakes were made, and there were always one or two imposters who got through. These are your weak links. And you're only as good as your weakest link.

When the stakes are high, and there's so much adrenaline, testosterone and steroids flying around, it's only a matter of time before the bullets start flying. At the end of the day, it's just maths. If you look at the statistics, the number one cause of bikie death is other bikies.

Leadership of an organisation like the Comos is a bit of a poisoned chalice. If you fuck up even once, then your chances of ending up knocked or incarcerated dramatically increase. Even if you don't put a foot wrong and never make a serious mistake, then someone else out there will make a mistake on your behalf.

Two years in, the Melbourne Comos were preparing for our national run to Sydney. We would leave on a Friday for the three-hour ride across the border to Albury, have dinner and some drinks, and just hang out together and talk shop before staying overnight. Some of the boys would cut loose and party most of the night.

The next morning we'd ride the remaining six hours to Sydney in time to celebrate Saturday with our New South Wales brothers. I couldn't leave on the Friday, preferring to stay back with my family, so I kept four members back to ride with me the Saturday morning. We could leave at 5 am, be in Albury by 9 am then lead the boys into Sydney. The first contingent drove into Albury around 4 pm on the Friday afternoon, then chilled out with some food and drinks.

Late that night, my second-in-command Sarge rang me from Albury with a disturbing rumour. He'd just been told by a member, Mexi, that the Sydney Comos were planning to ambush us. According to Mexi, when we arrived in Sydney, we were going to get jumped and battered and thrown out of the club. The inference was that me and a few others were out.

Sarge wasn't happy. He was somewhat reluctant to push forward. If I'm being honest, I thought he had a good reason to turn back. The Sydney Comos counted some of the most formidable cunts ever to ride a Harley among their ranks. Direct confrontation with them would not be good for anyone's health.

I thought about it for a sec, dissected all possible reasons for the existence of this rumour. Went over my actions and methods that could have triggered this type of reaction, and concluded it just was not possible. If orders had been given for me to have my vest snatched, they would have come from the very top, and Mick Hawi was too smart for that. Even if he had a problem with me – which I had no clue about – then it would have been easy to invite me to a meeting on my own, then deal with me without the rest of my crew there to interfere.

It's not that I trusted Hawi not to turn on me, but I knew him to be a better chess player than to lead me into a fight with all of my best soldiers by my side. It would have been carnage all around.

'Maybe we should turn back?' Sarge suggested. I detected a hint of panic in his voice, and fair enough.

'No chance, we don't turn back, bro. We keep nudging forwards.'

I jumped onto my bike at 4 am in the rain and rode to Albury where the boys were waiting, and then led them into Sydney, as per the plan.

I had my boys with me, my good boys. Everyone was on their toes. We stayed tight and vigilant, one in, all in.

At the celebration we stayed sober the whole time, ready to throw down at the slightest hint of trouble. None came. We gave the ambush rumour a bit of a nudge, but nothing came up. No-one said anything in Sydney. I tried to flush it out a little bit without saying too much, and I grabbed Mexi, the member who spun a really good story — a very fucking farfetched one, in fact. Turns out Mexi was an ice addict; that explained the text messages he'd been sending that read like the ravings of a paranoid. Wasn't unusual for ice addicts to dissect and recreate delusional situations in their mind. Mexi was an interesting guy but was clearly off his head and had to go. Sarge had relied on information from an ice junkie who really didn't make much sense. Not good.

The Sydney run worked out for us. We didn't blink, and nobody made a move. We rode away, unclear if this rumour had any truth to it. Could have.

There was a bit of to-and-fro going on leading up to this event. Some of my boys were spending time in Sydney and I just didn't know what they got up to and didn't report. Wouldn't be hard to stir the pot and create friction. All it takes is a couple of gossipers running their mouths with some he-said she-said shit to get people offside. When someone wants to try to knock you down a peg or two, they'll take the opportunity to believe anything.

To be the alpha you have to fight to get to the top and keep fighting to stay there. There are always ambitious people who want to be you. Have what you have and take what is yours. I did it to Adam even though it wasn't my immediate ambition. He started to slip up and was ultimately replaced. Granted, I had inherited fuck-all, but I still took it when I had the chance.

With these rumours of ambush circulating, now it seemed cracks were starting to appear in what was once an impenetrable vault. We were stronger when we were a smaller team of ten. At the inception of the Victorian chapter, all members were on the same page and moved in unison. With growth came loss of absolute control. You can't micromanage every individual. I had to rely on my chapter presidents to run their chapters and manage their members. Which let the rot set in.

12

BAD APPLES

When we returned to Victoria, I tried to flush out a guy who I figured was feeding Hawi. I tracked them down to the Williamstown chapter of the Comancheros, a formidable club just 10 kilometres away from our South Melbourne clubhouse.

Turns out the Williamstown chapter had some hang-arounds who were also frequently visiting members in Sydney, all the while talking shit about me and my Melbourne Comancheros. Stirring the pot and starting shit.

I heard from Hajasi, a senior member from Sydney who was in turn speaking with Hawi daily, and discovered that these two hang-arounds sold themselves as being proper hard cunts and that they had Hawi's ear.

The Williamstown sergeant-at-arms had brought them into the club and introduced them to Sydney, so I figured he should deal with it. I passed down the order to grab these clowns and bring them to my South Melbourne clubhouse. I waited a few days for the call that never came. Frustrated, I summoned everyone to the boardroom for a please explain.

'Where the fuck are these hang-around cunts?' I wanted to know. My questions were met with lies and excuses. The president of the Williamstown chapter who I respected didn't want me to issue a punishment for his sergeant, who I did not respect.

This was a big ask, as this cunt needed to be taught a lesson for two reasons: firstly, bringing dogs to the clubhouse, and secondly, for avoiding responsibility or doing anything about it after having been given the order.

Worse, he held the position of sergeant-at-arms. He was meant to be looking after the club and dealing with these issues, not fucking starting them.

I'm not going to lie, it got a bit tense, and guns were produced. Could have gone either way. It's a tricky situation when all of your members are present and watching. It's easy to get caught up in the testosterone-fuelled frenzy and go kung fu on a guy. But that would have caused other problems. A dilemma: brutality on my part would have been bad for club morale, but letting it go unpunished might have been even worse.

I let it slide but concluded that the sergeant had to go. Back at my HQ, I gathered the South Melbourne chapter and got my boys onto the job. Find that cunt and bring him to me.

The following day I got the call. They had him in their sights in Craigieburn and were following at a distance, waiting for an opportunity to grab him. I jumped into my car, a very fast Maserati, in anticipation, absolutely ropeable. This cunt who I didn't even know was creating drama in my club, so I couldn't wait to get my hands on him. I started driving north when I received an update from my team. The dog cunt must have seen one of my boys following him, because he suddenly slammed on the gas and shot through the red lights and over the raised kerbs between lanes to flee. Nevertheless, my guys stayed on his tail.

In a desperate attempt to save himself, he drove to the police station and literally parked on the nature strip outside.

'What the fuck!' I yelled, very frustrated. 'This is the same cunt who convinced Sydney he was a proper gangster.'

I pulled up alongside and called out, 'Hey, bro. Why don't you come join me over here?'

He ignored me, not having any of it, so for a minute we just stared at each other across the road in front of the cop shop.

I couldn't exactly start wailing on this dog under police cameras, so thinking quick, I dialled Hajasi's number.

'Phone your mate in Melbourne and put us on a three-way call,' I demanded. Hajasi did it right away, called the dog, and the idiot answered.

'Hello, you dog,' I said pleasantly down the phone. 'Why don't you tell Hajasi where you are? There you go, Hajasi, that's your hard cunt crying. This is the source of the intel you guys are getting. Didn't you say he was proper?'

Safe to say, Hajasi was taken aback and chimed in with his contribution. 'You weak dog. We will get you. You'd be smart to run.'

The dog did run. Don't know how far he got. He left the country and was not seen again.

The sergeant was retired and lost his bike. But it didn't matter. The damage was done.

Things didn't go the way I'd hoped from a national point of view. I don't believe I ever got ahead of myself; I knew where the real strength in the club was, and it wasn't Melbourne. We were good men and good soldiers, but we couldn't match the warring capability of the Sydney crews.

Those guys are next-level hectic, don't hesitate, possess no fear.

Last thing I wanted was a problem with Sydney, as my members were not equipped for that type of aggression. We all looked good, fit and strong, rode mad bikes, trained regularly, caught up once a week for meetings and paid our dues, then went back to family and work. I could have selected a different type of member, since there were many violent and willing men looking for a home and a brotherhood who would have jumped on, but I chose carefully not to bring that energy into the club. I couldn't be fucked with the drama and headache.

I'd had enough of all that while I was incarcerated. Ten years of war trapped inside with the most violent gangs in Victoria – next-level crazy, with no recourse but bloodshed. We didn't need that type of savage atmosphere in the club. We were good as we were. I kept running the club the way I thought best, and to keep things nice and civilised, while all around me the bikie game got wilder and wilder, until it got so high-stakes that something had to break. But that's a longer story.

When I first joined up, the Comancheros only existed in New South Wales and Victoria, with the capital city chapters managing issues sensibly so everything just worked, everyone knew their place and acted accordingly. Two years on and we had expanded to Perth and South Australia, and those guys were at a different stage and seemed to attract a lot of issues and constantly had dramas with other clubs. Sort of took the fun out of being involved – some of the shit that went down was too much even for me to have to deal with. Being a bikie started to become hard work and a lot less fun.

My intuition is not bad. It's not great, but not bad either. Most of the time, when I've got a bad feeling about something coming down the pipeline, it's turned out to be a shitshow. Look at ANOM.

Bit of background: Around 2018, the encrypted app that everyone in the underworld used to communicate was shut down. Suddenly, dudes needed a new way to keep in touch.

Someone who knew someone who knew someone recommended a new app that was supposed to be untraceable called ANOM. It was relatively cheap and worked on Android phones, and it was supposed to provide instant, anonymous communication between players.

Of course, what we know now is that it was all going straight to the law. The whole app was a Trojan horse, a sting operation designed and built by the FBI and distrib-uted by the FBI and AFP. The cops built a listening device and handed it to the crims who put it straight in their fucking pockets.

Every operator who used the app had all of their messages stolen and archived by law enforcement, and then the hammer came down on them. Mafia, Triads, outlaw motorcycle clubs, drug rings. Aussies, Albanians, Germans, Dutch, Swedes, Americans and many more – they were all smashed.

I took one look at ANOM and ran a mile. Back in the day, I never talked on the phone, and I wasn't going to start now. I've had six BlackBerries over the years, and I never used them for club business. I never trusted them. Never.

I put out a bit of bait once, as an experiment. Years ago, in a conversation with a friend, I mentioned something that would be, as the police say, of interest – some information about an underworld event. Completely untrue, just something I made up on the spot, but it was spicy enough that I knew that the ears of any law enforcement eavesdropping on the conversa-tion would prick up.

Sure enough, pretty soon I received information from a friend who had a friend within the police force, and sure enough they were investigating my bullshit lead. It was some-thing that could only have come from this conversation because this is the only time this particular piece of infor-mation had ever been discussed. I knew then that the devices were no good, because the cops had told me in their own way. So I threw away all the devices, and never touched them.

However, heaps of crooks ran their whole operation though

ANOM, and they were immediately fucked. I was in Europe recently, talking to a friend who works in private security for government agencies, and he says that the cops are overwhelmed by how much evidence they collected and continue to collect from the encrypted devices, all the encrypted devices, not just ANOM.

There's apparently a ten-year backlog of information that's so dense with incriminating evidence, the agencies are throwing stuff away. They literally don't have the time and manpower to respond to every crime, so they have categorised them according to priority and seriousness, from murder down to huge drug shipments and so forth.

Unless it's a murder or a huge drug deal or the exact location of an active door, they just don't have the resources to investigate and prosecute, so bin it. There's still so much pain coming down the pipeline for so many people.

These days, bikies are getting bailed up and incarcerated at shocking levels, but there's always been the risk of incarceration. And with that comes the risk that a member will start working with the police to avoid their jail time. Even back then, I was starting to realise that although my boys were solid, very few of the outlaw fraternity shared my old-school beliefs on doing your jail time. Where I came up, if you broke the law and you were caught, you served your sentence without incriminating anyone else.

But the new generation of villains coming up behind me were different – they crumbled at the prospect of a few years under lock and key and would chase after opportunities to inform for the police like a dog after a treat. Most of these crooks would opt for a deal when they are looking down the barrel of a bit of jail time.

Meanwhile, the papers were all over me, really smashing my name in the media, putting the spotlight on me every time a bikie on the east coast sneezed. The cops have a very cosy relationship with the press, and it started to feel like I was being set up for something big.

My understanding was that Cheesman and Echo didn't like how fast the Melbourne chapter had grown after moving into the city. The rumour was the police weren't happy. Personally, I think they should have thanked me. I kept things peaceful, which wasn't always easy to do. You'd think that would count for something. But every peace has to end.

All the while, life in the club was changing. The politics between chapters and the business decisions that other chapters wanted to take were moving in a different direction, which meant it seemed like a good time for me to leave on a high note.

I started to enjoy the club less and talked it over with my wife. 'Well, I've had a good run, perhaps it's time to move on.'

I thought I'd go overseas – get away for two years, let things calm down in the press and then see how we go. Getting hassled by the cops is one thing, bikies another, but I was getting grief from my wife. I was in the newspapers a lot, and she was growing embarrassed by the coverage and worried what the community would be saying about our family.

My daughter had just started attending Melbourne Girls Grammar, and my rising profile was causing tension there. I was in the papers most days and usually on the front page.

Before too long, rumours reached us that some other mums were trying to get our girls thrown out of the school. Sam was very concerned by this. I thought it was concerning. I thought to myself, *Do your best, ladies. What do you think happens next? I'll have Comos on every school gate greeting the mums and children as they arrive. Nobody's getting in or out. Take that to the Parent Teachers Association, geniuses.* Fortunately, the school didn't have a problem with the Malkouns and treated us as we presented, with respect and courtesy.

Still, none of it sat well with Samantha, and our fear was that it was never going to end and become such a huge distraction that the girls' performance at school would be affected. We didn't want to embarrass our children or cause them to be ostracised because of my bikie–underworld involvement and associations.

Our dream of having children and doing our best for them, providing a good education and everything else associated with developing well-rounded, smart, sporty kids was being hindered by my club life and gangster shit and all-round bad decisions.

It was clear to me that I had made an epic mistake, that despite my guaranteeing it would not interfere with my family life, club life was having a huge negative impact. Ultimately it was isolating my children from schoolfriends, and any associated activity – such as birthday parties, play dates and all the stuff we take for granted – was at risk. I really fucked up.

I couldn't ignore that it was becoming harder and harder to balance family life with the responsibilities of leading the Comancheros. On one hand, I felt like the king of the mountain. I could have gone on, and grown more and got stronger, but I never took advantage of it. Not really. My family came first. It was time to look for other opportunities.

My wife had an interest in advanced education for kids, and was really into Shichida, which is a right brain-training program for kids aged between six months and six years old. We did it with our girls, and she wanted to become an entrepreneur, open up her own franchise and teach young students to reach their potential. I fully supported Sam.

'Why don't we do it in Dubai?' I asked her one night. We loved Dubai, and we would spend a month there every year with the kids just to holiday. If we could make our holiday destination our day-to-day lives, why wouldn't we?

The perks for expats in Dubai are crazy. If you're employed in Dubai, you get a 60,000 dirham allowance to educate each of your children. For most people, the job pays for private school; everybody has a driver and a nanny.

The Shichida program involves hour-long 'whole brain' training sessions between the infant and parent or a nanny. You really have to sit with the child and engage with them to achieve best results. It seemed like a no-brainer. Why wouldn't you want to send your child to early learning and get them ahead of the game – especially if it costs you nothing, and you don't even have to participate, the nanny will do it. The more I thought about it the better it felt.

'Let's go,' I said to my wife.

And I wasn't getting any younger. I was well into my mid-fifties and thought I should really give all that bikie shit a rest. I loved running the club, but if I had to choose between bikie shit and my family? Not even a choice.

I saw the writing on the wall and took the lesson. Gave that life away and gave away all the shit that came with it. For a while, friends of mine who stayed in and went with the new way of doing things lived well. Very, very well.

But the government was relentless. With all the resources of the Australian police against you, not to mention the Greek and Turkish police and Interpol on your case – it's a gamble I wasn't willing to take.

You may as well be living in a casino. Eventually, the house is always going to win. Time to deal myself out. I packed up and made plans to move my whole family to Dubai to start an early learning centre. Fuck, when I say it out loud it sounds ridiculous. But at the time it seemed like the right thing to do.

Maybe the police presence and constant pressure got to me, maybe I made it sound better than it was to myself. I don't know, but I did know that the bikie life had a use-by date and the only way to avoid it was to retire.

We decided that I would retire from the Comancheros and move overseas for two years, long enough for shit to settle, we reckoned, and then we could return and continue our family life in a normal capacity. This was a tricky situation. I had to ask myself – 'Who do I trust?'

My concern was that because the cops had such a boner for me, they would stop me from leaving if word reached them about my plan. I decided to trust no-one, except for my wife and brothers. Two weeks after I went on a trip, I announced I was not returning and retired from the Comancheros.

Technically speaking, you're not supposed to be able to leave a club. They'll tell you that once you're in, you're in for life. If you leave, or if you patch over to a rival club, that's seen as a betrayal.

You're supposed to cover up your tattoos by inking them out completely, or the brothers you've abandoned have the right to remove them with blades and blowtorches. Both methods are painful. Using fire is brutal. You'll never be able to order roast pork off a pub menu again if you've seen it happen. Blades aren't much better – you've got to go an inch deep to make sure you've completely removed the skin.

I didn't leave the club: I retired. That meant I was still able to access the clubhouses as a retired member but no longer had a say in the running of the club.

I had, over the past few months, discussed retirement with Dax and Sarge, who was the natural person to replace me. Sarge had been in it with me from the beginning, and together we'd built the Melbourne Comos. He had his ways and I had mine, we didn't agree on everything, but we did always get along. Sarge was champing at the bit to take over the club; after our first chat about me retiring he got excited at the prospect of running the club his way.

Sarge had been a strong and loyal offsider, but deep down he'd always wanted the leadership. I couldn't think of anyone better to lead the Melbourne Comos.

We'd started the real history of the chapter together, and built it from three amigos in an empty shed to a truly awesome MC chapter. We were a powerful chapter of the number one club, and he was my number two through it all. There's no way the club could have grown the way it did without him.

I wanted him to have the leadership, but I didn't tell him I was moving to Dubai permanently right away. Not until I was safely out of the country.

I went on tour with Sarge and ended up in Dubai. While there I told him I was not returning.

'You want to be the state president?' I asked him.

'Yeah, sure.'

'There you go, you're the boss. I'm staying here. The Comos are yours now.' I folded up my vest and handed it to him.

'Oh,' he said. 'Fuck.' I could see he was panicking. It's one thing to want the crown; it's another thing to wear it. 'You're not coming back from Dubai?'

'I'm out,' I told him. 'I've got my personal reasons.'

'What if I've got a problem?'

'You can sort it.'

He thought about it for a minute and then made a counter-offer: 'I'll only accept the leadership if you promise to be my sergeant-at-arms.'

'Sergeant? What are you talking about? Why would I move from boss to sergeant? How the fuck is that supposed to work?'

In the end, I promised him that if there was a problem, I would help sort it out.

'But there won't be any problems,' I reassured him. 'You'll be the leader. Just keep doing things the way I have been. You've got four chapters in Victoria, and Sydney backing you up. You've got seventy men you can drop on any issue. You don't need me. Do you want it or not?'

'Yeah. I want it.'

'Well, that's that, then. Take the colours. The Comancheros are yours now. Congratulations.'

Then I handed my colours over to Sarge, which was my final act as leader of the Comos in Victoria. Sarge was excited to be the state president and wanted the position but also wanted me back there with him. I could not, I told him; I had my family to consider. At a certain point, a man has to choose his family, and, honestly, if you're a man at all, then it's not really a choice. Family always comes first. Not even a question.

I wish I could have given Sarge more of a warning that I wasn't coming back, but I had a feeling that if the police knew I was migrating they may not let me out of the country. On reflection that would have been a better scenario, so much better than how it all played out.

Travel was becoming harder and harder for members of bikie clubs in Australia. Peter Dutton, who was the Immigration and later Home Affairs Minister for Australia, had gone to war on bikies as easy targets so that he could get a quick solution to the problem of bikie violence and crime. Deportation was the solution: send them back to the country of origin.

The federal government started deporting bikies to their home countries based on the '501' section of immigration law Dutton created where people could be removed on the grounds of 'good character'. All of a sudden you had members getting arrested and shipped off to Manus Island in the prison camps where Australia kept refugees.

It hit the Comos hard, because we had a lot of Kiwi, Māori and Islander members in Australia. Basically, they were rounded up and deported to their countries of origin. Some of these guys had been living in Australia since childhood. Peter Dutton had told the press he was taking the trash out, to make Australia a safer place. This minister was not fucking around. They deported hundreds of bikies and many more crims who were considered undesirable.

All of that was on my mind when I had to deal myself out of Como business. I knew that if I flew to Australia to help Sarge sort out his issues, then I might end up in a fucking offshore prison camp.

I was at that stage of my life where I'd be travelling for work, and my daughter would phone me, already calling the shots: 'Daddy, you must come home right now. I miss you.'

And I would drop everything. Finish my work and get on a plane straight home. I am just so in love with my kids. The time I spent with my children when they were so young and happy? Priceless. There's nothing that comes even fucking close to that.

Things got hectic for the Comos after I left. You can read all about it in the papers, so I don't need to go into it now. Sarge and the guys he led were the best mates you could ever ask for, and I wish things could have been different, but I had to give away the bikie life, and make a new life for myself and my family in Dubai.

13

DUBAI

DUBAI WAS HEAVEN. Or hell. It can go either way over there. It really depends on how much cash you have at your disposal.

Dubai is a city where the past has to run that little bit harder to catch up with you. If you're making 5, 6 million a year, and your work has a way of making enemies, then Dubai is a relatively safe place to live.

If you arrive with a stack of cash, it doesn't matter how you acquired it. You can blend in. If you're driving a brand-new Bentley, you may as well be taking the bus. If you've got a fleet of twenty cars, that means nothing there because everyone's got a fleet of twenty cars. If you're living in a penthouse in the Burj Khalifa, the world's tallest luxury skyscraper? No big deal. The next guy owns the floor above you.

If you can pay for it, the world is your oyster in Dubai. Private schools, drivers, security, household staff. You could go out of an evening and drop a few hundred thousand dollars having a good time and nobody would blink, because the guys to your left and right are dropping a few hundred more.

This level of wealth was normal, and it meant that money movers inevitably were prevalent in Dubai. In the Emirates' glitziest state, you could live in a way that would put a target on your back in any other city in the world. It made it easy to relax, and that meant you would meet like-minded people from all over the world kicking back and enjoying life. That's how I met Wayne Schneider. He was a high-ranking Hells Angel who had a reputation as an international kingpin. On a financial level he was well-respected, the most significant member the Angels had produced from a money-making point of view.

Wayne had left Australia in February 2012 for a stint in Thailand after police busted two meth labs in south-west Sydney that they wanted to pin on him, and he'd then moved on from his Thai apartment to Dubai with his wife and kids. He kept his family in the Burj Khalifa and his mistress in a villa on Jumeirah Beach. It was hard to say for sure who had the better deal – each an incredible property. I suppose Wayne had the best of both worlds. That's the way he liked to live – the best of everything.

He was huge, tough as nails, but you wouldn't know it to look at him. Smooth skin, sharp haircut, he had a bit of a baby-face that gave no clues to how hard he went. Tall, handsome, articulate – Wayne was The Boss in every sense. He wasn't arrogant or flashy. Just an Aussie bloke having a good time who happened to just have it all. However, tall poppy syndrome being what it is, a lot of people were jealous of his success. For many, he was easy to hate. For me, he was easy to like.

A mutual friend, Simon Main, introduced us – he told me that he wanted me to keep an eye on Wayne and watch his back in the new city. Later on, I found out that our mutual friend had told Wayne the same thing about me.

We caught up now and again to train and have coffee, but kept it nice and casual; he did his thing, and I did mine. It was impossible for me to keep up with Wayne on a night out – to split the bill I would need to take out a second mortgage. I thought he was pretty cool. Carried himself well.

I learned early in the friendship to keep the catch-ups out of the clubs and limit them to daylight hours – breakfast, maybe lunch or the gym. Nothing with bottle service, because that became dangerously expensive quickly. He dropped big money every time he went out, one of those outlaws who has no limit, and the hosts of Dubai all knew it. When you went out with Wayne, the red carpet was laid out to another level.

In Dubai the bars open at midnight and close at 3 am. No-one arrives before 1 am, so you get two solid hours to have some fun then take the party home. Still, Wayne knew how to spend a staggering amount of cash in that short window.

I caught up with him for breakfast one morning, and he brought along his good friend Glen, a Hell's Angel who'd just arrived from overseas the previous day and exchanged all of his money, $30K, to dirham in cash. He'd been carrying it all on him. Then he'd gone out with Wayne. When I saw them the next morning, Glen was looking very hungover and sorry for himself.

'Did you have a good night?' I asked Glen. 'You look a bit dusty.'

'Wayne got me, bro,' he replied, and, in between skulling bottles of water, told me about the night. They'd decided to have a few drinks in the club downstairs at 1 am. Wayne ordered bottle service to the table, then two hours later, Wayne handed him the bill.

'Your shout, mate,' Wayne yelled to Glen over the music. Those two hours cost just about all the cash Glen had in his pocket.

What the fuck, I thought. *You could buy a decent car for that.*

After hearing about a couple of incidents like this, I knew not to go out clubbing with Wayne. He was a great guy but a bad influence on a night out, and he was not alone. Dubai seems to bring out the Las Vegas in people; they suddenly start spending obscene amounts of money, usually during a short stay or holiday. Louis Vuitton and Hermès become the go-to shops to grab a few items. Tourists would easily drop $100K on a shopping spree without raising any eyebrows.

I knew of blokes who would arrive in town for twenty-four hours on their way home from Europe, book a room at the Burj Khalifa at $7K a night, check in, drop the bags, go shopping and spend a $100K stack, drop $15K on dinner, hit the club, spend $20K, back to the room, shower and straight to the airport. Only used the room for a wash and to store their things for the night. Unreal, right? Not in Dubai. There it made sense to spend $7K on a shower and a storage locker.

★

In November 2015 I went to Bangkok for medical reasons – I had a lump in my throat that I needed to get biopsied to check for cancer. I booked into the Bumrungrad International Hospital for the consultation and surgery. I landed on Wednesday, had some samples taken from my throat and lymph nodes, and then expected to receive the results on Saturday.

Wayne flew into Bangkok to keep me company for the duration. In those years, he was spending a lot of his time in Pattaya, the Thai resort and party capital about 140 kilometres outside of Bangkok. There are good parties to be had in Pattaya – it's a certain kind of paradise, if you're into that sort of thing. And in those years a lot of bikies and underworld types set up lives there. Wayne kept a villa there, and whenever I was in Thailand I'd give him a call and we'd catch up.

He booked a three-room hotel penthouse and we had a pretty chill few days. Thursday night we went out to dinner, got up early the next day to train, nothing that exciting was happening. Wayne had a girl with him and was on his best behaviour.

But then on the Friday, Michael – my lawyer mate who I'd travelled with to London and who loves a party as much as any gangster I've met – flew up from where he was living in Phuket and took the third room in the penthouse apartment. He started playing up, getting on the piss, and called some girls up to the room. Next thing you know, there's a full-scale party going on all around me. Wayne got on it, then I got on it, but it was all pretty civilised, very PG-rated.

But then Wayne cracked out the liquid GHB. Next thing I know, it's two in the morning, there's us three and maybe ten girls all running about, and Wayne's lost it completely. It was like he was possessed, just totally insensible, screaming like an animal and throwing himself around the upstairs bathroom, all six foot four and 120 kilos of him.

Hotel security was a bit alarmed by all the screaming, so they were calling up the room wanting to know what was happening, but I shunned them; I told them it was all good, thanks for your concern. I could handle it, but my mate Michael nearly shat himself when he saw the state of Wayne.

'What do we do?' he asked me. 'He's gone fucking crazy!'

'You go,' I told him. 'You're a lawyer, you don't need to be around this. I'll deal with the mess.'

Michael left immediately and checked into another hotel, and I spent the next hour just hosing Wayne down in the shower, trying to get him to come to his senses. Dude was like something from a horror movie. It was fucking weird, and I'd never seen anything like it before – he was up and moving, but there was just nothing behind his eyes. By the time I finally got him to settle and go to bed, the sun was coming up. I decided to stay up for my results at 10 am from the hospital. The call came in – all good, no cancer – and when Wayne woke up, he wanted to celebrate.

'Come to Pattaya,' he kept urging me. 'I have some international guests coming, it will be a lot of fun.'

'I don't want to go to fucking Pattaya, I'm not in the mood,' I said. 'I want to get the fuck out of here and go back to my family in Dubai.'

But Wayne was relentless, giving me all these reasons, and after a while it seemed like it would be easier to just go to

Pattaya for a minute than to keep resisting, since Wayne was not taking no for an answer. So we went to Pattaya, to Wayne's villa. There were another couple of blokes there, just hanging out, training, partying a bit. Wayne introduced me to one of them, Antonio.

Antonio 'Tony' Bagnato. I'd never met him before, but he seemed like a pretty cool bloke. He was a proper hard cunt. He and Wayne trained together and hung out; Antonio was a kickboxer and was living full-time in Thailand. They say water finds its own level, and these guys found each other.

I wasn't feeling good at all, as you can imagine. I'd been up all night hosing down an out-of-his-mind Hells Angel, and I was feeling pretty shit. Nevertheless, I went and met his guests, shook some hands, put in an appearance and then made my exit, back to the villa for a rest.

I crawled into bed, took a Xanax and passed out. I woke up to someone hammering on the front door. I assumed it was the cleaners or a delivery guy or whatever, so I lay in bed, a bit groggy from the Xanax, yelling for them to come in. I lay there waiting and waiting but the hammering only got louder, so in the end I mustered the energy to go to the door and open it and was confronted by about twenty Thai coppers.

Well, fuck, I thought, and out of reflex I did a quick scan of the room. There was a little rack around from the night before, so my first thought was: *I hope they don't make me do a drug test.*

While I was looking, I could see Tony's wallet and cigarettes and his manbag on the coffee table, but I didn't have much time to think about it, because the cops wanted answers.

Apparently, the villa security guards had reported a bit of commotion the night before.

'There was a disturbance here last night,' the lead police officer told me. 'And there's blood out here on the landing. What happened here?'

'I don't know,' I said. Honestly, I didn't know. One minute I'm asleep, and now I'm surrounded by the Royal Thai Police. They weren't giving me much information either – I explained why I was in Thailand, showed them the medical records that proved I was there for medical reasons, and they were satisfied with that. But they still detained me all day while they carried out their investigations.

It wasn't until 4 pm that afternoon that I discovered that Wayne had been kidnapped. He'd disappeared, with everything pointing to a kidnapping. I relaxed a bit when I heard that. Wayne had told me about a guy who'd been kidnapped previously in Pattaya and was released after paying a $7000 ransom.

I thought that must have been what had happened here – some young hothead snatched Wayne knowing the Angels were good for a ransom, so this was a temporary situation with an easy solution. I'd find who'd done it, pay whatever it took, and bring Wayne back. Easy.

But I was still under arrest pending the investigation, although not restrained, at least. No cuffs, no cell – they were fairly polite about it, as cops go. They told me I had to check out of the villa and get a room in the Hilton across the road so I could sleep for the night, but in the morning I'd need to head back to the cop shop while the investigation continued.

I had my phone though, so I contacted my Comanchero brothers in Europe to let them know the situation. Just quickly: A, B and C had happened, and the police were holding me in custody without charges. Not too big a deal.

'No worries,' the boys told me. 'We'll send someone to help you.'

Later that day when I was at the police station, a call came through. A Thai national – a man of influence – entered the holding area and asked which one of us was Jay. I stuck my hand up, and he wandered over.

'The boys told me to get you out of the country. You're in my custody now. I've got strict instructions to get you out. Let's go to the airport and get you on a flight out.'

Wow, this is kind of full-on, I thought. *And handy if I had been guilty of anything.* 'I'm not going anywhere,' I said. 'I haven't done anything wrong. I can't bail on my mate – he's been kidnapped.'

I explained to my new Thai friend that leaving was not an option. He said he was given strict instructions not to leave without me. We were at an impasse, so he said he would stay until Wayne got back.

At this point I didn't understand the extent of what was happening. Wayne and Antonio had both vanished. I called Sam in Dubai and asked her to phone Wayne's wife, let her know what had happened, and to get a hold of Glen, the Hells Angel mate of Wayne's also living in Pattaya.

Glen came to the police station, taken aback by the reality of what was going on, but neither of us had a clue as to how bad things were about to get. Best we could establish is that both Wayne and Antonio were missing.

Adding further confusion to the circumstances, Glen had a number of missed calls around 2 am from Antonio but had slept right through them. Had they both got into trouble? Were they calling Glen for help? We didn't know.

I watched the rest of the investigation from inside the police station. It was all hands on deck. A whole area of the station was dedicated to the case, and what must have been seventy cops worked the case – undercover, uniforms, marked cars. The works.

From where I sat, I saw all the undercovers coming and going on the street as they gathered intelligence. They were actually very, very on the ball. I've seen investigations where the cops don't know shit from clay, but these Thai police were good at their jobs.

But I still didn't know what was happening. By the third day, I had a quiet word with Glen to discuss the fact that the cops seemed to know more than they were letting on.

'Apparently the Thai police move things a bit faster if you offer them a reward,' Glen told me. That made sense to me, so we offered them a couple hundred thousand baht (about $30K) for good luck. Sure enough, within *six hours* of receiving the incentive, they closed the case.

They'd actually had the whole case unwound quite quickly. They knew exactly what was going on. Witnesses had placed a hired Toyota HiLux in the compound outside the villa. The crew in the car had been acting suspiciously, and the police tagged it immediately – a modern hire car that already had a tracker on it. They knew exactly where it had been and where it was now. Within hours of it being called in, they'd tracked the ute, cross-referenced CCTV, made phone calls, identified the crooks, and found the shallow roadside grave where Wayne had been buried.

I still don't know why it happened or have much more knowledge than they reported in the news. Some associates grabbed Wayne and took him to a safe house they'd set up for the kidnapping – two chairs with restraints and the bottoms cut out so you could keep victims tied up for days on end. All the tools for a long kidnapping and interrogation. Clearly there was a second target, who I heard was supposed to be Glen. Fucking horrific end for my poor mate Wayne.

But after all that commotion I was free to go. The Thai cops drug tested me just to see if they could land a charge there, but it had been five days in custody so by then my system was clean. I left Thailand with the police's blessing, confident that I had nothing to do with what had happened.

The underworld, though, was a different story. You have to appreciate that the Comos and the Hells Angels were fierce enemies. A lot of blood spilled on both sides, going back a generation. The fact that a Como leader like me, albeit a former one, had been in the house when an Angel was murdered wasn't a good look. Everyone thought I'd knocked him – both sides: Comos and Hells Angels. On the day I walked out of the police station, there were probably a lot of Angels who would have liked to see me in the ground too, but Glen relayed to them that I wasn't the problem.

I left the country without incident, but I'd never know if my being there in Wayne's final days would come back to bite me.

You could easily come to the conclusion that I had in some way been involved. The media went to town, with some outlets saying I was arrested for his murder, which wasn't helpful reporting. I was getting calls from all over the world: Did I kill Wayne? Were the Comos at war with the Hells Angels? My brothers in London, Spain, Lebanon, Sarajevo and Australia all bridged up with anticipation of a war they thought I'd started.

They were like, 'Oh yeah, no issues. We get it, he was your friend. *Wink wink.*'

It was difficult for Comancheros and Hells Angels in Australia to believe or accept that me and Wayne were mates. I suppose when you do the maths, our friendship really didn't make sense, but that was the beauty of it – we were very different people, but we had one thing in common, which was the capacity to look past the issues and move forward peacefully.

Luckily, I had kept senior Comos informed of my friendship with Wayne, and despite the old issues they got it. It was unorthodox for Comos and Hells Angels to hang out purely because we got along and were in similar circumstances. We hung out simply because we liked each other's company. Wayne was genuinely a likeable rogue, he ran his own race and stood out alone. We had no business together; we were just mates. I lost a friend, and he was actually a really good bloke. He lived hard and fast. Gone too soon, but how many of us manage even a fraction of the living he did in a weekend? To this day every time I see a handsome fucking contender with a bird on his arm order bottle service at the corner table, I think of Wayne, and I smile.

14

THE CONSULTANT

IF YOU WANT TO get shit done, there's no place like Dubai. There's not as much tall poppy syndrome or the bullshit jealousy of success that you find in Australia. If you are ambitious and work hard, then you can make anything happen.

The banks are discreet and open twenty-four hours at the airport, the laws are the right shade of opaque, and the culture rewards big swings and smart investments. It made it easy for me to work on projects all over the world and step in to help things happen where necessary and financially rewarding.

Here's the thing: what they don't tell you when you're a young kid running around smashing cunts and hustling and dreaming of the good life is that the lives of the one-percent elite business heavyweights aren't that different from the lives of the one-percenter outlaws.

The same set of skills that made me a leader of the Comancheros – reading people, striking a balance between hard and fair, finding the way both parties could benefit from a situation and making that happen – well, the corporate world needs them as much as the underworld. Probably more so because corporates are used to fucking around without anyone finding out. Some of them are very easily startled when consequences come knocking at their doors.

When I'm brought in to fix a corporate situation, it's extra satisfying. At the end of the day, the only real difference between the two worlds is the amount of money on the table. In some ways, my life in Dubai was a more sophisticated version of my years in Melbourne straight after I was released from prison. Again, I found myself running around directing traffic, solving problems for people in high places. People in low places, on occasion, of course, because everyone deserves a fair mediator.

My social circles were even more diverse, because in the cosmopolitan mecca of Dubai, I was mingling with the most diverse and interesting people from the far corners of the world. In Dubai, I made some unlikely friendships. Wayne was one end of the scale. His Highness was the other.

Me and LK would fly into Dubai for his corporate meetings. Dubai was a great meeting point, accessible to players no matter where they lived. LK had a lot going on, usually with projects in various countries. People would fly in from all over the shop; London, Africa, Australia and the US to meet with him, including his friend The Lebanese Lawyer, who handled some African and Middle Eastern stuff for LK. I would watch

LK work, impressed by how he never wasted a moment. You never saw him watching TV or chilling out, or doing anything that didn't relate to work and success. I mean, we would hit the mall now and then for a bit of a shop, but mostly it was only about work. Even our dinners were corporate meetings disguised as mealtime.

While in Dubai with LK, we attended an Arabian horse show in the neighbouring emirate of Sharjah that was being held by His Highness (HH) Sheikh Sultan bin Muhammad Al-Qasimi. I struck up a conversation with a woman named Julie, the manager of the Arabian Horse Facility at the palace in Sharjah, who had been working for HH the ruler of Sharjah for more than twenty years.

HH has a world-class Straight Egyptian breeding program and some of the finest and rarest bloodlines in existence. Straight Egyptian horses make up only about 5 per cent of the Arabian horse population. Only the purists breed Straight Egyptians. I had inherited a few Straight Egyptian horses from a friend and loved everything about them. If there's one thing more beautiful in this world than a chopped Harley with ape hangers, it's a noble purebred Arabian horse.

I was blown away by the high standard of Egyptian Arabian horses in competition and asked Julie if it would be possible to visit the palace stables and see the horses. I didn't have any ulterior motive and I just wanted to visit the horses.

'It's difficult to get into the palace,' Julie told me. 'However, write me an email request and I'll fax it to HH in the morning.'

I did. I wrote that I admired HH's breeding program and that I also bred Straight Egyptian horses in Australia, and went on to say that I would be grateful for the opportunity to visit the stables and meet his horses.

Later the following day Julie phoned me with an invitation to visit the palace the next day at 8 am. Along with strict instructions on how to conduct myself around HH: no touching, no profanities, don't sit before he sits etc. I had to send a copy of my passport for security reasons.

I arrived bright and early to be greeted by HH and full staff with a breakfast banquet laid out and the horses ready for display in the arena. HH knew each horse like a good friend and had great affection for them. He took great pleasure in regaling me about each one and its heritage – which mare was bred with which stallion and the reason for selecting this match, the qualities of the foal that was ultimately produced. This was far better than any horse show I had been to. Those events are great, but always a bit formal and stiff. Here I was talking horses with an Arabian royal in the grounds of a palace. It would have been surreal, except for the fact we got along like old friends.

He showed me one of his prized horses, Ansata Iemhotep. HH had purchased Iemhotep for US$1M years earlier, and the stallion had sired many foals in that time. But now he was no longer being used as a breeding stallion and therefore was living out his retirement at the stables. He was just as you would imagine the perfect Arabian stallion to be – curved face, big nostrils, small ears, long sinuous neck – and he galloped with attitude with his tail thrown up and over his rump. I loved to watch that horse trot about. Such an elegant creature. I admired him nearly as much as HH did.

We talked for a long time in both Arabic and English, and, after we'd seen all the horses, HH dismissed the staff and took me first for a tour of his gardens and then a tour of the palace. It was incredible, opulence I had never seen before. HH is renowned throughout the Middle East for being a generous and fair leader. For a while he'd served as the minister for education and has written a number of books, and clearly enjoys sharing his wealth of knowledge with like-minded people.

At the end of the day, I asked Julie in passing if HH would consider retiring Iemhotep to Australia, 'You know, since he is no longer breeding him.'

'He may . . .' Julie said. 'Write HH a letter and I'll fax it to him.'

So, I did. I wrote about my family farm and its rolling green pastures, with over 60 acres of paddocks for the horses to enjoy. That it would be a fine life for Iemhotep, and that Australia would benefit from having the prize stallion available to breed with the local horses.

I couldn't believe my luck when Julie called to say HH had gifted me the horse.

Unreal, I thought, *I'm now a serious breeder. Or at least half of a serious breeder; I have the stallion but not the mares to match.*

This new relationship I had with HH grew and we became friends for a while. He gifted me and my children many more horses over the next few years. You just never know who you're going to hit it off with in this life. Life always finds a way to surprise you.

★

Whenever I fly in to consult on a corporate situation, I seem to run into people I first met back in the day.

Case in point: let's go back to 2010, when John Kizon called me. Said a couple of blokes wanted to catch up in Sydney. He dropped a few names, I didn't know them, but I knew of all of them. All serious people. Not the sort you go along with if you can't handle yourself. But I knew John well and that he was not about setting up an ambush, so along I went.

We met at a restaurant, the Cosmopolitan in Double Bay. I had my mate Simon Main drive me and keep watch from a distance, just to be on the safe side. Simon is six foot seven and formidable. Incredibly fit and fast, he should be the scariest dude in the room, but is way too good-looking to be intimidating. You couldn't catch a break around this guy, women just threw themselves at him. Simon used to visit the Comos a lot in Melbourne. The men would be very nervous around him if they had their girls with them; you couldn't trust they weren't sneaking off with him the first chance they got. But I trusted him to watch my back in a tense negotiation.

I walked into the restaurant expecting villains, and I wasn't disappointed. The main dude I was there to meet was Greg '25' Keating. An intimidating leader from the Finks, he ran a lot of security on the Gold Coast. He'd put his hand up for the security at the potential Gold Coast strip club we were looking at buying and expanding Spearmint Rhino, and I considered him to be the natural choice. Normally I'd like to keep the door gig with my teams, but 25 and the Finks had the Gold Coast locked down, with all the knowledge you need to run a tight operation. Who the local teams are, who to let in, who to fuck off, etc etc.

Second guy with his hat in the ring was Troy Mercanti. Troy was the sergeant-at-arms of the Coffin Cheaters, who had been the dominant club in Perth for some time. Troy was their most notorious member. He was a force on his own, feared by most and for good reason. Troy didn't take a backward step ever. Always surged forward with aggression.

The Comos had butted heads with him once or twice. Somewhere around this time, the Comos had a friend in Perth who was kidnapped by people that rode motorbikes and looked a lot like Coffin Cheaters. Our friend was bashed and told to leave town. The thing is, he had loyal friends within the Comanchero hierarchy, and they don't fuck around. They sent a couple of boys from Sydney to leave a message. A very clear message: they burned down the Coffin Cheaters' club-house and the twelve motorbikes that were inside.

Soon afterwards Troy parted company with the Coffin Cheaters and became the state president of the Mongols. He was regular face in the papers for quite a while, and moved in and out of prison. Good bloke. Great sense of humour. For example, not too long ago he made headlines for copping a $9000 fine for attending a mate's funeral and thereby breaking WA's anti-consorting laws, which were put in place by Attorney-General John Quigley to prevent bikies from socialising with each other and wearing their patches. He fronted up to court to cop the fine wearing a T-shirt that said 'Mr Squigley, fcuk your laws.'

So he was at the meeting in 2010. The other guy there was Roger Rogerson, the infamous ex-cop that ran Kings Cross for many years. He ruled with a shotgun, killed and maimed many. He's since died in prison while doing a big whack for killing a Chinese drug dealer in what may have been a rip.

Among the men at that table were some of the toughest characters Australia has produced. Any outsider looking in and seeing the heads on that table wouldn't believe for a moment that the main point of discussion was going to be something as ordinary as who would get the bouncers' job at a new nightclub.

And the host was John Kizon, who knew everybody relevant in Australia, the go-to guy in Perth who could make most shit happen. Hated by the police, embraced by the media, John is a no-grey guy who's played by the rules and stuck to his code of ethics.

Needless to say, I did offer the security work to 25, and I am sure his boys would have done an excellent job had we bought the place and established a Spearmint Rhino on the Gold Coast. But negotiations ended up breaking down and we walked away from the deal. Simon had acquitted himself well back then, and years later, when he was kicking around the Middle East, we connected again and did a few jobs together.

Case in point: I was in Dubai in 2014 when I got a call from Simon. He had been living in Lebanon for more than a year working with a group on developing an online gambling platform. He asked me if I could help transport a container of US dollars from Iraq through Syria and into Lebanon. They were apparently being stored in a shipping container and belonged to Simon's new friend from Qatar – a guy named Mustafa.

Mustafa, according to Simon, was a very wealthy hotel owner and businessman who needed to outsource this job for his own personal reason, namely a divorce that required him to be discreet with his assets. *Bit of a stretch*, I thought. *But these days who the fuck knows what the truth really is?*

Simon directed me to Mustafa's hotel website. I had a quick look and found a picture of him and a spiel on him being an Olympic taekwondo champion. The hotel claimed to have seven stars, with a fleet of Rolls-Royce vehicles available to guests.

Impressive, I thought. *This cunt is proper.* Then thought no more of it.

A few days later Simon was at me again, 'Bro, Mustafa will put up 2 million to put a team together, then another 2.2 million on delivery.'

Not a bad offer: US$2M to do a bit of groundwork and pull together a squad of military guys.

First step was to work out the logistics and get a clearer idea of the cost to transport such goods. The costs were high – ballistic vehicles and a small army, and that's before we even got to the bribes at the borders that are typical business expenses in that part of the world. Wouldn't it be easier to charter a commercial plane and fly directly into Lebanon? Do we have enough connections all the way up the food chain to get us clear passage at the airport? Would the ongoing civil war in Syria complicate matters? All these questions and more needed to be answered. But I was interested.

'Okay. If he's putting some coin up, it's worth a catch-up at least,' I told Simon. 'Tell Mustafa to fly to Dubai.'

Straight up Simon objected: 'No, bro, he wants us to go to Qatar.'

'Qatar? No, bro, fuck that.'

Simon insisted. 'We go to Qatar, stay in Mustafa's hotel, work out some magic, bank the fee and hit the road.'

'Okay.' I thought it was a compelling offer: 'Two million is two million, right?'

I agreed to do a same-day in-and-out. My instinct told me to spend as little time in Qatar as possible. By this point I'd been in the game long enough to know when a job wasn't entirely kosher, plus factor in being overseas where there were eyes everywhere, so it felt right to be wary. In the meantime, I reached out to some ex-military mercenary guys I knew and discussed the possibility of doing such a job. I had contacts at the Lebanon and Syria borders, so that was straightforward enough. However, nothing in Kuwait.

My guys started to research both ground and air travel to discover our best and safest options. Air cargo was definitely the best method at that stage – that's without sighting the cargo and discovering if the container was hot or cold. 'Hot' meaning that the package was under surveillance and vulnerable to an ambush.

We didn't have an accurate location, only that it was a few hundred kilometres from the Iraq–Syria border. Which was complicated, but possible. My read on the situation was that the whole thing was doable but I needed more information.

With all this in mind, Simon and I made arrangements to fly to Qatar to meet with Mustafa. This was back before Qatar won the hosting of the World Cup and started spending big on infrastructure and its airport. We landed at a small airfield that had military staff doing all the airport work:

customs, border control, all of that. Military everywhere, as well as police who carried wooden canes to smack anyone who was behaving inappropriately. In Qatari culture, inappropriate behaviour included men wearing shorts. Capital punishment is part of normal life there. Not a place you want to get caught playing up, so finding the place crawling with police wasn't relaxing.

We made it through customs and were greeted by Mustafa in the arrivals hall. Not what I expected. Limited English – heavy accent where the heavy 'T' and 'D' sounds were a little mixed up, which made communication just that little bit harder.

I thought for sure being the billionaire entrepreneur that his website made him out to be that he would have an entourage, or at least a driver. Nope, neither. He was behind the wheel.

Wait, it gets better. He walked us to his car – guess what it was? A Rolls-Royce? Maybe a lowly S-Class Mercedes? No, Mustafa was driving a fucking Toyota LandCruiser. The car of a Qatari billionaire this was not. *Hmm. Bit suss*, I thought.

I turned to Simon and said in a low voice, 'Look at this cunt and how he stands. Straight upright like he's on parade. I don't know any billionaires or millionaires that stand to attention like that. This cunt's a cop setting us up.'

Fuck me. What had Simon got us into? I worried it was going to be hard to escape this country. My mind was running flat out trying to figure how the fuck we were going to get out of this trap.

Mustafa clearly did not watch *Miami Vice* enough to get an idea of how undercover is supposed to work. It requires genuine backdrop and performance to snare your prey. This cunt was giving us dinner-theatre matinee. Mustafa continued his piss-poor efforts by taking us to a three-star restaurant for our meeting. *At least take us to any five-star hotel and buy us a nice lunch before you bust us, bro.* But no, nothing like that at all.

We sat down and I asked Mustafa, 'Why don't we go to your hotel for lunch?'

'It's too far.' He waved the question away. 'You won't get back in time for your exit flight.'

We had five hours. The whole Qatari peninsula is a hundred miles long. We could go full *Gran Turismo* in the Toyota LandCruiser and still have time to eat. By now I knew for sure this was a set-up. I wasn't sure in what way yet, but had no choice but to play it out. Simon as always did his best by cracking jokes and left the heavy lifting to me.

We started with some introductory talk; I mentioned I did some logistics work and gave some examples of my accomplishments. All above board and nothing illegal. I showed Mustafa pictures of my family and particularly my children, who were waiting for me in Dubai, and let him know I had to get back to them which was why we were only staying a few hours in his country.

Mustafa in turn showed me photos of his children. I noted that none of the background details implied a wealthy man. Mustafa started on about the money; he said there was a lot of money left over from Iraq since President Saddam Hussein had been bowled. He said he had access to over a billion dollars sitting in containers and wanted it transported to Qatar. Not Lebanon, as I'd been led to believe.

'A billion?' I acted surprised. 'Who has a billion? I thought you had 20 million in cash and assets in Syria you wanted to transport to Lebanon. I thought you were going through a divorce and wanted to move your assets. And Qatar? I don't know Iraq. For Syria I can help – we have governments and military friends and relatives in both Syria and Lebanon. This is achievable. But Qatar, I'm sorry I cannot help with that.'

He wasn't happy; his face looked a bit puzzled and annoyed. His accent was a bit thicker now that he was getting upset. 'But what about trucks?' he said.

Now I was puzzled. 'Trucks?'

'Yes, trucks.'

I turned to Simon. 'What's he on about, bro? Why the fuck is he talking about trucks?'

'Not trucks,' said Simon. 'Drugs.'

And there it was. That was my cue to exit. I said to Mustafa in an angry tone, 'Did you say *drugs*?'

'Yes, *drugs*!' Mustafa said, more cheerful now. 'I've been watching Simon in Lebanon and I know you people are involved with *drugs*.'

Abruptly, I stood up. 'I have nothing to do with drugs and will not participate in any conversation related to anything illegal. Especially drugs.' I was, very angry now. I turned to Simon. 'You told me this was all above board, that Mustafa was a businessman who needed some help moving his assets. I'm going outside. Take me back to the airport.'

I waited outside while Simon had a quick chat to his mate. I wasn't sure at that point if we were going to the airport or to a police station. Could have been either. They came out and

Mustafa drove us to the airport. That was a long and quiet drive. My thoughts were running wild. *What if we get locked up? Do we run? If I run, how will we get out of Qatar? I have no-one here. We are fucked.*

Mustafa dropped us at the airport. He didn't seem to give two fucks. Now that he'd worked out I wasn't involved in drugs he'd dropped all pretence of giving a shit about us. In a way, I was grateful. This was his ball game. He could have fabricated evidence and had us locked up on anything, no matter how far-fetched. Once you're in their system, good luck getting out.

Our three-hour wait at the airport was intense. I shrugged off Simon and made it clear that I was annoyed at him. I knew that we were likely being watched, probably recorded. Until we were in the air, I wasn't going to say anything that could possibly come back to bite. I didn't breathe a sigh of relief until the plane took off and we were out of there.

Turns out Simon had procured Mustafa some coke in Lebanon a few times through a connect he had. Not for profit, just as a friend. Mustafa for sure was some kind of American asset setting up drug dealers for a big bust, a tale as old as time. That part of the world was flooded with CIA money because of the war on terror. I was more than happy to dodge that particular bullet, but hoped Mustafa was paid enough for his troubles to buy a decent car for his next set-up.

Not every consultation came with a payday, but when one did, it more than made up for those that didn't. My old friends

Mick and LK had kept me on speed dial ever since mediating the deal between the Coffin Cheaters and The Midget, and they called me in over the years to mediate this issue or that.

LK had an office building in South Perth that his team worked out of – all mining people. One of his projects was a Western Australian diamond mine that he'd secured from the Jewish mining magnate Joe Gutnick. I believe at some stage during the mine's working life with Joe, a famous rabbi in Israel had blessed the mine, sending the stock price north.

LK had made a packet, and ever since was always on the lookout for the next literal diamond investment opportunity. Which often meant complications. The problem with mining is half the time when you think you've hit paydirt it turns out to be quicksand. And the cunts who dragged you into it are now trying to drag you down with them while they sink.

The miners in LK's Perth office always had some situation that needed a careful negotiator on it. There were a lot of pirates in the resource industry who needed to be smacked down once in a while to maintain order – which meant I was often flying between Dubai and Perth on this job or that.

Fast forward a few years and the mining cowboys were at it again. My guy Mick had been robbed for seven bricks by The Turk, a partner in a mine near the Georgia–Russia border, through a company called Straits Oil and Gas.

We started with a quick chat and a please explain in Dubai with Mick and The Turk's guy Alen. Alen was a corporate type who was focused on keeping the mine going and getting his wage and dividend. Didn't seem to have any priorities beyond the dollar, and we really didn't get much traction talking to Alen. The Turk was nowhere to be found so we let it lie for the minute.

A few months later Mick called to let me know they were having an annual shareholder meeting for the Georgia company in London and The Turk would be there. He'd finally surfaced, but now he had a bodyguard with him 24/7.

Quite savvy, I thought. Alen had clearly given him the heads-up. I booked a flight to arrive the day of the shareholder meeting and arranged for two of the boys to accompany me for backup in case we found ourselves in a situation. One flew in from Spain and the other from Turkey. Both serious people. Both ready to escalate if necessary.

As fate would have it, I was sitting in business class, working out a plan of attack on my way to London, when I heard a loud and familiar voice. It was Peter Landau – a mining and exploration guy with a lot of irons in the fire – getting drunk, having the time of his life on the same flight. I couldn't believe my luck.

He was a few seats in front, so I waited for an opportunity to have a quiet word. This was an Emirates A380 aircraft with a small bar and lounge for business-class guests, and that's where I caught him. As he ordered another round, I said, 'Hello, Peter. Small world.'

I put a few questions to him and found out he was speaking at the same shareholder meeting, and that he knew The Turk, who was also scheduled to speak. How convenient.

'Give us the address,' I told Peter. 'I'll see you there.' He wasn't that drunk, and he stalled, telling me that he would arrange a meeting with The Turk for 7 pm at the May Fair Hotel, my usual haunt in London.

I arrived at the hotel at 5 pm, where me and my two boys sat and waited until 7.30 pm. No Peter and definitely no Turk. I called Peter a few times with no result.

Shit, I thought. *I look like a dick to my two brothers who have gone to a lot of trouble to be here.*

I kept calling Peter and he kept ignoring my calls. At 9:30 pm I sent Peter a text: FORGET THE TURK. WHERE ARE YOU!?

He understood that he'd fucked up and offered some bullshit excuses. He promised he would get me the hotel details for The Turk. Not optimal, but at least I had a lead. None of this was going the way I had mapped it out in my head.

A few hours later, Peter called with the following infor-mation: The Turk was staying at a boutique hotel around the corner in Mayfair. He would be eating breakfast in the hotel restaurant at 7 am, with his bodyguard. I would recognise them by the guard's ponytail. I couldn't miss them. Result.

We went straight to the hotel, an old building, the kind where they lock the doors late in the evening so you need a room card to access the lobby. Frustrated, we called it a night. We returned the next morning at six-thirty and posi-tioned ourselves in the dining room. Me at one end near the main entrance and the other two at the only other exit. I was humming with anticipation, ready to absolutely unleash on The Turk for the epic chase. Seven-thirty came and went, and nobody that resembled The Turk or his bodyguard came to breakfast.

By now I'd endured more than enough fucking around and wanted a quick, firm chat with The Turk. I went to reception

and asked them to call up to The Turk's room. The receptionist smiled and checked her records.

'I'm sorry, sir,' she said, 'your friend checked out at 2 am.'

What the fuck. I'd been played by Landau; the cunt gave
The Turk a heads-up and shielded him from me. I was fuming
and paid my boys their airfare and some change to cover the
cost of the hotel. We all left for home. Mission failed.

Well, not completely. The Turk knew he had a problem,
and I would see him in due time. More urgently for me, Peter
Landau had made himself my personal problem.

I flew to Perth to see Landau and recover my expenses.
I was out of pocket for flights, hotels etc. because he'd caused
me great inconvenience in my efforts to grab The Turk.
Worse, he'd blocked me and given The Turk the heads-up.
I was adamant Peter would compensate me and had a figure in
mind, but I was not saying anything about an amount. I had
learned a long time ago when negotiating that it's usually best
not to name your price first.

I set up a meeting with John Kizon, who invited Landau
around. He rocked up all smiles but soon changed when he
realised we had ourselves a situation. I said a few words to him,
but to be honest I didn't get to complete my version of the
events and my demands, as he blurted out an offer to transfer
X number of shares in his company to cover everything. He was
a bit generous. I would have been happy with the $50K. Even
covering our hotel, air fares and a bit of walk-around money,
my costs would only have amounted to $35K.

★

I had a good track record of sorting problems out for Mick. He had a short list of associates who could only talk to him through me. I managed the noise.

In one particular scenario, Mick was contemplating removing this guy called Anthony Herb from the board of a listed company. He was removing him from his controlling position and putting a trusted person in his place. By the way, Anthony, it turned out, is a brilliant businessman; he just wants to get the job done and look after his investors, the shareholders. I heard him ask on at least a couple of occasions regarding the direction of his companies and investments, 'Is it beneficial to the shareholder?' He took his responsibilities seriously.

I was in Dubai at the time with Mick and LK when Anthony got in touch, pleading for a meeting with Mick. He'd got wind of Mick's plan and wanted to put forward his case. I was happy to be involved so I told him to drop $30K into my account and to fly to Dubai so Mick and I could hear him out.

We held the meeting in Mick's suite at the Burj Al Arab. Tony made his case with Mick, telling him he had a buyer for an asset that was owned by Cape Lambert for $400M. He had a Chinese group that were heavily invested in iron ore and wanted to buy this iron-ore asset that was owned by Cape Lambert. He just needed six months to get all the moving parts in place.

Mick agreed to let him stay on for a short while on a performance basis, with a warning that if he did not conclude the deal within the next few months Anthony would be removed from the board. We all agreed that Anthony would sign an undated resignation letter as insurance. Basic shit.

Anthony went on to successfully sell the asset for $400M and keep his job. Rumour has it the selling agent was paid a huge commission – $40M for his trouble.

Once the sale was concluded it turned out to be a flop. It emerged that the site is difficult to mine because of an important railway that was inconveniently built over the section where the minerals lay. That wasn't a problem for me, Mick or Anthony, but it was for the buyer's agent. Rumour has it they killed the agent back in China and sold his organs.

A year later I heard Anthony was talking a bit of shit about how the whole shemozzle had gone down. He told anyone who would listen that I held a gun to his head to make him sign the resignation. When John Kizon recounted this to me I laughed, thinking it was just a metaphor. I didn't even lean on the cunt that much, let alone pull a bit on him. Some guys just have a low threshold for negotiating, I figured.

Fast forward to 2009 and I was in another meeting with John Kizon. This time we were in London doing a corporate mediation between some mining people who were having an internal dispute over stock and control of their company.

The other mediators present were Mick Gatto and John Khoury – both brilliant mediators and highly successful at getting results. Mick needed no introduction. His larger-than-life presence demanded respect and attention. John was a master negotiator, swift and deadly in his fast-talking tactics, not one for giving decision-makers enough time to think or breathe, which usually achieved the desired result.

LK and FV were also present, the latter representing Mick S. FV was a heavyweight corporate consultant, he feared no-one and often ran the ball for Mick, especially when things got a bit heavy, such as on this occasion, when FV and John Kizon went toe to toe. Tables were thrown and words were had, until LK launched himself in between them and settled shit down. FV was not backing down on principle and would not accept any outcome but winning the argument. This left no other avenue but the threat of violence to get the negotiations back in their favour. The old one-two.

There was big money on the table for all sides and we began negotiations.

We did our job and achieved the result we needed in two days, for which we were paid $3M. Not bad for two day's work. But not that good either.

To be honest, I thought we were underpaid. Ultimately we facilitated a handing back of a company with a few hundred million dollars in cash to spend. If the parties had chosen to solve their dispute using lawyers, it would have taken years and cost far more. Most likely the lawyers would not have succeeded in achieving the result we did, and definitely not as swiftly.

I wasn't upset at my share of the 3 mil, but a year later when we were all together again in Melbourne, I expressed my bitterness towards the corporates for underpaying us. I suggested we go back for round two. The others disagreed and said a deal is a deal. However, they were not aware of what we had actually pulled off and the financial gain the corporates enjoyed as a result of our efforts. I dug in and said, 'I'm going back.'

I asked John Kizon to arrange the meeting, since the UK guy loved John and kept in contact with him. Mick and John agreed if a meeting in London was scheduled that they would come but insisted it would be a long shot. John organised the meeting without saying too much but enough to keep them on their toes.

Off we went back to London and the May Fair hotel. We caught up with the two corporates and the main guy, Big Frank Timmis, an ex crim turned legit heavyweight worth over a billion.

We all squared off at the May Fair, and it wasn't long before everybody bridged up. Frank dropped the fact that he had a team of Chechen mercenaries at his disposal. I wasn't afraid of a few Chechens when I had my 300 Comos ready to run amok both there and back in Australia, and I told him as much. Threats on both sides were subtle but accurate as a smart missile. I knew what he was capable of, and he knew the shit I could get up to. There was healthy respect on both sides. But all of that aside, we had business to discuss.

It was just him and me talking, neither of us smiling or making polite talk. The problem I had with digesting the amount we were paid was with the fact that we were paid $3M from a $9M dividend, so it wasn't a direct expense to these guys, and in return they carved up *a few hundred* million dollars. Plus, they kept the remaining $6M from the dividend that should have been ours by rights. I didn't receive a thank-you note or Christmas card. We clearly were not friends, so we needed to get paid, and they knew it.

This meeting took all of seven minutes.

'Why the fuck am I even talking to you?' Big Frank wanted to know. 'After you put a gun to Anthony's head?' I was confused for all of a second, thinking, *What is he talking about?*

'This shit again?' It hit me like a smack in the face. He was talking about that meeting I'd arranged in Dubai between Mick and Anthony when Mick was having Anthony removed from the board, and Anthony signed an undated resignation. That cunt Anthony was going around saying I forced him to sign by putting a gun to his head.

I looked over at Anthony. I was clearly in a rage. When John Kizon had mentioned the rumour, I'd thought it was a metaphor for me being an adept negotiator making an offer that was too compelling to refuse.

Turns out he meant it literally – that he told people I'd actually pulled a bit on him. I jumped up ready to launch at Anthony when he threw his hands in the air and declared it was a lie. 'Jay didn't hold a gun to my head. I made that up. There was no gun.'

Now it was Big Frank's turn to throw his hands up – in frustration. 'Fuck you, you little cunt,' he growled at Anthony. He stood up and pointed at me, Mick and John Khoury in turn, telling Anthony to 'pay him a million, him a million and him a million'.

'What about John Kizon?' I objected. 'There are four of us.'

'Don't worry about John. He's with me and we'll look after him,' Big Frank said, which I took to mean, 'Fuck John for dragging us into this meeting in the first place.'

So, we shared ours with him. Equal to the cent as always.

I learned that lesson from Mick Gatto years earlier when we did a quick recovery for a builder who was owed $400,000 from a concrete company in North Melbourne. I knew the owner of the company so Mick asked me to bring him to a meeting for them to settle their differences. My guy fessed up to the bill and admitted he didn't pay only because he didn't like the builder. This is where it could have become a bit tricky, as my guy had recently sold his business to a public company and the debt now belonged to the company.

Mick called the MD of the company and made an appointment. Me, John and Mick attended armed with the bill. Mick had a chat with the guy and explained the situation – that he understood that the unpaid bill was a headache, and he sympathised, but still, the bill needed to be paid. My guy confirmed the debt, and we walked out with a checque for $400K. Our end was $200K. Fifty per cent – standard for recovery. To us anyway. That was our price.

And Mick was no different now that we were playing in the millions. I was transferred the exact amount of $66,666. Mick didn't fuck around like that. Me? I probably would have rounded it off to 65K or 66K or even 60K, but not Mick. With him, what's yours is yours.

I was in Dubai with Mick S and LK. We were cruising around in a new Range Rover with LK's driver. Mick and LK had a lazy $400K they wanted to give to a charity. The driver was from Somalia, and they got chatting to him about the situation back there, and how many people were suffering from the years of war, famine and poverty that had done a number on the country.

Mick and LK wanted to donate the $400K and asked the driver to find a charity in Somalia who'd accept it. It happened that one of the driver's friends knew the president of the Somali town of Bosaso so he made some calls and arranged for an appropriate charity who he felt would put the money to good use. In time, the president of Bosaso flew to Dubai to receive the cheque. We had a big lunch, some speeches were made from each side and the money was handed over. During the lunch, the president of Bosaso offered access to historical surveys that had been carried out many years earlier by exploration companies looking for oil and other minerals.

Somalia is positioned on the Horn of Africa and if you look in an atlas you can almost make out where it was once attached to Yemen and Saudi Arabia. With Saudi being a huge producer of oil, it struck us that there was a good chance there was a fortune in oil waiting to be tapped under the Somali soil. Mick and LK exchanged looks, thinking the same thing: this could be huge. Long story short: Mick and LK invested $20M through a company called Range Resources and sent geologists in to have a bit of a look around. They discovered some interesting sites. Some of them had evidence of potential oilfields, which made them very fucking interesting sites indeed.

They then sold 80 per cent of that company for $300M to a Canadian company who could fund further exploration and extraction. This all happened quite quickly. The president would often fly to Dubai to lunch with LK and Mick, and of course I was also present. During one of these lunches we discussed the pirate problem off the coast of Somalia. Somalia has almost 3000 kilometres of coastline that was being absolutely pillaged by foreign powers. Italy had a bad habit of dumping barrels of uranium waste into deep Somali waters in the Gulf of Aden and Indian Ocean. It had been a long time since they'd tried to colonise that part of Africa, but they were still carrying on like colonisers.

The Chinese weren't much better. The ocean was being depleted of fish by illegal fishing, particularly from the Chinese, who would use the barbaric technique of dropping miles of nets and grabbing and killing everything they could get their hands on.

Between countries acting like pirates and the actual Somali pirates who were raiding ships sailing these waters, the Somali coastline was a free-for-all. Without a coastguard, any sort of offshore operation would be uncomfortable at best.

Which was a problem. We couldn't exactly ship in oil rigs while dudes with RPGs and speedboats were hanging out on the waves looking for a ship to rob and a crew to kidnap or kill. The Somali government and businesses looking to invest in the country were fed up with international fishing and shipping using the Somali waters without financial contribution.

During the course of this particular lunch, I was asked to help develop the coastguard. So, we started to look at what sort of investment it would take to establish a proper coastal police force, which entailed extensive travel around Somalia, including expeditions from a compound in Bosaso: a fully fortified, half-lux/half-military-style deal with razor wire and machine guns all over the place. I thought it was all a bit over the top until we went out for a drive and were shot at the first time we left our quarters. We had an appointment to see a minister to further discuss the coastguard proposition and were riding in a vehicle with two military guys kitted out and tooled up to the back teeth. As we were walking back to the car after the meeting, shots suddenly rang out. I heard an automatic weapon go off and then felt dirt spattering my outfit as lead hit the ground right alongside us.

We dropped to the ground and moved quickly to position ourselves behind the car – a pretty basic thing that managed to get us from A to B but wouldn't stop many bullets if we didn't get out of there pretty quick. We waited for a minute, sweating and looking out from behind the car to locate the shooter and figure out the play, but nothing further happened. The military guys we were with shrugged. They reckoned it was probably someone just having a laugh. Happened every day around there.

I've got no problem with guns, but Somalia was too much of a good thing. A few days after we were first shot at, we were driving into town when a Toyota HiLux with a 50-calibre machine gun on the back tray and a cracked-out soldier basi-cally holding himself up on it came flying towards us.

We shat ourselves, because although we could all do fine in a gunfight and were tooled up, there's not much you can do against a weapon designed to crack tanks open. It would have been an impossible situation – game over. All we could do was stare death head-on as . . . it drove straight past us.

What a relief it was to see them keep driving away from us. To be honest, if they had had a proper crack we would have been killed for sure. We decided to take sensible precautions by buying three ballistic Toyota troop carriers to be our go-to rides while we were in Somalia. We drove to an industrial province in the emirate of Ras al Kamar that manufactured ballistic vehicles to place our order for our new rides.

On the way back, Mike Povey, a mining engineer we'd been knocking around with in Somalia, drove with LK in the passenger seat while I took a nap in the back. It was 50 degrees outside so the aircon was on max, windows closed. Both decided this was the perfect moment to start smoking cigars – with the windows closed. I woke to a car filled with smoke and Povey doing 120 kph on the freeway, cigar in his mouth with one hand on the steering wheel and the other fanning the smoke so he could see through the windscreen. Needless to say, I made him pull over and drove the rest of the way back with the windows cracked open for some air.

With proper military hardware on our side, I continued to investigate setting up a coastguard. On closer consideration, I discovered that it could be achieved on a small scale around Bosaso but would need a huge investment to secure boats, drones, personnel, training and every other aspect required to guard a coast and territorial waters 200 nautical miles out, as dictated by Somalia's sovereign ownership laws. Altogether we estimated a start-up of $50M would cover a good base. But who would fund it?

Peter Landau from Range Resources wanted security for the ships bringing in the drilling equipment, so we explored the option of contributing $20M towards a coastguard who would guarantee clear passage. But that project was benched for a few years.

Still, I got some good experience with mercenary and marine forces that came in handy when, sometime later in my career, Mick asked me to meet him in Dubai to discuss something he had on the table. Along with Peter Landau and through a company called Black Mountain, Mick was going to salvage a sunken ship that had $1.4B in gold bullion in its cargo.

The ship, SS *Arabic*, was owned by White Star Line and was one of the authorised passenger/cargo ships to carry gold to New York during World War II. Its cargo was believed to be a vast fortune in gold destined for American Express and Guaranty Trust NYC, when it was sunk by a Nazi torpedo launched from a German naval submarine that was hunting Allied ships in a major shipping lane in international waters south of Ireland on 19 August 1915. The ship – and the gold, more pertinently – had never been recovered.

Mick was planning to invest a few million into the project to make it viable, and I was all-in. I thought it was such a sexy story, like something straight out of a movie.

My role would be security and logistics. Assuming the expedition retrieved the gold and could haul it up onto the deck of an expedition ship. I drew up plans to have the gold secured and transported off the mothership via helicopters to the Isle of Man – a nice, self-governing place with favourable tax laws for entrepreneurial types – then flown out directly to Dubai on a jet. There, it would go directly to the Dubai mint and be secured in bank vaults before being melted into 12-kilogram bars and transformed into easy-to-transport, safe, stable, universal currency.

I did about nine months' work on this project. My Dutch mate Mark arranged an on-ship team out of the Netherlands, helicopter sea transport from the ship to the Isle of Man, and a commercial jet company for the final leg of Dubai. It was going to be magical, this $1.4B in solid gold, wrapped up like a Christmas present. I looked into buying a penthouse in the Burj Khalifa and turning one of the rooms into a vault to accommodate gold and currencies.

We got to the eleventh hour. Peter had booked the expedition ship and paid a huge deposit to mobilise it. I had all of the logistics worked out, people recruited, boots on the ground – literally. We had six Navy SEAL types in a Norwegian hotel waiting to board the ship to take us to the site of the wreck. All good to go, locked and loaded, but there was a bit of a delay when one of the main investors couldn't come up with his end of the investment.

A week passed, then two, with the soldiers just waiting around in the hotel. Ultimately, after two weeks of messing around, the main investor, who had to dump a quick brick into the account to cover the cost of the expedition, pulled out.

What a nightmare that turned out to be. I recovered some expenses, a couple hundred thousand. Ultimately, a good payday for the soldiers and a few others, but me and the other players came up short. I could see that both Mick and Peter were devastated. We all believed in this project, or at least wanted to believe in it. But it is what it is. I paid the bills and moved on to the next project.

Imran Khan was elected president of Pakistan in July 2018 and quickly began spending money on tweaking his military – throwing a bit of military cash around in the name of national pride. I was offered, through a mate in London, a contract to secure a dozen second-hand Mi-24 attack helicopters for

Pakistan. You would think that would be an impossible task for anyone outside the military. But I like challenges.

I found a guy, an Aussie actually, living in Europe, who bought, reconditioned and then sold helicopters. Through him, you could get your hands on old Russian gunships that had been Houdinied out of the collapsing military when the Soviet Union fell apart. Easy money if the deal went through. The only real problem was the sanctions on selling war-fighting vehicles to Pakistan.

My guy in London had government connections in Pakistan and thought for sure he could get the sanctions lifted and sell the helicopters through an intermediary. He was convinced that President Khan – a former international sportsman and playboy who'd lived in England and married Jemima Goldsmith, a wealthy model – would have western capitalist values. It all seemed to line up, and it seemed we could move forward with a small but healthy deal on the Mi-24s.

I had a few meetings with some pushy Pakistani dudes who really wanted some military hardware. It all seemed good, so I made a couple of trips into Turkey to put things in place through my Comos connect.

We were close to pulling it off, but it became rocky when we couldn't get all the parties to commit to the order. Everyone wanted it to go ahead, but legally it was still a grey area. It could be done, but not until some sanctions were lifted, which would have meant getting the UN over the line.

Ultimately, we pulled the pin at the eleventh hour, and I had to let it go. It was getting a bit too tricky, and part of doing business is knowing when to walk away. I was just glad we knew the outcome before I'd taken receipt of the helicopters. No harm done, from my point of view, but the Pakistanis were not too happy. Neither were the Russians. And if I've learned one thing in my lifetime, it's that pissing off the Russians usually results in bad luck for somebody.

I learned that lesson a couple of times firsthand, in fact. In January 2019 I'd been in discussions with some Russians over a transit deal. They wanted a hand to move some funds out of Russia without getting too much attention. They were talking big numbers: over US$500M. They suggested buying expensive items like diamonds or gold, then on-selling them, and wanted to know if I had access to such things. Given the amount of money involved we put our thinking caps on and decided a good way forward would be to buy some oil from Iran and on-sell from there.

The oil would go to a friendly port, then move to a fresh vessel with no ties to Iran. It would be sold to a buyer in the west and all the funds would find themselves in a nice neutral account in Hong Kong. It's done all the time.

And a lot of Russians were trying to move money and avoid local attention back then. A Russian billionaire who wanted to relocate some of his money discreetly was not exactly a rare animal, and these guys made out that they were working for one of the oligarchs. Naturally, I thought it was their boss's money, so I thought it would be rude to pry.

I hooked my new Russian friends into an Iranian crew out of Dubai that could facilitate the purchase of the oil, and so off they went to Dubai to meet my Iranian friends. These guys don't fuck around, and they were not big fans of the Russians, but money is money. I've found that religious, cultural or historical hostility between groups that goes back a thousand years can always be put aside when there's enough cash on the table.

Sadly, this venture turned to shit quickly, after a couple of weeks of back and forth, as when things got close to an actual transaction the Russians insisted on keeping one of the Iranians in Russia as surety. Let me tell you that request was not received well. Threats were made, chairs were thrown and the transaction was cancelled.

My phone blew up with calls from both the Russians and the Iranians. Wasn't good, but what did I care? I didn't give a fuck about the Russians and their medieval fucking way of doing business. Turns out the Russians could be quite nasty. I put a call into the crew that had brought these guys and this problem to me, and I was surprised to learn that they weren't actually working for the Russian billionaire like I'd assumed.

The money they implied they wanted moved was purely speculative. The plan? Glad you asked. It was going to be acquired by kidnapping the billionaire and his family, and forcing the transactions by torture and/or murder. Working with these people was clearly not a healthy option. I peaced out. Let the Russians kill and maim each other until the cows come home. I would stay in Switzerland on this. Nice and neutral.

I didn't sweat it though. Such was life back then in Dubai. Opportunities were everywhere. If you kept your eyes open and knew how to stand your ground, the possibilities were endless.

15

GREECE

Dubai offered endless scope for pulling in the cash if you weren't afraid of a bit of push and shove. But if the chances to earn were unlimited, they came at a price. While you were free to spend and enjoy your life in ways the west frowned upon, it meant swapping out other aspects of being free. Things that I began to miss more and more as time went on.

It was such a strict society. There was no tolerance for aggressive behaviour, for example. If you had a problem with another guy, you couldn't punch on or even raise your voice at him in public. Which was an adjustment for me, because I've had a lifelong need to make sure things are fair and even in the way I operate.

If I've got beef with someone, and I can't work it out with even a gentle smack? Not the end of the world, but not optimal, either. I'll seethe a bit on it, but I'm not going to upset the culture of the place just because I'm used to doing things another way.

My team, though, was a different story. I'd assembled a great crew around me to deploy on jobs and mediations. They were smart, hectic, aggressive units – valuable in a stand-off or a firefight or whatever situation I threw them into. Except for peacetime. They were far too aggressive for polite society in Dubai, always playing up and punching on whenever they were insulted. As time went on, each one had been arrested multiple times for brawling like teenagers in the bars and clubs.

It wouldn't be too long before they ended up in a proper Dubai prison, which is the last place in the world you want to be. My friend His Highness had told me some eye-opening stories about Arab Emirate justice that he'd seen growing up – dudes being beaten to death, starved, whipped. From what I heard, modern Dubai prisons weren't much better. Same brutality, just electrified. They'd hang you from the roof and taser your balls. Those aren't jails you want to be in.

You have to know when to tap out, and I tapped out at the right time. I had a bunch of reasons to move on, truth be told. The ostentatious way that cunts live in Dubai started to get a bit old. For a few years it was fun to wild out and throw money around, but it wasn't sustainable, no matter how much cash I pulled down.

It had been an adjustment. In Melbourne Sam threw the best parties, ate at the finest restaurants, drove expensive cars, had more than we needed and did well – then she found herself starting again in one of the richest cities on Earth. It was a challenge and a huge adjustment. In Australia, anything we wanted we got, to a degree. We lived very well, because we were established. I had done a forty-year apprenticeship on the streets and in prison and had a bit of a name around town. Big fish in a small pond, in a way. Then we moved to Dubai, where unless you've got a few hundred million dollars and a fleet of cars and you're rolling hard every night of the week, you're just an average tourist. It's fucking weird – you can be very rich yet poor compared to the sort of lives people live in Dubai.

The excitement fizzled out really quick. It feels pretty shallow after a while – I lived in a nice home and had a driver and a level of luxury in all aspects of life, but none of it actually was making me truly happy. Trying to raise three well-adjusted kids in that environment, to give them the life their peers enjoyed and expected, and still operate on a certain professional level was tough. I was working all the time, and Sam's own professional goals for her early education centre didn't turn out to be what she expected, so we ended up relocating to different countries – she back to Australia, me to Greece.

When we left Melbourne, I went literally from hero to zero. I didn't rate in Dubai, where I was just a standard guy and had no pull. It was worse for Sam, as her attraction to me was for that bad boy who was constantly in the middle of the action and getting the respect that came with it. Now she had a house dad who was striving for normal, life looked very different. Two years into our Dubai life and we separated. We're still good friends and we have each other's backs – and are doing our best to co-parent. But it's not lost on either of us how hard it's been on our kids.

She returned to Australia to be near family and enjoy stability in an English-speaking environment, and I had to stay in Europe to keep the lights on. My plan had always been to wait two years, let the dust settle with the Comos in Australia, and come back. But at the end of those two years, the media were still targeting me and writing so much nonsense about me that I felt 100 per cent the police were getting a jury ready to convict me on something they were setting up. Australia wasn't on the cards.

It was tough, but those are the breaks. I moved to Greece to set myself up, and in time my kids joined me. There were many things in Greece's favour. It was a lot more affordable and a lot freer. But my number one reason was to put my family first. To live a quiet life. That was the plan, anyway.

Our townhouse was five levels internally plus a rooftop terrace. It had all of the bells and whistles: a heated pool, two kitchens, six bedrooms and a private elevator that the kids often used as a cubby house. We overlooked the golf course in Glyfada, a beachside town on the edge of Athens, so everywhere you looked was green and blue and the endless Mediterranean sunshine. None of it was cheap, but that wasn't a problem.

The thing was, my reputation arrived ahead of me, and there was always a job that needed doing. That part of Greece is a playground for the rich, and now and then someone managed to lose part of their fortune and needed someone with a very particular set of skills to recover it.

Not long after I first moved to Greece, I was called to help recoup assets to the tune of $16M. My client was being pursued by authorities over some fraudulent activity and had asked a German national trustee, Carl, to hold all of his assets in trust until his situation improved.

Carl the German trustee had a different plan, and just decided to keep it all. He'd simply taken off with the loot, including a small collection of exotic cars and a chalet in Austria. I had a few clues to go on tracking him down. Rumour was he was living in Geneva. I had his parents' address in Germany and his offsider's address, also in Germany. I secured some working money (€100K) and began to hunt.

I reached out to my Dutch mate Mark, who'd helped put together the security team for the shipwreck gold expedition. He engaged a couple of his freelancers with surveillance skills to track down the trustee in Switzerland. As a first step, they flew across to Switzerland and staked out one of the addresses on my list. They found him almost immediately and started following him, sending me photos of his location – and proof that the cars he'd ripped off were parked in the basement of his building.

'Excellent,' I told the freelancers. 'I'll grab a flight from Dubai and be there this evening. Keep watching him until then. We'll knock on his door, introduce him to my gaffer tape and have a long chat to discover how to get the asset pool back.' That was the plan.

But I was delayed that afternoon when my mate Nick – a good friend who loved to punch on a little too much – got into a fight by the pool at the Jumeirah Beach Hotel in Dubai and smashed some English guy who was harassing his girl. That was okay, no big deal, but Nick was full of booze and as he tried to exit the scene, he slipped down some stairs and broke his arm. Unreal! What a mess. I had to miss my flight and stay to help sort Nick out.

No big deal, I thought. *I'll grab the German tomorrow.*

Wasn't going to be that simple, of course. While I was in transit to Switzerland, the German managed to lose my guys who were tailing him.

Turns out he noticed the two dudes on his tail taking pictures, got paranoid and jumped on an aeroplane. They watched him go into the airport terminal and he never came out. Vanished. He could have gone anywhere – Swiss airports are a very good place to go when you want to disappear.

We kept Mark's two surveillance dudes posted at the apartment, and Mark and I drove to Frankfurt to another address.

The offsider, Anton, held the chalet in his name with a fake loan from Carl. I had Anton's Frankfurt address so we headed to a block of flats and knocked on the door. No answer. We spoke with neighbours who told us that apparently, Anton worked in media and travelled a lot. I slid a note under his door with my full name, my number and the chalet address plus a request he please call me. Or I would be back.

We also had an address for Carl's parents in Frankfurt. We watched the house for a bit then knocked on the door and talked to his mother but didn't get much traction, so I wrote a note asking him to call me and gave my full name and number and the name of the client.

We then drove to Austria where the German had a chalet halfway up a mountain, purely on the off-chance we would find someone there who could give us a lead. A beautiful spot – amazing view of the Alps. Would have been stunning in winter with the snow. But right then, no snow, and no fucking German.

Again, no success; new plan. We started calling all of the numbers on my list, including the German's wife. We got the wife on a call, who again had nothing to offer. The Frankfurt guy received my note, did his homework, and called. He refused to meet with me and was being a bit tricky. Still no traction. If anybody knew where the German had gone into hiding, they were staying schtum.

We let it go for a few weeks before I decided to bring in the German Hells Angels. At the very least, these guys could speak German and their presence would help open doors and grease wheels.

I had a Hells Angel connect in Greece with guys in Germany, so through him we met a German Hells Angel who was president of a chapter. He knew of the Comancheros and our hectic reputation, and my being a friend of Johnny the Greek (a Hells Angel I knew) opened doors for me. I was proposing a rare cooperation between two clubs that were historically enemies.

There was a time in Australia when the Angels and the Comos would take up and go to war at the slightest provocation. The bad blood ran long and deep. But Johnny was a respected member and managed to get his Hells Angels brothers to look past the old issues and focus on the earn ahead. I did stay on my toes, however – I always had a tool close by. I figured the best way forward was to start with the dude back in Frankfurt who was proving to be evasive. My instincts told me that he had information he wasn't giving up, and the Angels would be helpful in extracting it. We drove in convoy from Hamburg to Frankfurt in the Angels' vehicles. A couple of lovely Mercedes G Wagons carried the muscle, and I rode with Hans, the sergeant-at-arms, in his Bentley GT. I was happy to see the German Hells Angels had similar taste to the Comos and drove lumpy cars.

We got to Frankfurt around 7 am and headed to the block of flats. No-one was home, so I asked the sergeant to phone the Frankfurt guy and get him to a meeting. Hans called and introduced himself as Hans from the Hells Angels.

The dude was delighted to receive the call and happy to catch up at a cafe around the corner.

Fuck, that was easy, I thought. *These guys are good.*

He rocked up all hugs and smiles and started talking in German. Turns out the German guy I was hunting had reached out to the Hells Angels in Switzerland when he heard I was looking for him. He must have googled me and saw I was a Como, and so he'd reached out to the traditional enemies of the Comos for protection. He thought the Hells Angels were at that meeting for his protection. You couldn't make this shit up if you tried.

We were all a bit puzzled at first, but soon realised the reality of the situation. I started talking. We had spoken on the phone a few times, so he knew my voice and shat himself. After some dialogue I got him to call the trustee, the trustee agreed to return assets and cash minus some expenses and bits and bobs. We arranged a meeting with his lawyers in a few hours in Frankfurt to work out the details. The trustee Carl would not be present but would be on the phone.

It was an interesting meeting; the lawyers were a bit tricky but at the end of the day had nowhere to go. This turned out well, easier than I anticipated. The client took a hit on some of the money in the bank accounts but secured his assets.

What I didn't know at the time is that there was a girl in the equation that both my client and the trustee were keen on, and this was the reason for the fallout. The trustee fell in love with the client's girlfriend and the girlfriend wanted to be with whoever had the money. Not exactly a classic love story, but still a tale as old as time. The girlfriend ran off with the trustee, however that didn't end well. Hearts were broken, potentially more than hearts, but after we intervened the money and assets were returned. Could have gone either way. The trustee could have run. In the end we got the job done.

Ultimately, a civilised discussion. Nobody was hurt, nobody disappeared. Everybody won. Admittedly, some won more than others. That was about as hectic as I got at that time. In my line of work, if everything goes right, nobody gets hurt. A bit of theatre always beats a bit of violence. You just need the right team.

I had a really good team in Greece. My offsider, and best friend, was Cain. Ex-military and a former bikie, he was half-Mexican, half-Canadian, half-soldier, half-bikie. Very capable. We used to go to the shooting range together to practise, and I never saw him miss. He'd accompany me on international mediations – Singapore, Spain and Dubai – where it helped to have someone with that skill set to watch your back. These days he's got his own team – a high-ranking leader of a motorcycle club that covers Russia, Ukraine and most of Europe, one of the top five most powerful clubs in the world.

While I was in Greece with my family, I didn't play up. A little consulting work, assistance with a mediation here or there, but I kept everything legit and above board. The media were speculating away back in Australia, and the cops in Greece weren't thrilled that I was there, but I just wanted to keep my head down and be a good dad. People would come up to me all the time with offers they wanted help with, and if it was piss easy and bordered on illegal, then I was good to go. But if it was highly illegal and hard work I always turned them down. I was approached a few times with invitations to assist with things that were out of my comfort zone: drugs, cigarettes, things of that nature. Stuff that can – for a short time – make you king of your world but always with a use-by date and a bad ending. I always declined and made a point to avoid people who brought me those offers. Don't get me wrong, if I were a twenty-year-old cocky kid with a limited future, I most likely would have taken the risk, but now, at my age and with three children to look after in a foreign country and no real family support, it was not even a consideration.

I'd sometimes go to the gym at 6 am before my kids woke up and even the short drive away from them made me uncomfortable. Because say something did go wrong – an accident that resulted in a hospital stay – who would look after my children? There was no extended family nearby and my closest friends were five hours away, Peter in Spain and LK in Lebanon.

There were plenty of operators from all over the world who'd got too much heat back home and had moved to Greece. Some, like me, for peace; some for a piece of the action. The best of them was John Macris.

2019 was a crazy time in Greece. It was especially crazy in Glyfada, where the people with money and influence rubbed shoulders. Stunning beaches, some of the fanciest seaside clubs in the world, and the most beautiful women. The shopping strip was crowded with boutiques and designer stores. They catered to the models who vacationed there, who in turn catered to the businessmen who flashed their money around. All sorts of businessmen, with all sorts of ways of making money. It was a second home for a lot of Aussies who'd had some trouble with the law back home and wanted a place where they could operate in peace.

But the Greeks weren't looking for peace. The economy of Greece was broken, and grinding poverty was on everyone's doorstep. All these flashy, loud-mouthed Aussies who were king shit back home were now kicking back in beach clubs, ordering bottle service, scoring local chicks – but if they jumped in their Lambos and drove five minutes across the city, they'd find families so poor they were struggling to feed their kids.

That rubbed a lot of people the wrong way. The local gangsters had had enough of the cocky Aussies moving in on their turf and started unloading on them. Lots of people were getting hurt or knocked.

Most of the Aussie expat gangsters who lived in Athens fled to Dubai or Turkey. Or they caught a bullet. I had no idea: I barely had time to go to the gym every day and was focused on looking after my three children. Between school runs and after-school activities I was so far removed from that shit that I actually had no clue so many people had even left. Those who could leave were already long gone, until by 2018 there were only two remaining: me and John Macris.

John was a champion. Your classic Greek-Australian success story. A sharp dresser, well spoken – an alpha male but one with the gift of the gab. And for seizing a business opportunity. He owned restaurants, developed property and owned a nightclub on Mykonos. In 2005 he'd done a little time over a drug bust but bounced right back and built himself an empire.

That empire brought him into conflict with another ambitious young bull, John 'King of the Cross' Ibrahim. Not surprising. In some ways they were cut too close from the same cloth to get along. Two handsome, confident, sharp business-men, both hugely successful operators who came up against the odds in the then skippy-dominated underworld of Sydney. Both had egos the size of a building and neither would back down. Ibrahim owned the clubs in the Cross, but Macris enjoyed them like they were his own.

The Cross was glamorous, lucrative – but too small a town for two kings. When you've got that much power and ambition in the hands of two talented operators, then conflict is inevitable. That's just human nature.

Around 2006 there'd been a little war going on between the two Johns. While they were busy fighting over Macris getting into his clubs, Ibrahim was buying the buildings, quietly taking over the assets and establishing his property portfolio.

Things got hectic, family got involved, people got shot. From what I understand, it never became too serious, but at the height of it, Macris had the support of the Comancheros. This was way before my time, so I never saw any of that beef. Personally, while my loyalty is naturally with the Comos, I like John Ibrahim. What a guy. He built his wealth literally off the streets of the Cross and safely navigated through the worst types of killers and hustlers to be the last man standing, the King of the Cross. You have got to love that success story.

Historically, however, the Comos were drawn into the war, and they chose to side with Macris. The Comos were looking after Macris, so technically he was protected, but that didn't stop John Ibrahim or his family, as they were fearless, ruthless and very capable of getting the job done. In 2011 two of Ibrahim's brothers stood trial on conspiracy to murder Macris, but they were acquitted. Like I said, things got hectic.

Ultimately, John Macris decided to move to Greece in 2013 and was living large, calling the shots like an Onassis. Whenever the Comos came to Greece, John would catch up with them, as he was a supporter of the club and everyone knew that they reciprocated his support. They still had a solid relationship all these years later – and a mutual dislike of John Ibrahim.

The boys arranged a catch-up meet-and-greet between me and Macris when I first landed in Athens. Just a matter of mutual courtesy. We got along. In all honesty I didn't have much to do with him, but on the few occasions we ran into each other it was always good. He was an easy guy to like, and I was always impressed with his sharp mind, which saw opportunity everywhere he looked.

John was the exception to the Aussie tourists who try to set up shop in Greece. There is no shortage of young wannabe gangsters running around Greece – men with big ambitions, big mouths, but no brains.

One of the worst was this guy Nick. He was a low-level crook who hung out at my gym in Glyfada. Whenever I was benching, he would always appear and be available for a spot and a quick chat about nothing.

I like a good chat, but I always felt he was too enthusiastic by half. A bit too keen on the details. My gut told me he was no good, even if I couldn't put my finger on why. I asked John Macris about him, who shrugged. 'He can be a shit-talker, but he's okay.'

'Are you sure? He dropped your name and was trying to steer the conversation in directions that make it seem like he's gathering intelligence.'

'He's not that smart. He's okay. He is good for a coffee catch-up, but I wouldn't get into bed with him. He's a weak cunt.'

'If you say so.' I wasn't convinced, but it wasn't really my business. In all practical ways, I was retired from that world. I had a few visitors here and there from places like Russia, Turkey, Spain, London and other spots around the world, but they were mostly passing through.

I won't elaborate on it too much, but he was no good, this Nick cunt. Bit of background on him: he came to Australia

318

to do some work a few years back. He was supposed to be collecting money from some dealers and moving it overseas. He lasted maybe three weeks. The idiot started spending the money, flashing it around, having coffee out in the open with the people he was collecting the cash from. So, he fell onto the radar of the police; they started to follow him and established what he was up to, then they raided him and found $900,000 under the bed.

The cops confiscated the money, he signed it over to them and did a year in prison. Stupid, right? It gets worse. When I first met him, he told me this story. Like it was something to be proud of.

He was on the payroll of the cops in Greece for sure. This Nick guy tried everything to uncover nefarious activities or get me involved in them to zero result. He was my entertainment; I had a quiet laugh at his stupid attempts to get information or get me into a job. I did have a crack at him a few times, but he would just shrug it off and stay on the job trying to set me up. Must have been money in it for him, I assumed. It's a challenging balance keeping your friends close but your enemies closer.

Once in a while I'd throw out a breadcrumb and see if he picked it up. Eventually, he did. My visa was about to expire. I told Nick it had expired and that I had to exit Greece for a short time to renew my three-month visa – standard stuff.

To renew it, I decided to head over to London, take the kids on holiday with Sam while I was at it. Catch the ferry to Italy, plane to London, get a visa, see some culture, head home. I got Nick to drive us to the ferry, we joined the line for the boat, and an undercover police officer approached and asked for my passport.

'Why do you need my passport?' I asked.

'You've overstayed your visa and are in Greece illegally.'

'No, I haven't.'

'That's the information we have.' *Hmm*, I thought, Nick was throwing the towel in, couldn't get me on anything so settled for a visa overstay.

'Here then, have a look.' I was ready for this and pointed to page six of my passport. 'Here's my visa which will expire on 26 March. Today is 22 March. I've got four days on the clock, and I'm leaving right now.'

The cops did not like that, not at all. Since I'd landed in Greece, they'd been trying to get me, but the dogs had nothing. This was the best they could do. So, they arrested me anyway. Held me just long enough that I missed the ferry, then let me go. Sam waited for my release, then we caught a taxi home for a couple of days, then flew directly to London. Idiots should have checked my bags: I had €25K in my backpack. They could have taken that.

It was a pain in the arse, but that's how I clocked that Nick was working with the cops. He was the only person who thought my visa had already expired, but because he was incompetent, he'd obviously given the cops the wrong information, and they'd acted on it.

That's standard practice for Greek cops. They'll get some weak dog to roll over, put him on the payroll, steer him towards crooks to penetrate whatever they have going on, then report back to the police. Every time this Nick guy got into something shifty, the whole crew he was working with ended up getting arrested, and he'd walk.

I figured it was better to have someone like Nick close, because people like him can be useful if you play them the right way. So I kept him at arm's length, tapped him now and again to play chauffeur, and invited him to harmless social activities. For example, I carried my bit around in Athens, and I was spending a lot of time at the shooting range. You have to put in a certain number of hours at the range to qualify for your licence. Nick kindly arranged access for me as technically you needed a residence visa to participate. That way I didn't have to listen to him yammer when we hung out together – I was wearing ear protection and unloading rounds the whole time.

Macris was always up for the next big business move. He did his thing, did it well, and was rolling in cash. He would hit the gym in his Lambo Aventador with custom alligator seats, and all the Greeks would fall over him, desperate for his attention. They'd flock to him like seagulls around a chip thrown on the beach. He had that walk, the Aussie strut that exuded confidence, and a smile that lured people in. It didn't hurt that he was a genuine Greek success story, could navigate the language and the culture in a way most Aussies couldn't.

These skills, along with his contacts and the money, meant he could achieve a lot. Doors didn't stay closed for Macris for very long. He had established himself well within the Greek financial community and employed a lot of people. He drove very flashy cars and usually rolled with a small team of just two or three guards. Bodyguards in Greece were quite normal, as many people with money had to be protected. It was not unusual to see multiple teams of bodyguards waiting for their clients outside the gym or restaurants. They would stand and observe, looking out for kidnappers or straight shooters or even the savvy killer with a remotely activated bomb that could be placed under a car. I never had guards and thought it would attract too much attention.

You'd spot them by the cars they drove – old bombs that stood out in the affluent neighbourhood where luxury sports cars lined the streets. Or you could tell at a glance: these big units standing around smoking who carried themselves in the way that told you they could handle themselves. Ex-military, usually, or even police moonlighting on their day off. The average income for a policeman in Greece was €1000 a month so part-time work as a guard was in high demand. I'd see them and make a mental note in case any shit popped off. Macris, though, saw opportunity.

Security was a big business in Greece, and particularly in Athens, where ostentatious wealth rubbed up against some of the poorest people in Europe. Bodyguard business was a normal thing in Greece, since poverty and a broken economy made it dangerous to have money – they made you a target. It was a fairly regular thing for rich cunts to be kidnapped and tortured for a ransom. That's if you were lucky. There was always someone desperate and ruthless enough to go for your wife and kids if they couldn't grab you.

My neighbour from a wealthy oil family, for example, had a security team comprised of ex- and current police officers run by a formidable ex-cop. That meant three cars switching over in three shifts for 24/7 protection. The vehicles were strategically positioned to secure the house from outside, while another two guards patrolled inside the house.

That was standard practice for a monied family in Greece. Impressive to see, but a bit annoying for me that the street parking was always taken by these teams of security guards. It led to some conflict between me and the neighbour over a parking space in our shared lock-up garage, and I may have said some heated words to him.

When the family left the house, the security would move with them. I would often see the young mother go for a walk literally surrounded by over-enthusiastic guards. The cost for this service for this family was €28,000 a week. Big money.

John Macris, being the savvy businessman that he was, saw an opportunity. He teamed up with the mayor as his business partner and worked towards starting a security business. His ambition was to build a modern, flashy business based in a huge office on a main road with signage and proper branding advertising '24/7 security'. He bought a fleet of a dozen small cars that displayed the logo as a show of professionalism. A bit like the security firms you see driving around the streets of Australia, only with real guns and real issues to deal with.

Macris was warned off trying to tap into the personal protection business. The market was covered by a Greek ex-cop who had a lot of police working for him and a lot of trained guards. These guys were serious and tooled up, the right people for the job. Sometimes, the only difference between a gangster and a cop is the badge. Sometimes, in a place like Athens, they don't even have that difference. Nobody knows how to be above the law like the law.

The way I heard it, there was a bit of a battle being fought over the security of the party island Mykonos. Both the ex-cop and Macris were Greek and saw Mykonos as their rightful territory. Up until the new kid on the block blew into town, the ex-cop had the monopoly of Mykonos security, and he wasn't about to share. But some other security firm was looking willing and able, and wasn't going to back down.

A local club owner in Mykonos was unwilling to bend to the ex-cop's monopoly and engaged a third security firm — an entirely different crew to Macris' — to secure his clubs and restaurants. Thus, war began and ended quite quickly.

The problem wasn't that the club owner engaged others. The problem was that the outsider dared to work on the ex-cop's island. He didn't have long to enjoy the successful expansion of his business, though. The outsider was ambushed and gunned down by four killers as he left the port returning from Mykonos.

Serious stuff that could have possibly been worked out with a mediation, but it was too late for that. You would think the death would have been the end of it but nope, the outsider had friends, family and associates, and one of them took the initiative and gunned down the ex-cop not long afterwards as he left a restaurant in Athens. Eight bullets in the chest and head. The cop had €20K cash on him when they brought his body in, so it wasn't a robbery. It was business.

Threats were made on both sides. The ex-cop had family, friends and a large staff that relied on the security income, some of whom stepped up to fly the flag and keep the business going. Macris, seeing the opportunity, decided to fill the void with a new security firm with all of the bells and whistles including the fleet of cars, smart uniforms, a brand you could trust. He was warned not to proceed.

Macris the Aussie knockabout wouldn't take a step backwards. You would do better with a kind word than a threat with John. He'd never faced a battle he hadn't won. Back in Sydney he had the allies to make anything happen. In Athens, his team included the mayor. That's substantial in the business world but meant nothing on the streets.

He was gunned down that November while leaving his mansion to attend the grand opening of his new security company. He'd invited half of Athens for champagne to celebrate, and he must have let his guard down at exactly the wrong minute.

Two shooters who'd been tailing him for weeks saw their chance. The killers waited for John to jump into the car (that being the most vulnerable position) then started shooting him from behind, too quick for John to react. He always had a bit on him, but he never had a chance to use it.

A 9mm pistol caught him four times: chest, stomach and shoulder blades. He was hurt badly but managed to stumble out of the car and make it a little way down the road. Fatal wounds, dead at forty-six. His elderly father was the first to find the body. The whole thing was captured on CCTV. It was a hot night – crickets chirping in the background the entire time, that only stopped singing for a moment when the shots went off.

Your first instincts would tell you that John became a casualty of a turf war. The strange twist on it all happened later that evening. The business – '24/7 security', which was supposed to be a 24/7 security operation – was closed down within hours. All of the signage was removed and the cars garaged, eliminating evidence of a business and all before midnight. Almost before Macris' body had time to grow cold, his business was entirely shuttered, signage vanished, and the office closed forever.

The Comancheros were not happy. My phone was ringing off the hook over the following days, the boys keen to discover who the fuck had killed their friend. I was tasked with hitting the streets and finding out what I could about the killing. Me and my offsider Cain started making a bit of a fuss.

Cain had been living in Greece for more than ten years. He was known to a lot of the local gangsters, shall we say. We started asking questions, poking around, got some pushback from a local team that seemed a bit 'how you going?', but mostly no-one had anything solid to say.

On the face of it you could have thought that maybe John was caught up in the security turf war, but scratch the surface and things would get weird.

Bulgarian brothers Yuliyanov J Raychev Serafim and Milen Raychev were arrested after Greek police put it all together. They found clothes matching those in Serafim's hotel room along with a receipt and evidence that he rented a Nissan Pulsar in his name, which was caught on CCTV footage six times in the vicinity of Macris' home before the murder. Greek authorities went on to link the hit to a Canadian chapter of the Outlaws motorcycle gang.

Why the fuck did they have two professional Bulgarian shooters fly in for the hit? That's not the Greek way. They use Albanian shooters, cheap and effective. Bulgaria, Albania, Romania – they're all on the border with Greece, and they are not wealthy places. You've got some of the poorest people in Europe next to some relatively wealthy countries. And until recently, everyone had to do compulsory military service. So, you've got whole countries full of hectic, trained-up, traumatised, desperate people who can cross the border to Greece – which has some very, very wealthy people swanning around – kill or kidnap them, and be back home in time for dinner.

For example, a few months prior to John's murder, two Albanian shooters sat outside a club in Glyfada and waited for the owner to walk out with his girlfriend and bodyguard. They sprayed the owner, killing him instantly, and put one in the leg of the bodyguard and one in the arm of the girlfriend as an extra service. Then they were back over the border within hours, never to be seen again. Easy-peasy.

To add to the mystery, the key witness to the Macris murder got knocked before trial by a Mexican cartel dude. So, what about that – could it have been work related?

Maybe a greedy partner who wanted it all to himself, or perhaps a situation gone wrong that was worth a lot of money? It's a mystery that I couldn't seem to crack. But it seemed that my questions were making someone nervous. Perhaps we were getting too close to discovery. Maybe that's the reason I became the target of a car bomb? Who the fuck knows?

What exactly happened we'll probably never know. Because the truth is, in this world you don't know you've got a problem until it's too late, do you? Honestly, it could be as trivial as gossip. Someone says something about you, someone gets worried, gets paranoid, gets inspired to do something about it. That's more often than not the likely sequence of events. And coming up soon after Macris got knocked, it could be that's what happened to me, one morning not long after Serafim pulled the trigger and Raychev drove the getaway car from outside John's house, when I started my car and the whole world exploded around me.

16

THE AFTERMATH

AFTER I WAS BLOWN up, I was dragged from the wreckage and rushed by ambulance to the Asklipieio General Hospital for urgent treatment. If I'm being honest, the whole experience immediately after the bomb gets a mixed review. Public hospitals in Athens, man – what a fucking mess. Three stars, max.

The windows were so dusty, no light got in. You could see the sunbeams trying to fight through the grime and just giving up. My body was too big for the first bed they put me in, and my foot was hanging over the side with blood dripping onto the floor. The doctors didn't fix it up straight away, either. Instead of, I don't know, bandaging up the bomb wounds so that they didn't bleed everywhere, their solution was this: every once in a while, a nice old Greek lady would come in and mop the blood up off the floor.

There were a few initial procedures to try and stabilise me, after which the doctors didn't see the point of trying to save the leg. They told me I was going to have it amputated. That was fine by me. I'd actually decided on that the first time I saw the wound. I had a look, saw the state of my foot, and thought, *That's a fucking mess, Jay. There's no fixing that.* Logically, I thought that I would cut it straight off at the knee and get a prosthesis, and I'd be up and about again in six weeks and just get on with it. In that instant I was prepared for an amputation.

I had a change of mind in the Greek public hospital – when the mop lady had just gone out and the surgeon came in. He told me that all he could do was clean the wound and patch it up instead of actually building me a new ankle and saving my foot, and that amputation was inescapable.

'Mr Malkoun, you're going to lose the leg. Infection is going to set in, and we need to amputate.'

It felt different hearing this concept from someone else. It seemed far better when it was my idea. My instinct told me to reject this offer of amputation and negotiate my way around to keeping my foot. 'Why?' I asked.

'It's inevitable.' The surgeon sort of shrugged. 'Look around you, this hospital is over a hundred years old and not in good condition. In this environment, we can't prevent potentially fatal infections.'

He wasn't lying about the condition of the place. The hospital was dysfunctional as fuck.

'Okay,' I told the surgeon. 'I'm leaving. I am moving to a private hospital in Glyfada. Arrangements are being made to leave today.'

Suddenly the surgeon had a change of tune. You could see in his eyes that he was worried what would happen if a private doctor saw the job they'd done on my leg. It felt like he wanted a second crack at tidying up my foot.

'You cannot leave today. I must do another surgery early in the morning and then you can go after midday.'

Right then, my fortunes changed. His bedside manner might have needed work, but it turns out that this surgeon was one of the best in the whole of Greece. If you were going to get your legs blown off in a car bomb, here was exactly the guy you wanted to patch you up. Incredible luck.

He managed to put my foot back together, salvaged what was left and did a proper patch-up job in readiness for my transfer to the private hospital. Second time around, the surgery was a different result – my foot was immaculately sewn up, the bandages taut and clean around the wounds. It looked amazing in comparison to the first semi-botched version. Twenty-four hours after the bomb, and I thought things had started to look up. I was wrong.

After a day or two in the public hospital, my brother Joe had me transferred to a private hospital, where like in all of Greece, cash was king. As is the way in Greece, I had the money and so received the royal treatment. The private hospital sent me their own ambulance, and two medics kitted out like doctors collected me from the room.

As soon as I arrived at the private hospital numerous tests were carried out to examine my entire body for impact damage from the explosion. Remarkably, my injuries were limited to my feet and right hand.

A team of surgeons went to work and placed a fixator on my right shin, ankle and foot to hold everything in place. The head surgeon was pleased with his work and the result. He came in to see me post-surgery with good news. 'It went very well, and we believe we have saved your foot. The heel was severely damaged, however we managed to save 50 per cent of it, enough to build on.'

The force of the explosion had blown a hole in my right foot and ankle, and caused lots of skin and muscle damage, so bone and skin grafts were necessary. But possible.

That was amazing news. I was elated. Twelve hours earlier I'd been certain of an amputation and shopping around for a prosthesis, now it looked like I was going to be able to walk out of there on my own foot one day. I was so happy to receive the news, and thanked the doctor effusively. He nodded and went on to say, 'Now, about the payment. Can you pay in cash?'

This isn't a strange question in Greece. You'll hear it a dozen times a day, from cabbies, waiters, cleaners, maître d's at restaurants and, as it turns out, surgeons.

'Sure. How much is it?' I asked.

Eh,' he said, shrugging his shoulders. 'Ten, maybe fifteen thousand. For everything. That's it. No more surgeries.'

'I don't need any more surgery? Wow, that's great.'

'No more surgeries,' he agreed, but added, 'If we have to do a little bit more, I will throw it in for free, no extra charge.'

'So that's €10,000 to €15,000 all up, for everything, no more?'

'Yes, everything.'

'Deal.'

I then instructed my brother, Joe, who'd flown in to look after me while I was being patched up, to give him €15K.

I couldn't put away my wallet yet, though. Standing behind the surgeon was a woman from the hospital also waiting to speak with me. I assumed they were together, and he sent her off, only for her to come back when he'd gone. Turns out she was from admin in the hospital and also needed payment. Another €3,2000. Fuck, lucky we had credit cards. The following day the anaesthetist came in to see me; she had not been paid by either the hospital or the surgeon. She wanted to be paid too – €500 for each ninety-minute operation and clean-up.

It was almost funny at this point, so I was happy to pay the anaesthetist. To me she was most important as she literally held my life in her hands, so I paid her for that and every other surgery – *best to keep her on side*, I thought.

That's how it was. I had to 'donate' money for mattresses to the public hospital to get anything done. Seriously, I had to buy blood by the bag. They didn't want to give me blood transfusions until I got my wallet out. Clearly there was no shortage of blood.

The frequent bribes aside, the Greek medicos at that place were professional, competent and calm, and came in every day to discuss how they were going to find a way to fix all the broken bones and missing flesh without amputation. On reflection, the Greek surgeons were second to none, and the cost associated with my recovery was cheap. Definitely underpriced for delivering a miracle.

Compare that to, say, Germany – where I would go on to have a lot of treatment – it would have cost at least four times as much. Having said that, I wasn't bargain hunting, just making a point that my biggest regret is not completing my surgeries in Greece. I would have saved myself a year of hard-going recovery and a lot of pain. The Greeks brought in the top private surgeons from the army and air force to assess the potential for skin and bone grafts. These surgeons had a plan, a good plan, but wanted me to wait a month until they could safely schedule the operation.

Fuck that, I thought. I needed to be up and about, making my moves and discovering who the fuck blew me up.

I was in the Greek private hospital for about a month, and the whole time, my offsider Cain was always there, always tooled up. Cain was in Bulgaria when I'd been bombed – his girlfriend called him and told him what had happened when she saw it on the news. He had immediately jumped on a plane and was by my side within four hours, before I even had my first surgery. For two days after the attack, he didn't leave my side, didn't sleep. He didn't let anybody in except doctors, and he kept an eye on their every move.

In that time, he got a team together of private body-guards and former Navy SEALs. A day later my brother Joe arrived and stayed with me for the remainder of the year. Nine months he put up with me. Looking back I must have been a pain the arse: I was highly medicated, stubborn and often making the wrong decision. Joe put up with a lot to keep me mentally and physically healthy. He would drive me down the mountain to the gym every day, roll me into the building in a wheelchair and help me train, which was one of the only things that made me feel better. Big effort, best brother, wouldn't trade him for the world. We are all close, me, George, Joe and Elie. It's the way we were brought up – to love and respect each other and always be available in a time of crisis.

The Greek cops were baffled by the bombing – and were still angry about the Macris hit a little while earlier. It was a point of pride for them that another Aussie ex-gangster didn't die on their watch.

It was a huge media event. I don't know if it was a slow news day, but when I was blown up it was all over the evening news in Australia and made headlines all over the world. The papers sent reporters to my Athens apartment to stake it out, so I was glad my kids were being taken care of elsewhere, first by my sister-in-law and then by Sam. People were speculating wildly about who was responsible, what sort of bomb it was, what sort of retaliation I would unleash on those behind the attack.

All nonsense. If I didn't know who'd tried to kill me, the media sure didn't. But they've never let the truth get in the way of a good story. The articles kept coming. If any killers wanted to track me down, they wouldn't have to follow me for weeks this time, they just had to read the fucking newspaper.

So, I wasn't safe in the hospital, not really. Greek gangsters are reckless. It's not unusual for a target to be taken out by a machine-gun sandwich. The target will be driving along when one car will turn and block off the road ahead, a second car behind, then two teams will get out, one from each car, all toting machine guns. Both teams take position off-centre so they don't hit each other, unleash from both sides, put a hundred holes in the target, then get in and drive away. It's a serious country. For such a beautiful place, they take their crime very, very seriously. If whoever came for me wanted to go for round two, they would have no problem taking out a whole wing of a hospital with a car bomb parked under the window.

I was even more vulnerable to ambush after I was made an outpatient about six weeks into treatment. My doctors moved me to a private room at the InterContinental Hotel, which was much more comfortable but would have made things much, much easier for a shooter trying to put a bullet in me. I could have my team around me while I was in the hotel, but every Wednesday for the next six weeks or so I'd need to travel back to the hospital to have the wound cleaned, drained and dressed. All that time on the road meant too many moving parts to have security up to acceptable levels.

That was a lot to have on my mind, and I didn't want to wait weeks and weeks for my bone and skin graft. I wanted to be up and about as soon as possible. So I started looking for surgery options that would get me on my feet faster. I got on Google, found what seemed to be the best possible private hospital – a facility in Germany – organised my stay and had the boys grab a car, and we drove 3000 kilometres in two days. I arrived on a Thursday and checked in, and they told me the surgeon would see me on Tuesday.

I don't have many regrets, but I can honestly say I regret leaving Greece for surgery in Germany. My German surgeon had nothing on the Greeks.

When they finally did see me, they took off the high-tech Rolls-Royce-level infection-control device I'd bought in

Greece and replaced it with this crappy little metal band that leaked everywhere. They removed the fixator that held my foot, ankle and leg in place and replaced it with an internal small plate, originally designed to be used for a broken wrist. Within six hours of surgery the bone slipped off the plate and fell apart, my foot and leg went from being dead straight and held in a precise position to now resembling an S-bend. Worse, they removed my entire heel, and with it all the work that my brilliant Greek surgeons had done to save it.

When I saw it for the first time after their operations, I cried out in horror, 'Oh my God! What the fuck have they done?'

These guys had no clue. I could say that given the previous three months' experience with the Greeks and how things were done, I was fucked. My options were limited, and amputation was back on the table. I couldn't believe it.

I needed another nineteen-hour surgery to try and correct the mess they'd made of my foot. I spent €100K on it, and they still fucked it up. By the way, the anaesthetist in Germany charged by the minute – €8000 for the anaesthetist for one surgery. That's just taking the piss.

It wouldn't have been so bad if they'd achieved good results, but they fucked things up royally. They'd left a gaping hole where my ankle used to be, which they tried to repair with a bone graft from my hip and a skin graft from my back. Neither of them took, so all the bone, skin and muscle went straight in the bin. Back grafts, I later discovered, were a primitive way of doing it. These days they just take a bit of the quad for muscle and skin grafts.

It was like I had pursued the most advanced and modern hospital with the best surgeons and somehow found myself teleported back in time to the 60s but with modern, excessive pricing.

My conclusion? Going to Germany was a huge mistake. I was there for a month in total and I left with my wallet much lighter. And my body lighter a fair bit of meat and bone as well.

I went to a private clinic in Lebanon where I ended up convalescing for an entire year until the damage the Germans had done could be repaired. All through that time, I had one of my most loyal guys, Nabs, watching my back.

Nabs – a solid bloke in every way. Big, ripped Leb – pure muscle, but agile, fast on his feet and his thinking. Ripped as he was, he moved like a featherweight, always up for an opportunity to prove how hectic he could be.

I'd met him about fifteen years earlier in a Perth gym training with John Kizon. Nabs walked up to me and introduced himself. *Hmm*, I thought, *bit keen, wonder what his intentions are?*

John explained that Nabs had been asking to meet me for a while. He had ambitions. Over the next year or two I got to know him. Good guy, reliable and with heaps of drive. If I needed a door knocked on, or a quiet word under the cover of darkness to a cheeky cunt in Perth, Nabs was always good to go.

After my explosion Nabs joined me overseas, as did a few others. He was clearly upset. These guys, the guys like Nabs who commit to a friendship the way that many others commit to a marriage, are distraught when a friend is hurt or attacked. They take it personally and constantly express a need for revenge.

I spent nearly a year in Lebanon, living in my friend LK's place in the mountains, the building that used to house the former Honorary Consulate of Australia in Lebanon. It was a palace. I had an electric wheelchair and I could race around like it was the Grand Prix without hitting anything. From there I'd come down for repeated surgeries in attempts to fix my right leg, ankle and foot. For the most part I was in a wheelchair or on crutches. One surgery was to extend my shin bone by 2 centimetres as I had lost that much leg in the blast.

I already had a fixator attached so it was just a matter of tweaking the fixator and separating the shin bone. Every six hours I would turn the four screws a quarter of a millimetre, giving me 1 millimetre separation of every twenty-four hours. This I had to do for approximately three weeks.

My surgeon checked the progress after twenty days and determined I had to do it for a further twenty days as the leg really had not lengthened. So back at it. That did not make me happy. What a fuck around. My plastic surgeon was on point, but the bone surgeon was a twit, a proper dumb cunt. Three weeks into the process I pointed out a lump in my shin to which he replied, 'Oh yeah I see that', then dismissed it.

This went on for sixty-five days before my genius surgeon realised he had not completely separated the bone, so rather than extend the length I was creating a bow in my shin. Doing more harm than good.

This whole time, Nabs and my brother Joe would take me to the gym every day that I wasn't in hospital for a session. Training kept me sane. Looking back it was such a hassle for Joe, getting me into the car, loading the wheelchair, driving down the mountain, then loading me back into the wheel-chair and into the gym.

Once there, though, we both enjoyed a good train. The members all thought I was mad, and maybe I am. Just a little.

I'd do everything I could, work out every part of my body that wasn't about to fall off, and I was feeling good. My sessions started at an hour and progressed to two hours. Granted I spent most of that time sitting, but I wasn't resting. I was grinding away, focused on my invisible enemy, wondering around which corner he would appear next. I slept with a shotty and carried a beautiful Walther P99 380 9mm short, eight rounds in the clip and one in the chamber – same one James Bond has in *Tomorrow Never Dies*, one fucking sexy gun.

LK has a huge collection in Lebanon and gave me the P99 because of its size, weight and accuracy. I would often hold it in my hand, feeling the cold steel in my palm and desperately wanting to let off a few rounds into an enemy, visualising the kill – two in the legs, two in the chest and one in the head.

Always finish with the headshot. You'd be amazed how someone with a couple of rounds in the chest and stomach still manages to get up for one last crack at you unless you make sure the job is done. *Tap.* These thoughts gave me comfort, acting out a scene of revenge in my head.

Nine months into my recovery I flew to Bali for a month with my kids. My right leg was held together with a steel fixator and my heel had not entirely healed so swimming was not in the cards. Nabs joined us on the trip and would jump in the pool to watch over my kids while they played and I hung out poolside.

That's proper loyalty, right there. He stayed with me from Bali to Thailand then Spain and Columbia and finally Sydney.

Once back in Australia, Nabs continued on with me for a year until I could walk and drive myself. Once he was satisfied I could hold my own he went back to his family in Perth. This is the Lebanese way. When we give, we give everything. Nabs, true to form, gave unconditionally. I only wish he'd been a doctor instead of a soldier – with his talents he would have had my foot sorted out in a couple of weeks.

It looked like I was going to lose the foot entirely, until Dr Peter Lewis and Mr David Young, my doctor and surgeon in Melbourne, came to my rescue. After a lot of discussion and planning they came up with a new procedure that might save my foot: an artificially made titanium heel. Brilliant idea. He 3D-scanned my left heel then had a company in New Zealand build a replica out of titanium for my right foot. The key to the success of this implant was designing pockets in the titanium heel to sprinkle tissue from a bone graft that could eventually grow and cover the heel with bone. So far, we have had success. So, whoever tried to kill me only made me stronger. Now part of me is indestructible metal. The other day a mate joked that I'm halfway to being RoboCop.

'I'm not a fucking cop, bro,' I told him. 'Not RoboCop. RoboCunt.'

But before then there was a lot of time in the hospital, and a lot of time to consider my other problem, which was working out who was behind the bomb.

From the day of the explosion my phone was blowing up with theories. The bomb had made international news, and friends and colleagues from across the world all had their own opinion on who'd tried to kill me. Cain, as well as keeping guard in my hospital room, was answering my calls. There were a million maybes and what-ifs. Everybody had a theory, particularly some senior Comancheros in Turkey and Dubai. The local guys had made it clear they had a problem with Australians and tourists coming in and operating in their territory, but I wasn't doing anything to put a target on my back. I kept my head down, in the shadows – that was the whole point of my move to Greece. There was nothing of substance. I couldn't think of anyone who had a problem with me. No-one.

I remember floating this theory with Cain while I was being wheeled in and out of surgery.

'Really?' He thought this was the funniest thing he'd ever heard. 'Nobody?'

When I thought about it – and there would be a lot of time to think while I lay in a hospital bed and the doctors rebuilt my body – there were actually a few people out there who would want me dead.

The Comancheros' leading theory was that it was the Hells Angels. There were more than a few reasons why the Angels would take a shot at me. Could it be the German chapter that assisted in the collection from the trustee? Maybe they were paid a bit more to turn on me.

Or could they be suspicious because I was in Wayne Schneider's apartment in Pattaya when he was killed? After all, Wayne was a senior member of the Angels in Australia. Although Wayne was my mate, and I'd been crushed by his murder, for a lot of Angels I guess the idea that a Comanchero leader being in the house the night he got knocked was just too much of a coincidence. The average Hells Angel probably still thinks I was involved in the murder of Wayne in Thailand. If you were not in the know then, how would you know?

It was just too hard for some of the old-school Angels to believe that a Comanchero would have been there without being a part of it. So that was a strong possibility. Or it could go even further back, to the beef with the Angels when I was making big moves trying to keep war from breaking out on the streets of Melbourne. That was what my old Comanchero crew landed on in terms of a theory. The leading media theory was that it was simply a series of hits against the Comancheros and their associates.

The fact that Macris had only recently been murdered and was allied with the Comancheros in a few conflicts with underworld figures was seen as just too much of a coincidence. It could have been a package deal, seeing as the Comancheros protected Macris. Personally, I didn't see it. Friendship aside, a car bomb in a foreign country is not from the bikie playbook. They keep it personal.

I like to think that the assassin was smart enough to put the device under my car when I went to the gym. It was parked there for an hour. Easy to do. The car park was just a gravel yard off the main road, completely open, and it would have been easy to access my car. It's possible the device had been there for days. They could have put it in my Merc at night; however, then they would have had to have access to the secure garage I parked in. Of course, those are easy enough to get into if you have the skills. It's a theory, but then that opens up a whole new line of questions. There are so many what-ifs.

What if it was the Russians who were still angry about me dropping out of their plan to kidnap and torture the billionaire? Those cunts were capable of anything. Pull that thread, though, and it unravels further. What if it's not the Russians, but the Pakistanis who were pissed at me for the helicopter thing? Or some cowboy from the mining world angry at me because I negotiated a better deal for my guys than for his?

Or, after everything I've seen and done in this world, what if it was some petty Greek expat bullshit?

I'd learned in prison how to read the play, look for the signs: two hands under the front of the jumper were usually concealing a shiv, and whispering in the corner while fidgeting and focusing their sights on a certain person usually indicated the victim. Or read the time of the day: if it was just after the muster, then for sure someone was about to be stabbed. I hadn't got the feeling like I was about to have a blade pulled on me, but something about this situation had made me uneasy.

When the ex-wife of the president of the Hells Angels snubbed me in the gym thirty minutes before I was blown up, I had that uneasy feeling that I should start carrying my piece again, keep it close by, that something was definitely up. Thinking back, maybe she knew I was about to be knocked and didn't want to be one of the last people to be seen talking to me?

Or maybe it was Nick? He was no good, he was a police informant. I had let him know that I knew he was no good and made it clear that he should fuck off. Was he savvy enough to ignite a situation to cause a reaction? He could have pitted someone against me, probably someone he set up or ripped off. He certainly was not shy.

When I really thought about it, the only person I had an active issue with was my landlord. We did a handshake deal on the apartment next door that I wanted to rent, then he rented it to someone else, all within twenty-four hours. Naturally, I blew up at him. In public, put it on him hard. For me a deal is a deal, we shook hands and that's settled. In my world, a man doesn't shake hands then look for a better deal, which is exactly what this guy had done. I may have spoken to him unkindly when he told me this.

We'd had words a few times and ultimately, he wanted me out. Tough shit. I had a contract, and he could do nothing but put up with my abuse.

If it were me and I wanted my apartment back, I would do whatever was needed to get it. Threats were made by both of us, and his life suddenly became uncomfortable. He didn't seem like a killer, but sometimes the most dangerous people are the ones you never suspect. He had the motive and the money and the connections. And access to the car park to install the bomb. Maybe it was as simple as that? Maybe it was him? Or maybe . . . Or maybe . . . Or maybe . . .

Maybe it doesn't matter. It's the sort of thing you could go crazy over if you spent too much time thinking about it, and I have better things to do. There's work to be done. Deals to be made. If there's scores to be settled, I'll get around to them in due course. Time's on my side. They blew my legs off at the ankle, and I'm still standing.

★

I've been through a lot, but it's all experience. Experience either builds character or breaks you. I'll tell you I'm experiencing more pain as a single parent than any act of violence that's been done to me. I've never killed a man in my life, but I'd kill for the chance for a decent nap.

Watching your kids grow and facing their own challenges? The fights they can only fight for themselves. That's brutal to go through. Trying to deal with issues and keep your kids well balanced and grounded and focused on their education and happiness?

Come at me with a blade, or a bit, or a car bomb? No problem, I'll handle it. But I've got no idea what to do about social media and all that shit. Trying to advise my daughters on navigating a girls' school? It's fucking brutal, bro. Give me Pentridge over private school any day. But I'm happy. I've got three amazing kids, and they are the greatest joy and greatest challenge of my life. The rest is just a rehearsal.

The bikie life was fun for a minute, but it's not something you can do forever. The walls are closing in, and they won't let the outlaw one-percenters live their lives. Nearly everyone from back in the day is either in jail or dead. There's a few still living in Dubai, but the world's a small place these days. It's not so easy to hide. The days of going to South America and living happily ever after, they're gone. So, I'm going to live happily ever after on my own terms.

They say live every day like it's your last. I've had plenty of days on Earth that should have been my last. I've changed a lot over the years, but in some ways I'm still that kid in the housing commission who made a decision to never back down and to defend what I feel to be right. I never learned the Bible verse for verse, but God gave me an unshakable sense of right from wrong. I'm just as spiritual as I was then, maybe even more so, because I've had a ride to the afterlife called on me more than once, and I'm still waiting for it to turn up.

I have been back in Australia for four years. A lot has happened in that time. I was denied entry into Columbia, arrested in Germany, held up on separate occasions in the Netherlands, Thailand and Bali – all while waiting to return to my home country.

Even when I finally made it back in, it's not the same place as when I left. The tides have shifted. The underworld keeps turning over, as old gangsters get out of prison and a new breed rises to challenge them. That or old scores – grudges that have waited out decade-long prison sentences – are settled. Seems like every other day I open the paper and read about an old friend/enemy/rival getting bowled pretty much the minute they stepped out for their first restaurant meal after being granted parole.

I have lost a lot of friends and associates to murder and incarceration. Big names, some of the biggest operators who I always thought untouchable, have recently either been locked up or killed.

The ANOM sting took a huge bite out of the underworld and the fallout is ongoing. Most of the big players have been caught up in an impossible situation where they are waiting to see whether or not a random message will be decrypted and for some crime or conspiracy to be pinned on them.

The world is changing, certainly getting smaller. Safe havens like Dubai, Turkey and Lebanon no longer offer the protection they used to. Dozens of Aussies in Middle-Eastern countries thought they'd live happily ever after. Recently, just under forty were arrested in Turkey in one hit, half a dozen in Lebanon and quite a few in Dubai. Even if I'd stayed there, playing up, chances are I would have ended up in a bad place.

All in all, the mediation game is not always as lucrative as it once was, but conflict is rife so demand is high. I'll always have my finger in the game while heading into greener pastures, with new adventures, new stories. Of course, once in a while the old life comes back around to visit me. The other day I was in a dust-up where a knife got pulled, I took a blade through the ribs, broke a leg, lost my spleen, almost bled out. No biggie. Shrug it off and keep moving. I'm back on my feet doing my thing without taking a backwards step. But that's another story. I'd need a whole other book to fill you in on what's been going on since that bomb went off.

The way I see it, in the underworld if people don't want to murder you once in a while, then you don't rate. Life is short, and I make the most of it. If the cunts have a problem with me, it's because I stand by my moral compass, standards and beliefs – and don't bend those for anybody. I'm at peace with the past – I'm not losing any sleep. Tomorrow's a new day. And that'll be a story all of its own.

And if whoever put that bomb in my car back in Athens wants to come at me for another round? Good luck to you. I don't like your chances. If it comes down to it, I'm going to bet on myself. Same as it ever was. Same as it'll always be. If that's something you think is a good idea to take to the table, then go for it. I'll be here. Ready as always.

GLOSSARY

Associate – Someone who is associated, socialises or works with a motorcycle club but is not a member.

To be backed up – To have one's hackles raised; to be on a war footing and ready to respond with force.

Bowled over/Bowled out – To be murdered: 'He caught a shot to the head and got bowled out of the game.'

Bikie – A member of a one-percenter club.

Brick – 1) $1M: 'I dropped a brick on an unwise investment.' 2) A ten-year prison sentence: 'He's inside doing a brick for theft.'

Chapter – A local franchise of a motorcycle club. Usually semi-autonomous, but often reporting to a centralised national or international authority.

Colours – The insignia or 'patches' worn by motorcycle club members on cut-off vests to identify membership of their club and territorial location. A status symbol only awarded after a series of initiation ceremonies.

Dog – To work with law enforcement, give statements to the police or work as an informant. See also 'Rat'.

Door – An infrastructural weakness exploited to allow drugs or other contraband across international borders. For example, a seaport that will allow through a shipment of contraband is considered a door, as are the individuals who facilitate – a dockworker, or a corrupt law enforcement officer etc.

Dropping a note on oneself – A prisoner who informs jail authorities that they are in danger in the current prison environment and at risk of harm, in order to be transferred to another facility.

Enforcer – The motorcycle club member who ensures the club laws and rules are followed by all members.

Fully patched – A full member of a motorcycle club with all the benefits and responsibilities of club membership.

Hang around – An individual who is interested in joining a motorcycle club. More of a social position than an official one; they attend meetings, socialise with and get to know members, might run errands, but don't have any real obligations or benefits.

Hottie – A stolen car.

Key – A killer: 'Whoever's got a door, needs a key.'

Knock – A murder, typically organised in advance.

Left-handed drop – When someone wants to dob on you, without dobbing on you. A prisoner will offhandedly mention information to their wife on the phone, who will relay it to the authorities.

Mail – Rumours.

Meth – Crystal methamphetamine. AKA 'Ice'.

Nominee – A man who would like to join a motorcycle club but still needs to earn his patch. He must be sponsored by an existing member and work pro-bono at beck and call for them for usually between six and twelve months. A low-rank low-status position that leads to full membership. AKA 'Nom' and 'Prospect'.

On the drip – To be extorted, or to pay money to a third party, syndicate or gang in order to avoid the consequences of past mistakes.

One-percenter – A member of an outlaw motorcycle club. Originally coined after media coverage of a Californian motorcycle riot in 1947 when the American Motorcycle Association (AMA) issued a statement saying 99 per cent of all bikers were upright citizens, with only 1 per cent being outlaws who caused trouble. The label was soon reclaimed as a point of pride by bikies and remains in use internationally.

President – The chairman and also the CEO of the chapter.

Rat – Someone who dogs to the police.

Road Captain – The motorcycle club member who plans all club runs, when members ride in numbers on their motorcycles. He is the ranking officer if the president and vice-president are not present and therefore leads the club formation on the ride.

Set-up – Betrayal or entrapment achieved by encouraging someone to commit a crime in order to gather evidence for law enforcement.

Sergeant-at-Arms – The motorcycle club member who defends and protects the club members and prospects, and ensures all the laws and rules of the club are upheld. Responsible for weaponry within the club.

Shiv – A makeshift knife, usually a sharpened piece of metal but a toothbrush sharpened against stone will do the trick.

Shotty – Shotgun.

Slot – Solitary confinement in prison: 'I played up and they slotted me for a week.'

Smack – Heroin. AKA 'Gear', 'White', 'China white'.

Soldier – A loyal club member willing to follow orders and use violence when necessary.

Tipped – Thrown out, released from prison.

Tool – Personal weapon, usually a handgun such as a Glock that can be easily carried and concealed. AKA 'Piece', 'Bit'.

Treasurer – The motorcycle club member who keeps all the financial records of the club, collects the income from all operations and is responsible for paying all the bills.

War – Conflict between motorcycle clubs.

ACKNOWLEDGEMENTS

THIS JOURNEY OF WRITING my story dates back to 1987, and runs all the way up to 2024, and I have a list of people I'd like to thank, who helped me along the way.

When I was first arrested, Charles Giglia was the first friend to encourage me to share my experiences. Charles is a film producer, and he was sure that my life, even at that stage, was an interesting story that people would enjoy. I didn't pause to share it then, which turned out well, as the following thirty years provided a lot more interesting content, including ten years in jail, navigating the underworld wars for seven years and becoming Victorian president of one of the most feared outlaw motorcycle clubs in Australia.

After the car bomb, my best friend Greg 'Doc' Roberts visited me in hospital and suggested that it was time for me to control my story. I was conscious that it could only be a matter of time before a news reporter-turned-author might write a book that included my story, and probably with a negative twist. I mean, I'm no angel, but I would prefer an account written from my perspective and how I lived my life, rather than from the viewpoint of a stranger.

Greg nailed it that day and that's when my writing journey began. Charles was keen to help me put pen to paper, so flew with his good friend Peter to Lebanon where I was recuperating, and we began to record and write. So I am grateful to Greg and Charles for encouraging me and helping me start the process.

The truth is, I would not have been able to continue without the support of many other people, especially my family. After the explosion my brother, Joe, sacrificed so much time and energy to get me up every day to continue the fight of recovery, when my leg was mangled and offensive to the eye. Everyone around me was telling me to amputate and get on with it, but it was Joe who hung in there and kept me focused on keeping my leg. This came at a cost to him as he would push me around daily in my wheelchair. He accompanied me everywhere to keep me sane and it was thanks to him that my recovery journey became bearable and doable.

I also want to thank LK for being present for seven months of my recovery, for opening his doors to me without rules or conditions. He tooled me up and we were ready for anything. I slept with a shottie and two pistols. He always got me to hospitals on time, even when battling roadblocks and fires. I'm grateful to LK for tolerating me and my idiosyncratic habits.

ACKNOWLEDGEMENTS

Looking back, it must have been a frustrating time for both Joe and LK, but neither complained.

Back in Australia, my gratitude goes out to my agent Alexandra at Rêve Agency for running with the ball and turning the concept of this book into a reality. I'm grateful to my publisher, Penguin Random House Australia, particularly to Alison for taking me on, having faith and trusting me to finish it, and to Clive for all his help.

Also, I'm grateful to my kids for putting up with me and allowing me to write without interruption each morning from 5 am to 7 am while they slept, as well as to Jasmine for encouraging me during the process.

And finally, I'd like to thank my man Liam, the coolest kid on the block and handy with a pen.

There have been many others along my journey so far – too many to name – but it's really thanks to all these people that this book has come to life. I hope you enjoyed reading it as much as I have enjoyed living it.

Powered by Penguin